THE BANTU PRESBYTERIAN CHURCH OF SOUTH AFRICA

Scottish Religious Cultures *Historical Perspectives*

Series Editors: Scott R. Spurlock and Crawford Gribben

Religion has played a key formational role in the development of Scottish society shaping cultural norms, defining individual and corporate identities, and underpinning legal and political institutions. This series presents the very best scholarship on the role of religion as a formative and yet divisive force in Scottish society and highlights its positive and negative functions in the development of the nation's culture. The impact of the Scots diaspora on the wider world means that the subject has major significance far outwith Scotland.

Available titles

George Mackay Brown and the Scottish Catholic Imagination
Linden Bicket

Poor Relief and the Church in Scotland, 1560–1650
John McCallum

Jewish Orthodoxy in Scotland: Rabbi Dr Salis Daiches and Religious Leadership
Hannah Holtschneider

Miracles of Healing: Psychotherapy and Religion in Twentieth-Century Scotland
Gavin Miller

George Strachan of the Mearns: Seventeenth-Century Orientalist
Tom McInally

Scottish Liturgical Traditions and Religious Politics: From Reformers to Jacobites, 1560–1764
Edited by Allan I. Macinnes, Patricia Barton and Kieran German

Dissent After Disruption: Church and State in Scotland, 1843–63
Ryan Mallon

Scottish Presbyterianism: The Case of Dunblane and Stirling, 1690–1710
Andrew Muirhead

The Scots Afrikaners: Identity Politics and Intertwined Religious Cultures in Southern and Central Africa
Retief Müller

The Revival of Evangelicalism: Mission and Piety in the Victorian Church of Scotland
Andrew Michael Jones

The Bantu Presbyterian Church of South Africa: A History of the Free Church of Scotland Mission
Graham A. Duncan

Forthcoming titles

The Dynamics of Dissent: Politics, Religion and the Law in Restoration Scotland
Neil McIntyre

William Guild and Moderate Divinity in Early Modern Scotland
Russell Newton

Protestantism, Revolution and Scottish Political Thought: The European Context, 1637–1651
Karie Schultz

John Kennedy of Dingwall (1819–1884): Evangelicalism in the Scottish Highlands
Alasdair J. Macleod

edinburghuniversitypress.com/series/src

THE BANTU PRESBYTERIAN CHURCH OF SOUTH AFRICA

A History of the Free Church of Scotland Mission

GRAHAM A. DUNCAN

EDINBURGH
University Press

Edinburgh University Press is one of the leading university presses in the UK. We publish academic books and journals in our selected subject areas across the humanities and social sciences, combining cutting-edge scholarship with high editorial and production values to produce academic works of lasting importance. For more information visit our website: edinburghuniversitypress.com

© Graham A. Duncan, 2022

Edinburgh University Press Ltd
The Tun – Holyrood Road
12 (2f) Jackson's Entry
Edinburgh EH8 8PJ

Typeset in 10/12 ITC New Baskerville by
Cheshire Typesetting Ltd, Cuddington, Cheshire

A CIP record for this book is available from the British Library

ISBN 978 1 3995 0393 8 (hardback)
ISBN 978 1 3995 0395 2 (webready PDF)
ISBN 978 1 3995 0396 9 (epub)

The right of Graham A. Duncan to be identified as author of this work has been asserted in accordance with the Copyright, Designs and Patents Act 1988 and the Copyright and Related Rights Regulations 2003 (SI No. 2498).

Contents

Acknowledgements		vii
Timeline		ix
A Presbyterian Anthem		xiii
	Introduction	1
1	Background to this Study	4
2	The Origins and Early Development of Scottish Presbyterian Mission in South Africa, 1824–65	18
3	Rev. Tiyo Soga (1829–71): A Paragon of Early Indigenous Leadership	30
4	The Role of Mission Councils in the Scottish Mission in South Africa, 1864–1923	44
5	The Rev. Edward Tsewu's Dispute with the Free Church of Scotland Mission	57
6	The Mzimba Secession, 1898: A South African 'Disruption'	71
7	Presbyterianism in South Africa, 1897–1923: To Unite or Not to Unite?	85
8	Preparations for the Formation of the Bantu Presbyterian Church of South Africa, 1897–1919	98
9	The Formation of the Bantu Presbyterian Church of South Africa, 1920–3	111
10	Mission to Church – Church to Mission: The First Ten Years, 1923–33	123
11	Reaching Out: The Bantu Presbyterian Church in South Africa and the Presbyterian Church of South Africa and Ecumenism, 1923–39	137
12	The Bantu Presbyterian Church in South Africa and Ecumenism, 1940–99	149
13	The End of Mission Councils: The Church of Scotland South Africa Joint Council, 1971–81	161

14	A Young Church in Mission or Maintenance Mode? The Bantu Presbyterian Church of South Africa, 1923–99	174
15	The Bantu/Reformed Presbyterian Church and Socio-political Issues	186
16	Bantu/Reformed Presbyterian Church Women in Leadership in Ministry	200
	Conclusion: Indigenous Presbyterians and Missionaries – Transferring Contending Roles and Responsibilities	212

Bibliography 215
Index 232

Acknowledgements

This book is the result of the support, encouragement and co-operation of many colleagues in the church – far too many to mention individually. However, some have played such a significant role in my development they merit a mention:

Rev. Adamson M. Mxekezo, Moderator of the Presbytery which ordained me, mentor.
Rev. Abraham N. Maja, Moderator of General Assembly, 1979–1980.
The late Rev. Samuel B. Ngcobo, General Secretary of the RPCSA.
Rev. Blessing B. Finca, Manager of Lovedale Press, Administrator of the Ciskei, Member of the Truth and Reconciliation Commission.

These mentors and friends challenged, advised and counselled me with varying degrees of severity and care.

I constantly felt supported throughout the church and owe a great deal to all my colleagues. Much of my vocational life has been spent in ecumenical settings and I pay tribute to my colleagues at the Federal Theological Seminary in Southern Africa (1982–7), the congregation of Cumbernauld: Old, Church of Scotland (1988–98), the Faculty of African and Democratic Studies at the University of Fort Hare (1998–2001), the Faculty of Theology at the University of Pretoria (2002–19), the Department of Church History, Christian Spirituality and Missiology at the University of South Africa, St Augustine's Roman Catholic College, Johannesburg and the Baptist Theological College of South Africa, Randburg. I also pay tribute to my students at FedSem, Fort Hare, Pretoria, St Augustine's College, Johannesburg, the Baptist Theological College, Johannesburg, who have provided the greatest stimulus to my theological thinking and development over the years.

My former student, research assistant, colleague and friend Justin Taylor has provided constant IT support throughout this project. Rev. Mzwamadoda (Zwai) Mtyhobile, my colleague in ministry at St Andrew's Presbyterian Church, Pretoria, keeps me grounded concerning church matters. My wife, Sandra, has provided a home environment conducive to research and academic study, and many forms of material support.

Many of those who have helped me have now gone to join the communion of ancestors in heaven. They too deserve my thanks.

All of these people have enabled this work to come to fruition and deserve my heartfelt thanks.

Graham A. Duncan
University of South Africa
August 2021

Timeline

1795	The London Missionary Society (LMS) is formed.
1796	A proposal is presented to the General Assembly of the Church of Scotland to begin overseas missionary work. It fails.
	The Scottish Missionary Society (SMS) is formed.
	The Glasgow Missionary Society (GMS) is formed.
1779–1889	Wars of Dispossession.
1799	Dr Johannes van der Kemp of the London Missionary Society arrives in South Africa.
1816	The LMS send Rev. Joseph Williams to work near Fort Beaufort.
1820	British settlers arrive in Algoa Bay.
	Rev. John Brownlee settles at Tyumie Mission.
1821	Brownlee is joined by Rev. William R. Thomson and Mr John Bennie from the GMS in 1821.
1824	The Presbytery of Kaffraria is formed on 1 January.
	The General Assembly of the Church of Scotland gives its blessing to the cause of foreign missions.
	Thomson and Bennie are joined by Rev. John Ross from the Presbytery of Hamilton, Church of Scotland.
1829	Tiyo Soga is born.
1841	Lovedale Missionary Institution is established.
1843	The 'Disruption' occurs in Scotland and the Free Church of Scotland (FCoS) is established.
1846	The War of the Axe.
1847	The United Secession Church and the Relief Church form the United Presbyterian Church of Scotland (UPCoS).
1856	Tiyo Soga is ordained a minister of the United Presbyterian Church of Scotland.
	Edward Tsewu is born in Grahamstown.
1856–7	The prophetess Nonqawuse and the cattle-killing tragedy.
1857	Emgwali School for girls opens.
1861	Lovedale Press established.
1864	Mission councils introduced.
1866	Dr Jane Waterston arrives at Lovedale.
1867	Diamonds are discovered in Kimberley.
1870	Rev. Dr James Stewart becomes Principal of Lovedale.
	Theological education begins at Lovedale Institution.

1875	Pambani J Mzimba is ordained.
1877	Mission from Lovedale to Nyasaland commences.
	The translation of the Xhosa Bible is completed.
	Blythswood Institution opens.
1880–1920	The high imperial era.
	The high missionary era.
1880	The Free Church and United Presbyterian Presbyteries of Kaffraria prepare a preliminary report on the possibilities of union.
1880s	Gold is discovered on the Witwatersrand Reef.
1881	Mission councils disbanded.
1891	Rev. Edward Tsewu is called as minister to the Johannesburg congregation.
	A Presbyterian Federal Council is established to consider the possibility of union.
1893	Rev. Mzimba is sent to attend the jubilee celebrations of the Free Church of Scotland.
	The Women's Christian Association (WCA) is founded.
1896	Mission work is established in the Transvaal.
	Rev. Edward Tsewu secedes from the Scottish mission and establishes the Independent Native Presbyterian Church.
1897	The Presbyterian Church of South Africa (PCSA) is formed.
1898	Rev. P. J. Mzimba secedes from the Scottish mission and forms the Presbyterian Church of Africa (PCA).
1899–1902	The South African War.
1900	The Free Church of Scotland unites with the United Presbyterian Church of Scotland to form the United Free Church of Scotland (UFCoS).
1901	Mission councils are reintroduced.
1903–5	The South African Native Affairs Commission.
1904	First meeting of the South African General Missionary Conference.
1905	James Stewart dies.
1906	Rev. Dr James Henderson becomes Principal of Lovedale.
1910	Formation of the Union of South Africa.
	The World Missionary Conference takes place in Edinburgh.
1912	The South African Natives' National Congress (SANNC) is established.
1916	The South African Native College (later renamed the University of Fort Hare) is established.
1918	Black people are admitted as members of mission councils.
1920	United Free Church of Scotland FMC deputies, Rev. Frank Ashcroft and Mr Andrew Houston, are sent to South Africa to deal with the issue of uniting the two branches of the Scottish Mission in South Africa.

1923	The Bantu Presbyterian Church of South Africa is established.
	SANNC is renamed the African National Congress (ANC).
1929	The United Free Church of Scotland unites with the Church of Scotland.
	Amaculo ase Rabe, the Xhosa hymn book, is published.
1935	Discussions take place regarding the formation of an association for men.
1936	The Christian Council of South Africa is established.
1937	The Faith and Order Conference meet in Edinburgh.
1947	Partnership in mission becomes the policy of the Church of Scotland mission.
1948	The Nationalist Party comes to power.
	The World Council of Churches is formed.
1950	Group Areas Act passed.
1952	The Willingen Conference of the International Missionary Council meet.
	Passive resistance campaign.
1953	Bantu Education Act passed.
1954	The Girls' Association is established.
1956	Decision is taken to engage with the PCSA with a view to union.
1957	Native Laws Amendment Act passed.
1960	The ANC and PAC launch anti-Pass Law campaigns to be held on 21 March which leads to the Sharpeville massacre.
	The Cottesloe Consultation takes place.
1960–82	The forced removal policy is implemented.
1962	The policy for integration in South Africa is defined.
1963	The Federal Theological Seminary of Sothern Africa is established.
1964	The Foreign Mission Committee of the Church of Scotland is replaced with the Overseas Council.
1965	The PCSA challenges the BPCSA to ratify the resolution on union.
1968	The Christian Council becomes the South African Council of Churches.
	The Church Unity Commission is formed.
1969	The WCC establishes the Programme to Combat Racism.
1972	BPCSA affirms the CUC Declaration of Intention to unite.
	BPCSA withdraws from seeking union with the PCSA.
	University protests take place.
1973	The Church Accountant, Mr Matthew Stevenson, arrives in South Africa.
1974	Rt Rev. Gladwin T. Vika gives his Moderatorial Address, *Whither Bantu Presbyterian Church?*
	The Alice campus of the Federal Theological Seminary is expropriated.

1975	The BPCSA approves the union of the Congregational Adams College with the Presbyterian St Columba's College at the Federal Theological Seminary of Southern Africa (FedSem).
	A portfolio of Church of Scotland trust funds is handed over to the BPCSA.
1976	Soweto students protest against the enforcement of Afrikaans as the medium of instruction in schools.
1977	The BPCSA admits women to the offices of elder and minister.
1978	Rev. Charity Majiza is ordained on 13 May.
	Consultation between Church of Scotland and BPCSA regarding the disposition of assets derived from the sale of properties in South Africa.
	Matt Stevenson resigns.
1979	The Bantu Presbyterian Church of South Africa (BPCSA) is renamed The Reformed Presbyterian Church of Southern Africa.
1981	The Church of Scotland South Africa Joint Council is dissolved.
1983	The United Democratic Front (UDF) is founded.
1985–7	States of emergency are declared throughout South Africa.
1986	The BPCSA Ecumenical Relations Committee (ERC) is formed to oversee all developments in the sphere of ecumenical relations.
	The *Kairos Document* is published.
1993	The Federal Theological Seminary closes.
1994	The first democratic government is elected in South Africa.
1995	The Truth and Reconciliation Commission is established.
1998	Rev. Charity Majiza is appointed General Secretary of the South Council of Churches.
1999	The RPCSA and PCSA unite to form the Uniting Presbyterian Church of Southern Africa.

A Presbyterian Anthem

These words are generally believed to have been the first words Rev. Tiyo Soga uttered when he returned to South African soil from Scotland as the first black minister educated in Scotland (1857).

Lizalis' idinga lakho,	Fulfil your promise,
Thixo Nkosi yenyaniso,	Lord, God of truth!
Zonk' intlanga zalo mhlaba	Let all the nations of this earth
Mazizuze usindiso	receive salvation.
Amadolo kweli Lizwe	Let all knees in this world
Makagobe phambi kwakho.	Bend before you;
Zide zithi zonk' ilwimi,	Until all tongues
Ziluxel udumo lwakho	Confess your glory
Lawula, lawula, Yesu Nkosi,	Rule! Rule! Lord Jesus;
Koza ngawe ukonwaba;	Through you will come happiness,
Ngeziphithipithi zethu,	Through our confusion,
Yonakele imihlaba.	Lands have been corrupted.
Bona Izwe lakowethu,	Behold my fatherland;
Uxolel' izono zalo;	And forgive all its sins.
Ungathob' ingqumbo yakho	Don't release your wrath,
Luzeluf' usapho lwalo.	Let all its people die.
Yala singatshabalali,	Warn, so we do not perish,
Usiphile ukhanyiso;	you have given us light;
Bawo ungasibulali	Father, don't destroy us,
Ngokudela inyaniso.	For slighting the truth.
Nkosi, khawusikelele	O Lord, bless
Iimfundiso zezwe lethu;	The teachings of our land
Uze usivuselele,	Please revive us,
Siphuthume ukulunga.	That we may restore goodness.

Rev. Tiyo Soga: translated by Rev. Makhenkesi A. Stofile

Introduction

My first contact with the Bantu Presbyterian Church of South Africa (BPCSA, always known as the BPC) was in 1977. We had offered to serve the church overseas and had been approached Rev. Iain Moir, Africa Partnership Secretary of the Overseas Council of the Church of Scotland regarding a vacancy for Missionary-in-Charge of the world famous Lovedale Missionary Institution. Despite our initial concerns about working in apartheid South Africa we allowed our names to be presented to the BPC. I was about to complete my BD degree at Aberdeen University.

I was invited to go to Edinburgh to meet the Rt Rev. Jonas Khonyane, Moderator of the General Assembly of the BPC, who was on a visit to Scotland. Our meeting was cordial and I discovered some of the important background of the church I might go to serve.

The Overseas Council accepted our offer of service as a joint appointment and forwarded our names to the BPC which accepted us at their General Assembly in 1977. After a period at St Colm's College in Edinburgh (1977–8) we travelled to South Africa on 19 February 1978 and I was ordained a minister of the BPC on 12 March 1978 at Burnshill Mission by the Presbytery of the Ciskei. The rest is history . . .

This study is located within the discipline of the History of Christianity, a field that is broader than the traditional field of Church or Ecclesiastical History. The History of Christianity is a comprehensive field of scholarship that considers Christianity as an expression of faith that is found both within and beyond the institutional church. For example, in Africa, this is true of the phenomenon that is known as African Initiated Churches (AICs) which until recently were denied the name of churches and were often regarded as cults or sects and sometimes even as expressions of African Traditional Religion (ATR). As a discipline the History of Christianity draws on insights from the social sciences which moves it beyond its limited church theological definition. It also takes its relationship with the secular context seriously. Within the History of Christianity, this study engages the sub-field of the History of Mission Christianity. I believe that the history of Christianity is the history of the mission of Christianity.

I also believe, in line with the thinking of my Master's and Doctor of Theology (DTh) study mentor, the late Prof. Willem Saayman, in 'the intrinsic connectedness of unity and mission in the heart of the Gospel' (Saayman 1984: 2), following the thinking of Marty (1964: 102–3) who claimed that 'Unity produces mission produces unity produces mission etc.'. The dimensions of unity and mission became central to the design of this book.

Arising out of the Reforming tradition, Reformed churches are committed to the unity of the church. They never set out to disrupt the church during the Reformation period and remained committed to the principle of unity, despite the historical reality that they continued to engage in schism.

Mission is the essence of the church. My definition focuses on the activity of God in the world reconciling all of creation to Godself in which humans are called to participate. The main aim, therefore, is inclusivity and equity as opposed to some traditional dualistic bifurcations – superiority/inferiority, black/white, believers/unbelievers (*amaqaba*), good/evil and educated/ uneducated.

These together demonstrate the interdependence of mission and unity. However, historically this was not the case. With regard to Protestant missions, during the nineteenth century, mission had existed separately from the churches and resulted in a degree of estrangement and mistrust until, with the formation of autonomous churches in mission areas, there grew a desire for relationships with the churches of the West:

> The growing ecumenical impulse from the 'mission fields'. . . inevitably brought these missions to an encounter with the Church, being *the* theological context in which the interrelationship between unity and mission could – and must – be expressed. (Saayman 1984: 9)

The history of Christianity in Africa is the history of Christian mission in Africa. From the beginning of the Christian church, Christianity has been active in Africa reaching out, expanding the parameters of the faith, inculturating itself within the contexts where it settled. Mission necessarily implies migration. Christianity is a faith that is constantly *in transit* and Scottish Christian mission was exceptionally mobile, *en route* towards the kingdom of God. This was true of South Africa. Although there had been earlier Portuguese missions in South Africa from the fifteenth century, the first permanent mission was established by the Moravians in 1792 (Baur 1994: 17).

A Note on Sources

An important secondary source for this paper is David Burchell's 'The Origins of the Bantu Presbyterian Church in South Africa' (*South African Historical Journal,* 1977, 9: 39–58), which was the first attempt to trace the formation of the Bantu Presbyterian Church of South Africa (BPCSA). Although I have been interested in this subject since I studied for my Master's degree in 1995, I cannot verify several references in Burchell due to several reasons. The Lennox papers have been transferred from the Howard Pim Africana Library (HPAL) to the National Heritage and

Cultural Studies Centre (NAHECS), at the University of Fort Hare (UFH) and have been re-catalogued. The records of the Presbytery of Kaffraria and the Synod of Kafraria remain in the Howard Pim Africana Library, UFH. Several references could not be traced in the Henderson and Stormont papers at the Cory Library, Rhodes University. When Burchell was writing, the Henderson papers were unclassified. Classification has since been completed. None of the references to documents in the RPCSA Offices in Umtata could be traced either in 1996 or later. The material there was neither filed nor catalogued and several items have disappeared without trace since the references found in Burchell's work. Although attempts to contact David Burchell over the years have failed, there is no reason to doubt the integrity of his sources and references. Following the union of the Reformed Presbyterian Church in Southern Africa and the Presbyterian Church of Southern Africa in 1999 to form the Uniting Presbyterian Church in Southern Africa, the RPCSA office in Umtata was closed and the remaining church archives were transferred to the Cory Library for Historical Research at Rhodes University, Grahamstown, where they remain uncatalogued at the time of writing.

CHAPTER ONE

Background to this Study

Mission and Migration

Andrew Walls (2014: 19–37), the doyen of global mission history (Kalu et al. 2005: xi–xii), asserts the essential nature of mission as human participation in the *missio Dei*. Van Dyk (2011: 20) describes it as 'an irrepressible human urge'. People are called out from their secure situations to become 'perennial migrants' (Walls 2014: 20), agents of God's revelation, concurring with Richard Rohr's (2011: 21) assertion that 'someone has to make it clear to us that homes are not meant to live in but to be moved out from'. Coleman and Elsner (1995: 206) use the imagery of pilgrimage rather than migration, but with a similar understanding as: 'the experience of travel and the constant possibility of encountering the new . . .', while Műller (2011: 11) considers it a ritual engaged in by people 'who remain hopeful in the possibility of a future, preferable to the travails of the present'. All of these meanings indicate movement towards an end point – the kingdom of God.

Walls (2014: 21) distinguishes two types of migration; the Adamic and the Abrahamic models; the former indicates a situation of 'disaster deprivation and loss' through incurring a penalty as we discover in the biblical story of the Fall; the latter implies 'escape to a superlatively better future' through Abraham receiving a promise that through mission God would make him the father of the nations. Both types of migration model were present in the South African context. However, the result may not be so clear cut as the experience of the migrant in relation to the receiving culture is determined by the receiving community's 'own numbers and social cohesion'. Unfortunately, many migrants have discovered anything but a welcome in the global diaspora. Incoming missionary migrants to South Africa brought with them both their historical identity and memory and their differing theologies, factors which were determinative for the results of their mission.

Historically, Walls describes the 'Great European Migration' process in the modern period, which lasted from the beginning of the sixteenth century until the middle of the twentieth century. During its course, first hundreds and then thousands and eventually millions of people left Europe for lands beyond Europe. Some moved under compulsion, as refugees, indentured labourers, or convicts; some from lust for wealth or power. Most, however, were simply seeking a better life or a more just society than they found in Europe. Those of the original inhabitants (indigenous peoples, often a majority) unable or unwilling to adopt these traditions were effectively dispossessed and forced to the margins of a society that now lived by European cultural norms (Walls 2008: 193). Hanciles (2008: 119) attributes this more directly to 'the needs and purposive designs of European imperialism' facilitated by developing communication technology, ease of travel and the interstate system. The Marxist historian Eric Hobsbawm (1994: 119) describes it as:

> ... the greatest mass migration of history... Men and women migrated not only across oceans and international frontiers, but from country to city; from one region of the same state to another – in short from 'home' to the land of strangers and, turning the coin around, as strangers into others' home.

This mission was one result of the eighteenth century Evangelical Revival with its:

'acknowledgment of a society (Christendom) that while being Christian is insufficiently so'. It assumed the normativity of Christianity aligned with Western civilisation and aimed at conversion. It reflected a state of 'spiritual parity ... a consistent view of human solidarity in depravity [which] shielded the first missionary generation from some of the worst excesses of racism' (Walls 2014: 26).

Walls' statement: 'the missionary is a form of migrant' (Walls 2014: 26) can be applied both in a broad and specific sense of the definition of 'missionary' in the global and South African contexts (Williams 2008: 11). The South African Presbyterian mission, as is true of many others, was the result of '[t]he power wielders, in Christendom, once committed to the worldwide propagation of the Christian faith, now [seeing] the lands beyond Europe in essentially economic and strategic terms' (Walls 2014: 30). What Walls says about missionaries, became true in South Africa Presbyterianism:

> They often felt that western colonial governments failed to support them, or even actively obstructed their work. Where missionaries worked in the same territories as western migrants, there were often intractable problems in combining migrant and indigenous Christians in a single functioning ecclesiastical structure without subordinating the interests of the indigenous people to those of the migrants. (Walls 2014: 30)

In response to Walls' (2014: 22) affirmation in South Africa there were dramatic examples of migration leading pagan peoples to the faith – we will note later the impact of the Mfecane (Difiqane: forced removal) during the first half of the nineteenth century and the cattle-killing tragedy (1856–7) and their impact on the growth and development of mission in the Eastern Cape.

Presbyterianism in South Africa shares, to a degree, a similar history with those churches of European origin (CEO) which arrived in the early nineteenth century – Anglicans, Baptists, Congregationalists, Methodists and, somewhat later, Roman Catholics. The initial impetus was the desire to convert the heathen in a context where their mission would also support the expansion of the settler population and the colonial authorities with their quadruple aims of Christianisation, colonisation, commercialisation and civilisation. All of these were interlinked at different times, for varying periods and in numerous venues. In time, they all became part of the grand project of British imperialism in interdependent relationships. The prime focus of this book is to examine the role of Scottish Presbyterianism in this process.

This history of the Bantu Presbyterian Church of South Africa (BPCSA), which was renamed the Reformed Presbyterian Church of Southern Africa (RPCSA) in 1979, is represented by a long migratory journey which is ongoing although now within a uniting denomination. It offers a number of early examples of diaspora by means of migration which involves alienation from the home culture and integration within the adopted culture. This has been a constant in mission history. The original roots of the now Uniting Presbyterian Church in Southern Africa (UPCSA) are found in the Apostolic Church, the Swiss reformation and sixteenth century Scottish Presbyterianism. Like all of Christianity, its growth represents a migratory process. The largest part of present day Presbyterianism in southern Africa results from the coming together of two streams of Scottish descent, both of which had their beginnings in the Cape in the early nineteenth century. The PCSA stream began with the arrival of immigrant colonists and settlers in the Eastern and Western Cape, while the BPCSA/RPCSA stream began with the arrival of the immigrant Scottish mission in the Eastern Cape. It is this stream which is the primary concern of this study.

I write as a critical insider having been a minister of the BPCSA/RPCSA and a missionary of the Church of Scotland. This has enabled me to discern both the best and worst of this tradition of South African Presbyterianism.

At the present time, there is no history of Presbyterianism in Southern Africa and this work attempts to present the development of one significant Presbyterian church tradition in southern Africa – the Scottish mission tradition which led to the formation in 1923 of the Bantu Presbyterian Church of South Africa, which was renamed the Reformed Presbyterian Church in Southern Africa in 1979 and united with the Presbyterian Church of Southern Africa in 1999 to form the Uniting Presbyterian Church of Southern Africa. This study begins with the arrival of the Scottish mission and ends with the union of the RPCSA with the PCSA in 1999.

This is not a traditional chronological narrative as I have chosen to adopt a thematic approach. Those looking for details of individual congregations – their birth, development and current state – will not find them here. To provide such detail would have resulted in an unmanageable volume. The availability of sources has also been a determining factor here (see below). In addition, some chapters required more attention due to their relative importance to the overall subject of the book. This may explain the seeming discrepancy in the dating of the chapters and the varying lengths of the chapters as well as the ordering of events.

Following an introductory chapter, Chapter two examines the genesis of the Scottish mission to South Africa. Chapter three focuses on an iconic example of an early indigenous leader. The role of mission councils was important in the development of the mission and is considered in Chapter four. This is followed by a chapter which introduces the theme of resistance to missionary advance in the form of secessions. This theme is considered further in Chapter six in the rejection of mission Christianity which provided something of a stimulus to the formation of an autonomous church. Chapter seven discusses an early attempt to form one united Presbyterian church in South Africa with settler/colonial Presbyterianism while Chapter eight discusses the response of the Scottish mission and preparations for the establishment of an autonomous Presbyterian church. Chapter nine outlines the process of the formation of the Bantu Presbyterian Church in South Africa while Chapter ten describes the actual process of the inauguration of the new denomination. The early mission work of the new denomination is discussed in Chapter eleven and in Chapter twelve the relationship with the Presbyterian Church of South Africa is revisited. Chapter twelve considers wider ecumenical involvements of the BPCSA in the broad context of apartheid. The demise of the ubiquitous mission councils is the topic of Chapter thirteen paving the way for authentic autonomy. The life and work of the BPCSA is the subject of Chapter fourteen both internally and in multi-layered mission outreach. Part of the BPCSA's missionary outreach led to its engagement with socio-political issues as is demonstrated in Chapter fifteen. The phenomenal role played by women, often unacknowledged and unrewarded, forms the subject matter of the final chapter.

The Origins of the Mission in Scotland and the Eternal Land Issue

The Scottish Mission in South Africa has a distinguished history. This chapter traces the origins of the Presbyterian churches in Scotland's mission to South Africa by examining its antecedents in Scotland and its early development from 1824–65. It then considers the complex issue of land related to missionary activity.

The Reformation

The Preface to the *Scots Confession* (1560) states: 'And this glad tidings of the kingdom shall be preached through the whole world for a witness to all nations, and then shall the end come'. The Confession closes with the prayer, '. . . let all the nations cleave to the true knowledge of Thee' (Cochrane 1963: 184). This was clearly consistent with the *ad fontes* approach of the Reformation which sought to establish a link to the roots of the Christian faith and mission as exemplified in the early church. Clearly, it was the intention of the nascent reformed Scottish church that mission to the world *was* a priority. However, for more than two centuries, this did not materialise. The severe shortage of ministers may have been responsible, in part, for this state of affairs as well as the internal political situation in Scotland. While Ross (1986: 33) acknowledges the insignificant missionary impulse and indifference on the part of the established church from the sixteenth-century Reformation up to the late eighteenth century, he claims that mission has always been integral to the life of Christianity 'despite its high and low points'.

Prelude to Action in Scotland

The secular context

During the eighteenth century Scotland began to experience a substantial change in society. Intellectually, Scotland had become the centre of 'a cultural and intellectual florescence, reaching its peak between the 1750s and the 1790s. This has come to be known as the Scottish Enlightenment' (Erlank 2001: 142). The Industrial Revolution contributed to increased urbanisation, population growth, scientific discoveries (Hobsbawm 1962: 46), democratic universities (Hobsbawm 1962: 45; Devine 2011: 30–1) and political reform besides the ongoing effects of the highland clearances described by Mackie (1964: 315–18) as 'unhappy emigration and still more unhappy "Clearances"' (Mackie 1964: 315). Related to the Scottish diaspora, of which the missionary movement was a significant part, Thomson (2008: 51) has claimed: 'Of all the peoples of the United Kingdom it is the Scots' contribution to the empire that stands out as disproportionate. The Scots were the first people of the British Isles to take on an imperial mentality and possibly the longest to sustain one.'

The ecclesiastical context

However, it is impossible to refer to the ethos of the Scots without taking account of their religious values. Devine (2011: 191) counters a false view that the influence of the churches was declining by the nineteenth century: 'In fact, far from religious erosion, the Victorian era [1837–1901] saw quite a remarkable and hitherto unprecedented fusion between Christian ethos and civic policy'. And this ethos was fueled by evangelicalism which was to be a powerful contributing factor to the 'Disruption' in 1843 between the Moderates and Evangelicals in the Church of Scotland. This led to separation and the formation of the Free Church of Scotland (FCoS): 'It was evangelicalism above all which cemented the relationship between religion at home and the overseas missions' (Devine 2011: 192).

'Moderate' and 'Evangelical' Theology

But, the matter was somewhat more complex, as two views on mission had developed. Within the Moderate camp '[r]ational conviction had taken the place of the necessary intervention of the Spirit' (Maxwell 2001: 126) with the view that the rational superiority of Christianity was used to promote educational missions under the umbrella of economic development, social commitment and historical progress. James Stewart of Lovedale Missionary Institution in the Eastern Cape of South Africa was to declare in this regard: 'how important a part education plays for the gospel to pass through the intellect to the heart' (Monthly Record 1964: 482–3). For Stewart, education was a vital component of conversion (Erlank 2001: 165). This was in comparison with his predecessor William Govan's Evangelical approach (Thompson 2012: 142–3). Hewat (1960: 4) quotes John Buchan: 'They preached the forgotten lesson of the importance of the human reason in all human endeavour, and they strove to link religion to those other spheres from which it had been too long divorced'. Buchan further stated that: 'a religion without enthusiasm is a religion without life and without hope of growth'. This approach did not bode well for the missionary enterprise. The emphasis was on projects which were intellectually based and in tune with rational Enlgihtenment thinking, rather than the emotive approach to religion which was the preserve of the Evangelicals. This represented a providentialistic form of determinism.

'The typical Evangelical ... was strong where the Moderate was weak ... He was not afraid of enthusiasm, though his enthusiasm, as a rule, expressed itself in terms of thought and language that had more affinity with a past age than with the new worlds that were appearing' (Hewat 1960: 4). The Evangelical group favoured a strong unequivocal commitment to the preached word leading to an emphasis on translation work in missions (Maxwell 2001: 127). It argued from a biblical perspective that the proclamation of the gospel was the priority. Yet, either consciously or not, evangelical mission became instrumental in promoting Western imperial expansion (Bosch 1991: 288).

This debate continued until 1796, when a proposal was presented to the General Assembly of the Church of Scotland to begin overseas missionary work. Despite strong support, the proposal was defeated on the resolution:

> To spread abroad the knowledge of the Gospel amongst barbarous and heathen nations seems to be highly preposterous, in so far as philosophy and learning must in the nature of things take the precedence: and that, while there remains at home a single individual without the means of religious knowledge, to propagate it abroad would be improper and absurd. (du Plessis 1911: 182)

This was the case despite an earlier decision to encourage the collection of funds for work amongst American Indians. Du Plessis (1911: 182) attributes the formation of voluntary missionary societies (see below) to this disinterest on the part of the church. However, Hewat (1960: 2) points to the poverty of the Scottish nation rather than disinterest as the reason for lack of action. This is supported by the further decision of the General Assembly to pray that God's promise be fulfilled 'in giving His Son the heathen for His inheritance' though it was deemed 'highly inexpedient' at that time to accord such ventures financial support. It further agreed that it would 'embrace with zeal and thankfulness any future opportunity of contributing by their exertions to the propagation of the Gospel of Christ which Providence may hereafter open' (Hewat 1960: 6). The Moderates won the day at this point and as time progressed their view predominated as was clear from a sermon preached by John Inglis in 1818 which prioritised 'learning and education in order to hasten the civil societies [e.g. in South Africa] in question towards the historic moment of acceptance of Christianity' (Maxwell 2001: 135). However, the Evangelicals were a growing force and would soon emerge as 'more socially responsive and [they] blended science and evangelical Christianity into a theory designed to combat the social evils of the early nineteenth century' (Erlank 2001: 144–5). The evangelical leader, Rev. Thomas Chalmers, was a significant catalyst in bringing the two views together with his perspective that faith could precede civilisation. Early in the twentieth century, a senior South African missionary, Rev. David Stormont, offered his assessment of the situation:

> The rise of an enthusiastic religious life in England [the Evangelical Revival] which spread to Scotland gave that strength to the opponents of Moderatism that ultimately changed the attitude [sic] the public mind towards the spread of the Christian Faith in heathen countries. ('A chapter in South African mission work', *Daily Despatch*, 21 July 1910, Cory Library for Historical Research, Rhodes University, Grahamstown, PR2798).

Meanwhile, those who were motivated by a sense of urgency to inaugurate a global mission approach therefore had to do this outside the formal structures of the church. This led to the emergence and phenomenal development of interdenominational voluntary societies.

The voluntary societies

Bosch (2011: 327) argues that voluntarism, which influenced the development of missionary societies, had its roots in 'the Spirit of enterprise and initiative spawned by the Enlightenment'. The underlying ideology was that of 'social and political egalitarianism' (Bosch 2011: 328). Voluntary missionary societies developed in Europe and in the USA. They were essentially non-academic laypersons' organisations (Ross 1986: 38), interdenominational (at least at the beginning) and were 'humanitarian societies' (Hewat

1960: 8). 'This Protestant form of organisation – free, open, responsible, embracing all classes, both sexes, all ages, the masses of the people – is peculiar to modern times, and almost to our age' (Beaver RP [ed.] in Walls 1996: 242). Women played a vital role in these societies and found a place here 'far earlier than they could decently appear in most other walks of life' (Walls 1988: 151 in Bosch 2011: 328) if they were appointed as missionaries on their own merit. Pre-eminent among these in the United Kingdom was the London Missionary Society (LMS) formed in 1795. Despite what is said above, Hewat (1960: 8) claims it was because of the inability of people to stimulate the churches' interest in foreign mission that these societies emerged as a purely voluntary activity. Yet, Walls claims that missionary societies developed because of the organisational and operational inability of the churches. They had no 'machinery . . ., to do the tasks' (Walls 1996: 246–7). In this way voluntary societies may be considered subversive (Walls 1996: 249). And so missionary agencies frequently took the form of voluntary societies (Walls 1996: 260).

Following the General Assembly's negative decision in 1796, the Scottish Missionary Society and the Glasgow Missionary Society (GMS) were formed in 1796 and took up the cause of foreign missions. Their membership comprised committed Christian women and men who came, largely, from the lower middle and skilled working classes which also provided many missionaries (Ross 1986: 38). Women not only had a role but a place in the leadership of such societies (Walls 1996: 250, 253). They had been influenced by the mid-eighteenth century Evangelical Revival (Hofmeyr & Pillay 1994: 42) which had stimulated an increased awareness of sin and a 'joyful realisation of forgiveness' through God's grace in Christ (Burleigh 1960: 309) and had given a fresh lease of life to the churches. Ross (1986: 33) argues that the growth of the modern missionary movement 'coincided with the economic and political emergence of Britain as a dominant power in the world' through industrialisation and colonialisation which led to 'the simple identification of Christian missions as the cultural and spiritual arm of European Imperialism'.

The GMS held to an 'evangelical conservative theology that in the racial relationships of South Africa were regarded as "liberal"', i.e. they were evangelicals who held a '"liberal" view of missions' (van der Spuy 1971: 3, referring to a report drawn up by the GMS, dated 1 March 1796). Van der Spuy (1971: 4) believes this approach stimulated the hope of developing the potential of human nature through education and evangelism (keystones of Scottish mission) in opposition to 'a pessimistic view that regards human nature as unchangeable'. GMS liberalism is described as an openness to fresh ideas and an abhorrence of bigotry; it is related to liberalism in the political sphere in Scotland. Walls (1996: 242) asserts that:

> . . . such associations could only arise in countries which had an open, responsible form of government, where Protestantism had prepared

the way for civil liberty which arose from seizing the opportunities offered by a particular phase of western political, economic and social development.

In 1824, as the result of the tireless efforts of the protagonists of overseas missions, the General Assembly of the Church of Scotland gave its blessing to the cause of foreign missions. However, the internal ecclesiastical situation in Scotland was about to face problems which would have far-reaching consequences for the church both at home and abroad.

The 'Disruption'

The 'Disruption' occurred in Scotland in 1843 after ten years of conflict between those who adhered to the Establishment principle, i.e. 'the Church by law established' (Burleigh 1960: 266; Cheyne 1993: 1) and those who supported the voluntary principle. This dispute concerned the relationship of the church to the state. Arising out of the 1829 government proposal for a Bill for the relief of Roman Catholics, Rev. Andrew Marshall, Secession minister in Kirkintilloch, preached against ecclesiastical establishments as unscriptural and in support of the church and its mission being financed 'solely by the liberality of its faithful people' (Burleigh 1960: 325). Marshall attacked all forms of establishment as being contrary to the authentic mission of the church. This practice of the dissenting churches became the voluntary principle which promoted the idea of a secular state.

The two issues which brought the matter to a head were patronage and the 'Claim of Right'. The former concerned the right of a landowner to impose a minister of his choice on a congregation and parish on the land which he owned (Cheyne 1993: 3). It is interesting to note the ubiquity of land issues in matters of faith and religion as we shall see below in the South African context. The latter issue asserted the spiritual independence of the church. In 1843 the government refused to repeal the Patronage Act and to acquiesce in the demands of the Claim of Right. The 'Disruption' occurred when those who could not accept the privileges of establishment any longer left the Established Church of Scotland and formed the Free Church of Scotland (FCoS).

Rev. Dr Thomas Chalmers, leader of the Free Church body, claimed that the Free Church did not aim at voluntarism. He claimed it was a national church: 'We are advocates for a national recognition and national support of religion – and we are not voluntaries'. He aimed to produce an *alter ego* of the established national Church of Scotland 'relying on the resources which their faithful people would supply' (Burleigh 1960: 354). Saayman (1996: 32) has rightly said that the Free Church had 'a rigidly conservative and Calvinist interpretation of theology, and also had a tendency to regard itself as a national church'. Hofmeyr and Pillay (1994: 73) argue that the 'Disruption' 'ultimately led to the split in missionary work and the formation of the Bantu Presbyterian Church' in 1923. However, it would also be true to say it sowed the seeds of the Mzimba Secession from the Free Church Mission some years later in 1898. This newly formed Free Church of Scotland espoused the cause of foreign mission as the result of the influence of its voluntarist members and supporters.

Later developments

The FCoS supported foreign missions from 1843. At that time, almost all South African missionaries belonged to the Free Church; they were probably theologically conservative (Saayman 1996: 32), being evangelicals. In 1845, the GMS transferred its work to the Free Church's Foreign Missions Committee (FMC). In 1847, the United Secession Church and the Relief Church came together to form the voluntary anti-establishment United Presbyterian Church of Scotland (UPCoS). It was co-operation between the FCoS and the UPCoS in favour of disestablishment as well as in other areas of church life including missions that led in 1900 to their union as the United Free Church of Scotland. The clock turned full circle when the United Free Church joined with the established Church of Scotland to form the Church of Scotland in 1929.

But this is to bypass the situation in South Africa to which we now turn by considering the ubiquitous problems relating to land in both the secular and religious context.

Land as a Factor in the South African Mission

Missions, be they static or migratory, cannot exist without land. They require geographical bases where a process of inculturation can begin and from which they can migrate centrifugally. This sets the scene for our exploration. It is impossible to study these processes of development in isolation from the wider context. This is a story of the history of Christianity in Southern Africa which has deep economic, social, political, cultural and religious roots and implications. And nowhere is this seen more clearly than when we come to discuss the issue of land, which is also a spiritual matter for black Africans. Land is an issue where the sacred and secular cannot be distinguished. In Africa there was no such thing as individual land tenure; land was the property of the community, held under the supervision and stewardship of the chief who exercised both secular and sacred functions in this regard. Mofokeng (1977: 49) explains both the historical and contemporary value of land in an African context:

> The identity of agrarian people is tied to the land and expressed in the songs they sing, the art they create, their celebrations, their rituals and rites of passage. Religion is imbued with elements of life and the land, in the form of planting time and harvest festivals, sacramental rites of

water and grain and the fruit of the land. Land has the greatest moral and spiritual significance, and constitute[s] a way of life.

Prior to the arrival of Western influences, land was there for all to use as needed; it was a community resource. When it had served its purpose, the people moved on to greener pastures, leaving only their deceased ancestors to protect the fallow land as it replenished itself (cf. Gen 1: 28 where dominion indicated care for the land and human responsibility). This was voluntary migration. The land was described, not altogether incorrectly by a Reverend Impey during the 1850s, as 'one vast commonage where every man lives where he likes' (Peires 1989: 290). Life, by definition, was migratory due to the condition and fertility of the land.

When settlers, traders, civil servants and military personnel arrived, also as the result of voluntary migration, the nature of sacred land was transformed into a predominantly economic commodity:

> Small populations migrating to develop a territory considered void of settlement depending on historical setting, circumstances and perspective are referred to as settlers or colonists, while populations displaced by immigration and colonisation are called *refugees*. (Shiferaw 2012: 34)

Land was divided and subdivided and distributed to immigrants as the result of their previous migrations, and removed from the public domain. The authority and guardianship of the chief was replaced with title deeds. Much of this land was acquired under false or misleading pretences and differing understandings regarding the concept of the ownership of land. One example from the Presbyterian context on the perspective of land acquired for church purposes will suffice. Before the establishment of Lovedale Missionary Institution in 1841, Chief Tyhali gave the Free Church of Scotland a site in the Victoria East district for the work of the Church in education, medicine, agriculture and other missionary purposes:

> The land on which [the present University of] Fort Hare was built had originally been given by the Xhosa chief, Tyhali (together with his senior brothers, Sandile and Maqoma), to Scottish Presbyterian missionaries to build Lovedale, which began, as a boarding school open to all races, in 1841. The hope of establishing a university was conceived and cherished by James Steward [sic] and others at Lovedale, and a portion of the original Lovedale allocation was given for building the old Fort Hare [as a military establishment]. In 1961 another portion of the original grant was given for the [Federal Theological] Seminary, and it lies immediately below 'Sandile's Kop'. (Wilson 1974: 179)

Shepherd (1971: 12) aptly comments that 'For agricultural purposes over forty acres of good land, sloping down from the site of the seminary buildings, were obtained, thanks to the good offices of Chief Tyhali.' Writing in

1894, the Principal of Lovedale, Dr James Stewart, (1894: 1) commented: 'The site which the missionaries received was at first a bare hill-side and a flat valley'. Then, he commented: 'After education had been given free for many years, it was thought, some time ago, that the native people themselves should begin to aid the work and relieve the home church'. This change took effect in 1871 and although it was unpopular, it was accepted. There is a distinct lack of clarity regarding the original terms of occupation. One belief, propagated in the period leading to Ciskeian independence during the 1970s, though it may have had an earlier source, was that an agreement was made that the sons of the local chiefs would be educated free of charge. However, as costs rose, this agreement was reneged on by the missionaries, causing distrust between the missionaries and the chiefs. There is no extant evidence of this. Resulting from settler and colonial incursions, pressure on land led to 'alienation of land to whites' (Wilson 1976: 7). This view of land indicates the difference in land values. White migrants valued land as an exchangeable economic commodity, to be legally defined, demarcated, fenced, restricted, protected to exclude intruders, and passed on to future family members through inheritance. It had little or no religious significance. Howard Lamar and Leonard Thompson (1981: 7) offer an instructive view of a migratory frontier as:

> ... a territory or zone of interpenetration between two previously distinct societies. Usually, one of the societies is indigenous to the region, or, at least, has occupied it for many generations; the other is intrusive. The frontier 'opens' in a given zone when the first representatives of the intrusive society arrive; it 'closes' when a single political authority has established hegemony over the zone.

The earliest disputes occurred between Dutch and Xhosa stock farmers in the 1770s who encountered and either absorbed or decimated Khoisan hunters and herders with whom they had been trading partners and with whom they had also established political and social contacts (Switzer 1993: 43, 44, 45). This set the scene for further intrusion as the British assumed power in the Cape, as slavery was abolished, increasing:

> [t]he demand for labour, and the intra-tribal warfare among the between the Xhosa chiefs, Ngqika and Ndlambe. During the early decades of the nineteenth century, chief Maqoma was hounded continually by colonial raids and expelled from his territory in 1829 ... In 1834, faced with increased military pressure from the colony, Maqoma and Tyali had no alternative but to take up arms in an attempt to prevent further dispossession. (Stapleton 1994: 9)

This process continued for more than twenty years (Stapleton 1994: 164–5).

The Wars of Dispossession, which lasted from the late eighteenth century until the late nineteenth century, were an aggressive process of 'extirpating and pushing back the native inhabitants' (Hobsbawm 1987: 63) which led to the alienation of the people from their land, and have to be seen in the context of the geography of the land. From the Western Cape to Natal, the land is traversed by numerous rivers (Hofmeyr & Pillay 1994: xvii, 9, 48) – Breede, Gouriutz, Gamtoos, Sundays, Bushmans, Great Fish, Keiskamma, Chalumna, Buffalo, Nxerunhi, Gqunube, Khwelera, Great Kei, Gxarha, Mbashe, Gora, Mtata, Tugela and Pongola – all flowing from the north-west to the south-east where they enter the Indian Ocean. They provided natural boundaries beyond which, as the wars progressed, the local Xhosa and other Nguni peoples were forced to retreat or migrate in the face of the encroachment of the settlers and their military supporters: 'Cathcart, like Smith [governors of the Cape] had proclaimed his intention of chasing the Ngqika Xhosa across the Kei and hence beyond the bounds of British territory' (Peires 1987: 28). The landscape is also peppered with military forts, e.g. Forts Brown, Willshire, Beaufort, Cox, Frederick, Grey (Macgregor 2009: 1), Hare, Murray, Thomson, Peddie, England, Armstrong, White, Glamorgan, Selwyn, Murray and Fordyce – for the settlers' protection. Thus, the indigenous people became refugees in their own land. Lord Charles Somerset, Governor of the Cape, viewed the settlers as a solution to intermittent raids:

> The farms of 100 acres allocated to the settlers were substantially smaller than the 6,000 acre *trekboer* farms. The idea was to provide a comparatively dense settler population on the banks of the lower Fish River. (Villa-Vicencio & Grassow 2009: 50)

Individual land tenure was introduced to the Eastern Cape *amaMfengu* people by governor Cathcart and further promoted by Sir George Grey during the 1850s (Peires 1987: 60) with the intention of 'completing the economic liberation of the individual from the communal authority of the chief' (Peires 1987: 32).

The *amaMfengu* themselves, along with the Thembu, were migrants from the north who as a result of the *Mfecane* (crushing, disruption, scattering, forced dispersal, forced migration) had been settled in the Eastern Cape, mainly around the Peddie area, from the 1820s following the 'African Great Trek'. Their name is derived from the Xhosa *siyamfengusa,* meaning 'we are wanderers seeking refuge'. They became grateful and willing supporters of the colonists and missionaries who saw them as potential allies on whom they capitalised. This policy was a divisive issue and undermined the authority of the chiefs. It sought to prevent those with communal land tenure before the 1856–7 cattle-killing tragedy, and those whose labour contracts had expired, returning to their land, from repossessing it (Peires 1987: 290–6). The intention was to force people into village compounds composed of inhospitable land (Peires 1987: 294). This was achieved in October 1858 (Peires 1987: 295). White immigrants were settled on farms of 2,000 acres while blacks, for the most part, received 4-acre plots. For the whites, this was migration in the form of deliverance from encroachment in the Western Cape. Thus white settlement was facilitated and black dispossession assured (Peires 1987: 328, 329). The Scottish missionary Robert Niven, writing to John Philip, superintendent of the London Missionary Society's stations in South Africa, complained of the 'evil of depriving them of so much land and giving Europeans a position in the little that is left, which will, I fear, end in the Caffres becoming a nation of degraded servants on their own soil' (Quoted in Mostert 1992: 949). This situation is well summarised by Hobsbawm: 'if Christianity insisted on the equality of souls, it underlined the inequality of bodies . . . It was something done by whites for natives, and paid for by whites' (Hobsbawm 1996: 71). Villa-Vicencio and Grassow (2009: xv) summarise the outcome clearly:

> The missionaries, many of whom lived either on the contested margins of the colony, or, in some instances, beyond its frontiers, found themselves frequently caught between the interests of the peoples among whom they worked and the pressures exerted on them from the colony. As Europeans themselves, the conflict between these two sets of competing interests cut right through the consciousness of what they were doing. For the most part they sided with their colonial heritage and roots, but in some significant instances, their identification with the indigenous people led them to take extremely unpopular stands against both Boer and the British colonial authority.

Ultimately, black people became virtual refugees in the land of their birth and responded to missionary incursions by adopting and inculturating those elements which resonated with their own system of beliefs and institutions or requirements. Then government policy led to enforced migration through the policy of forced removals. So we can see how the land issue provided a backdrop to the development of the historic mission.

Conclusion

This chapter has introduced the topic and has given the background to the development of the Scottish mission leading to the formation of the Bantu Presbyterian Church in 1923 and its subsequent development.

CHAPTER TWO

The Origins and Early Development of Scottish Presbyterian Mission in South Africa, 1824–65

The Context

The South African context in which mission work developed, first in the Eastern Cape, was in the creation of a settler community where the indigenous peoples were forced to move eastwards and northwards to allow for the land needs of the settlers. These settlers were encroaching on land traditionally occupied by various ethnic groups and helped to create neutral territory between the Fish and Keiskamma Rivers between 1829 and 1835. This brought about a resistance movement often called the Wars of Dispossession which lasted for almost 100 years (1779–1889). This, along with the cattle-killing disaster of 1856–7, resulted in the destabilisation of the Eastern Cape for much of the nineteenth century (Cory MS 7514n). The authority of the chiefs was undermined if not destroyed and the change, allied to the diminution of chiefs' role in the allocation of land, produced a volatile situation in which missionaries sought to do their work in destabilised African societies. The main area affected was the Eastern Cape which was under pressure from the encroachments of white settlers expanding their territory eastwards from the Western Cape and from Algoa Bay, particularly following the arrival of the 1820 settlers. This was expressed in wars against the colonial authorities and accommodation with Christianity.

The African context of the Eastern Cape, in particular, was dynamic as it had for some time been accommodating itself to an ever-enlarging global domain through the intrusion of both British and African communities. It had incorporated the refugees from the early nineteenth century *Mfecane* (forced migration), the *amaMfengu* and the *amaGqunukhwebe* who became intermediaries and emissaries of the novel western symbolic universe or worldview as it was established. Lovedale Institution was one such site where the *amaMfengu* were settled and impacted on the new worldview. Despite this the *amaXhosa* inhabited a hitherto relatively static world where strangers and aliens were incorporated into a stable community. With the coming of white missionaries, settlers and colonialists, proselytisation became evident within the traditional African worldview helping to deny the validity of the new rival universe by promoting the values of the intruding dominant and dominating European colonial worldview (Berger & Luckman

1967: 130). Education was a critical means of incorporating blacks into the missionaries' universe; they also employed 'native agents' in this process. Christianising was the overt curriculum; civilising through character formation (see Duncan 2003b: 188–97) was the covert agenda. This was both a religious and a political agenda as many missionaries became government agents and advisers, and consequently collaborators whose function was to oversee the incorporation of indigenous peoples into the European worldview. This made the process ideological and the outcome of the 'collision' of the two universes was determined by crude military power (Ashley 1989: 36), rather than by negotiation, against which the *amaXhosa* could not maintain their traditional worldview and lifestyle. This produced the response which aimed to restrict the African victims within the boundaries of their new universe or worldview; deviant or innovative interpretations of the new universe needed to be contained as in incorporating misfits of Xhosa society into mission stations. The beginning of the success of mission education was presaged by the war of dispossession (1850–3) and the cattle-killing movement (1856–7). This led to education becoming the main tool in the destruction of the African worldview as children were taught to regard 'their customs as obnoxious to Christianity and civilisation' (Ashley 1989: 38).

Dependence and Independence in Mission

While it is not the task of the mission historian to read back into the past, Verkuyl (1978: 174) made a significant comment of missio-historical value in terms of dependency/independency within the Reformed tradition. He argued that it should: 'pay close heed to the cry of the various churches around the world for a greater opportunity to be themselves'. This relates directly to the issue of dependency/ independency in mission. This was not a novel issue during the formation of the Bantu Presbyterian Church of South Africa (BPCSA). It had been an emerging theme at the Edinburgh World Missionary Conference in 1910. Brian Stanley (2009: 91) has described it in the title of one of the chapters in his work on Edinburgh 1910: '"Give us friends!": The voice of the younger churches'. This call emanated from Bishop Vedanayagam Samuel Azariah and called for parity in relationships, for friendships cannot exist or develop where there are unequal stances. Here, in essence was the clarion call for the policy which was later to become known as partnership in mission.

Historians have increasingly emphasised that Africans were not passive victims of colonisation, oppression and segregation, but were involved in a wide range of inventive political responses and innovative forms of action (cf. Comaroff & Comaroff 1991, 1997).

> ... At the same time, the limits of nationalist and working-class organisation have been recognised. Africans could not mount any coordinated political action which might challenge the state. In many

senses, the rural areas rather than the cities were the primary focus of political conflict in the 1920s ... the incomplete transformation of African societies, together with the thrust of state policy, opened areas of compromise in the reserves where opportunities for African advance sometimes seemed more tangible. Some popular movements were actually separatist in character. The accommodation reached ultimately helped to defuse conflict in the inter-war years at the height of segregation. (Beinart 1994: 108)

But this was not only a socio-economic-politico matter, for it was also predominantly true in the rural areas that:

... the conversion of the heathen must be followed by the institution of a Church for the converts. Congregations must become self-supporting. Aspirations towards full independence would inevitably follow and the 'mother' Church must not try to frustrate them. Nor must it decolonise the converts or destroy their indigenous culture. Therefore, an independent and separate Church was the obvious answer. (Hinchliffe 1966: 201)

But this was not just a matter of converted indigenous people becoming self-supporting but also self-propagating and self-governing (Venn & Anderson in Bosch 1991: 331; cf. Reese 2010: 160). And more recently the call has been for indigenous churches also to be self-theologising (Hiebert 1985: 196) as an integral part of their missionary outreach. However, this was present from the earliest times as Africans sought, not just to reject mission Christianity, but also to forge a distinctly new form of African Christianity. It was in these complex political and ecclesiastical contexts, by 1923, that the time had arrived for black Presbyterian Christians to become and be a church denomination fit for purpose to continue God's mission in South Africa. Yet, the path towards achieving this laudable vision was complex and far from straightforward as issues of dependence and independence interpenetrated the development of the mission.

Our story of missionary advance is constantly characterised by the dependency versus independency syndrome. Veteran missionary Roland Allen concluded that:

... there are everywhere three very disquieting symptoms: (1) Everywhere Christianity is still an exotic [plant] ... (2) Everywhere our missions are dependent ... (3) Everywhere we see the same types ... So far then was see our missions exotic, dependent, uniform, we begin to accuse ourselves of failure. (Allen 1929: 141–2)

In every case it was a replica of the same-old, same-old model of the establishment and fostering of dependent Christian communities. Reese (2010: 1) defines dependency as 'the unhealthy reliance on foreign resources that accompanies the feeling that churches and institutions are unable to function without outside assistance'. Western missionary bodies imposed this on young missions and churches which became long term policy. This restricted the possibility of them becoming truly indigenised churches. It also prevented them from formulating their own distinctive theological emphases. This was fostered through the deployment of finance and personnel in pursuit of the aims and objectives of educational, medical, agricultural, industrial and other forms of mission, besides spiritual/pastoral mission. This need not have been so. Clearly, poor African Christians were dependent on external support. However, this was a weapon to dominate and control them as missionaries built dynastic empires (e.g. the Ross family in the Eastern Cape, South Africa). Control and dependence were two sides of the same coin.

It is suggested that: 'Dependency is an unintended part of the colonial legacy' (Reese 1985: 3); yet Reese (1985: 2) suggests that: 'the problem of dependency in mission churches remains a chronic one'. It is difficult to attribute innocence as part of the motivation for this practice when it was contrary to the sending church policy. Whether this is true or not, this facilitated the colonial exercise of power and control of indigenous peoples and foreign 'resources'. Secular historian, Eric Hobsbawm (1987: 5) confirmed this in his claim that the age of empire, also known as the 'high imperial era' and the 'high missionary era' (1880–1920), evidenced a world separated into:

> two sectors combined into one global system, the developed and the lagging, the dominant and the dependent, the rich and the poor . . . The (much larger) second world was united by nothing except its relations with, that is to say its potential or actual dependency, the first.

Independence, on the other hand, required that missionaries step back, where they remained in place, and allow local people to decide and execute policy with a minimum of interference.

Bengt Sundkler and Christopher Steed (2000: 621) have given classic expression to the dilemma by using the concepts of Time and Expectation:

> In the Churches the message about Time was largely that it was 'not yet'. Henry Venn's and Rufus Anderson's programme in the 1850s implied African self-government and eventual 'euthanasia' of missions, but when the question of self-government was brought up in the councils and committees of the Churches, the answer was 'Not Yet'. Not that this view was an exclusively White view. It permeated the African synods as well, enfeebling and debilitating.

Referring specifically to the impact of the Ethiopian movement, Steed commented:

> The Ethiopian Church Movement was an elemental protest against what was seen as delay and even deceit by the missionaries and against

a patronizing attitude of the White population in general. (Sundkler & Steed 2000: 835)

The lack of a facilitative, enabling and supportive approach exposed the deficiencies in the mission. The later decades of the nineteenth century and early decades of the twentieth witnessed the development of Ethiopian-type churches in response to the outcomes of missionary domination. Some retained the doctrine, liturgy, dress and polity of their previous masters but they chose this for themselves; it was no longer imposed on them. They also developed indigenous forms of expression and took great risks of failure in terms of administration of finance and property due to lack of training and inexperience. Duncan (1997) has claimed that secessions stimulated the movement towards the formation of autonomous churches. But secessions actually happened in accord with the three-self policy although this was itself an American/European concept. This was what happened with the formation of the Bantu Presbyterian Church of South Africa in 1923. But this is to pre-empt an intriguing story.

The Beginning of British Mission Work in South Africa

Reformed mission Christianity first arrived in the Eastern Cape in 1799 with Dr Johannes van der Kemp of the London Missionary Society who worked among the *amaRharhabe-Xhosa* for a short period. The name of Chief Rharhabe was adopted by black South Africans as the term for their African brand of Presbyterianism. Hence the church became a new focus of the people's loyalty and identity. Van der Kemp moved towards the Eastern Cape and settled for a brief time with Chief Ngqika. Conflict with the authorities and settlers led to him abandoning this work in 1800. He returned to Cape Colony and worked at Graaff Reinet before continuing his work amongst the Hottentot people at Bethelsdorp Mission. Part of the group embarked on a mission to the Bush people while others pursued a mission to the Bechuana, the Griqua-Hottentot and the Namaqua Peoples.

Political problems between Britain and Holland and the cession of Cape to Holland in 1803 led to the appointment of van der Kemp as Superintendent of the LMS' affairs in South Africa. However, he died before hearing of the appointment and James Read, a colleague, was appointed in his place. He was succeeded by Rev. George Thom, who was followed by Dr John Philip in 1819.

In 1816, the LMS sent Rev. Joseph Williams to work in the Eastern Cape near Fort Beaufort and in 1820 Rev. John Brownlee settled at Tyumie Mission. Brownlee was joined by Rev. William R. Thomson and Mr John Bennie from the GMS in 1821. These were the precursors of the Scottish Presbyterian church mission in South Africa. From the outset, land was an issue in which missions and missionaries became involved.

The Beginnings of the Scottish Presbyterian Church Mission in South Africa

Beginnings in the Eastern Cape

The early missions in South Africa became missions of the Free Church of Scotland, the GMS having transferred its work to the Free Church in 1845 following the 'Disruption'. According to Cheyne (1993: 12), the 'Disruption' had a positive effect on missions with the development of 'missionary endeavour on a scale and of a quality hardly surpassed by any other communion in the English-speaking world'. The Free Church stands firmly in the Reformed tradition and accepts the Bible as its supreme standard and the Westminster Confession as its principal subordinate standard. Central to its worship therefore is the preaching of the gospel – the good news of salvation through the sovereign grace of God in His Son Jesus Christ (Free Church n.d. https://freechurch.org/about/history:1).

Certainly, the Free Church mission emphasised educational work and evangelism, while the United Presbyterian Church came to promote evangelism and church building, reflecting their roots in moderatism and evangelicalism. The United Presbyterian Church was marked by a special zeal for foreign missions and by its constant opposition to all state aid to the church, holding that this led inevitably to state control (United Presbyterian Church https://www.britannica.com/topic/United-Presbyterian-Church:1). After a period of theological conflict the United Presbyterian Church came fully to share the forward movement of thought of the other Scottish churches. In 1837, the GMS divided over the voluntary principle. The continuing GMS allied its work with the established Church of Scotland and later the Free Church; the offshoot Glasgow African Missionary Society (GAMS) worked with the UPCoS formed in 1847. The GAMS was responsible for the work at Tyhumie and Igcibira and later at Mgwali and Tutura. However, until 1842, both societies' missionaries had worked together in the same presbytery. The cost of running these missions led to a move in Scotland to terminate their support in 1848. The intervention of the Glasgow members of the FMC of the Free Church of Scotland (FCoS) led to this conclusion being averted. Scottish indifference posed a greater threat from a reading from the correspondence of the Ross family of Pirie mission (Cory, MSS 7754, 3442, 7893, 7906, 7910). Problems in the mission defied the optimistic paradigm envisaged by the Moderates.

The voluntarist Glasgow Missionary Society (GMS) sent its first missionaries, William Thomson and John Bennie, to South Africa in 1821. They joined John Brownlee, a hardy Scot who had resigned from the LMS to start a mission at Tyhumie near Alice, as a missionary paid by the colonial government. The Tyhumie mission station provided both the centre for mission and military protection for missionaries and settlers and so contributed to the link between missionary and colonist. In 1823, the sacraments were celebrated for the first time and the *amaXhosa* worshipped with European missionaries. In 1824, Thomson and Bennie were joined by Rev. John Ross from Presbytery of Hamilton of the Church of Scotland. This enabled the formation of the Presbytery of Kaffraria on 1 January 1824 (Cory MS7514) and it organised the financial affairs of the missions until the 1830s supported by funds from the GMS.

In the same year Lovedale Mission was established, to be followed by Burnshill (1830), Pirie (1830) (Cory MS 7514n; Lennox 1911: 22), Balfour (1830s), Glenthorn (1840), Macfarlan (1853), Mgwali (1857), Adelaide (1861), Tarkastad (1869), Port Elizabeth (1899) and East London (1900). These constituted the Kafraria Mission Council area (Lennox 1911: 84). The Transkei Mission Council developed with congregations at: Cunningham Mission (Toleni 1856), Paterson (1868), Blythswood (1875), Malan (1875), Main (1876), Columba (1878), Somerset East (1878) Duff (1880), Tutura (1885), Somerville (1886), Buchanan Mission (Sulenkama, 1886) in East Griqualand, Miller (1888), Gillespie (1889), Ross (1893), Mbonda (Mount Frere, 1894), Rainy (1897), Ncisininde (1900), Ugie (1903), Kidston (1905) and Matatiele (1906).

Work also spread northwards into Natal under two missions established by the Free

Church of Scotland, the Mission Council and the Presbytery of Natal and missions were established at Pietermaritzburg (1867), Mpolweni (1872), Msinga (Gordon Memorial, 1870), Kalabasi (1896) and Polela (1905).

Mission work in the Transvaal began in 1896 with a meeting between Rev. William Mpamba and a group of male migrants who had been working in the diamond fields of Kimberly. These migrants constituted 'a leadership corps of those sons of the area who had been exposed to the gospel through [the] Native Congregational Church of Rev. Gwayi Tyamzashe, a Lovedale trained minister' (Manaka 1996: 1) while working in the diamond fields of Kimberley. Most of these missions concentrated on agricultural mission and evangelism. Initially, these congregations came under the care and discipline of the Kaffrarian Presbytery and included Donhill (Zoutspansberg, 1896), Stuartville (Zoutspansberg, 1902), Johannesburg (before 1890) (Duncan 2012a: 54), Gooldville (1905), Blaauwberg and Weirdale.

When the FC and UPC united in 1900, there were 28 congregations of the Scottish mission in South Africa with 14,402 members (Hewat 1060: 184). The mission was active in the Eastern Cape in the Ciskei and Transkei established by both churches, and in Natal under two missions established by the FCoS, the Mission Council and the Presbytery of Natal. However, work was not only established in congregational settings.

Mission Stations

Mission stations were the centres in which indigenous evangelists, catechists, pastors and teachers were prepared for mission. This was vital since most of the mission work was done by them and not their missionary mentors who often 'fretted within the confines of the mission station' (Elphick 2012: 24), which was not the original intention. They were intended to be the vanguard of mission.

Mission stations were one of the main means by which Africans came under the influence of mission Christianity and these were no mere accidental creations. As the missionaries developed the physical site for Lovedale Institution near to a source of water, they imposed their western Christian cultural stamp upon it and required those who sought its benefits, i.e. boarding school education, to conform to a pre-determined order which would, in turn, determine the nature of the person which it produces. The truth of the above statement becomes clear when it is realised that much of the surrounding population consisted of *Mfengu* susceptible to incorporation due to their loyalty to the British and were 'a ready field of evangelisation' (Shepherd 1940: 117; cf. Duncan 2003c: 18–19).

But these were not the only reasons the people were attracted to mission stations (Duncan 2003c: 18–27). They functioned as a refuge for many who opted out of facing the depredation resulting from *difference* which constituted them as the 'Other' in traditional South African society.

The Missionary Institutions

Educational work was fundamental to the work of the Scottish missionaries and this led to an inward migration from not only southern but central Africa. For example, the inward migration of the Galla slaves from the region of Abyssinia in 1890 to Lovedale brought a novel dimension to the institution (Shepherd 1971: 54–5).

The foremost FCoS institution was Lovedale, opened in 1841 (Duncan 2003c; Shepherd 1940, 1971). The original intention was to train teachers and evangelists but, in time, the work of the mission diversified as trades' training was introduced, especially in printing and publishing at Lovedale Press. To this was added agricultural and medical mission, theological education for the ordained ministry, a Bible School for the laity and the establishment of a 'native' University of Fort Hare in 1916. A practicing school and high school were also part of the Lovedale establishment.

A similar institution, but on a smaller scale, was opened in 1877 in the Transkei. It was called Blythswood and was mainly for the *Mfengu* people. The UPCoS had opened Mgwali Girls' School in 1857 staffed with lady missionaries. In 1868, the FCoS began Work at Toleni and called it Cunningham Mission. Other work was initiated at Buchanan Mission in East Griqualand (Sulenkama Hospital) and at Pietermaritzburg, Mpolweni, Msinga (Gordon Memorial Mission and Tugela Ferry Hospital) and Kalabasi. Most of these missions concentrated on agricultural mission and evangelism. Much later, Pholela Institution (a high school) was opened (1930s) in Natal by a Scottish missionary, Rev. Ben Jones. These institutions were not only neutral philanthropic places of education. The timing of their establishment and their location demarcated them as contributing factors in the broader policy of the colonial government besides their overtly missionary purpose. They specialised in developing a migration of the mind from traditional culture to the culture of the missionary 'civilisation' through the process of 'coercive agency' (Duncan 2003c: 22–3). More missionaries came, and the work spread until it embraced a chain of missions.

Eventually, these missions all fell under the Free Church of Scotland (FC) and the United Presbyterian Church of Scotland (UPC). The location of these mission institutions was not accidental. Mostly, they were placed in the Eastern Cape where the first British settlers arrived and where the nineteenth-century wars of dispossession occurred. The provision of education was for the mutual benefit of the black and settler communities. The missions provided a buffer zone between settlers and indigenous peoples and the educational institutions aimed to be places for the pacification of African people. They were co-opted into the plan of the Governor-General, Sir George Grey, with his plans to mollify the indigenous people through sponsoring the provision of trades training at mission institutions during the 1850s, so Grey's policy was not as innocent as Shepherd (1971: 22–3) suggests. There was little racial discrimination at Lovedale, for instance, in its early days. Mission stations became a means of gaining the support of local communities and transforming potential enemies into loyal friends. Education became a more efficient means of controlling and developing local populations than military might.

As it grew and developed, Lovedale itself became a significant mission centre to the African continent. In a sense, mission institutions resembled Medieval monasteries which were virtually self-sufficient communities. They were 'total institutions' (Duncan 2003c: 81–97) catering for almost all of the needs of their inhabitants.

Black Participation

We noted the efforts made at Lovedale in connection with the training of evangelists who were also interpreters for the missionaries. Yet, for the most part, they remain nameless despite the vast amount of work they carried out among their own people and their achievement on behalf of the mission. This is demonstrated in the growth of missions, members and congregations up to the end of the nineteenth century. The only credit is given to those exceptional people who either were the first blacks to achieve something such as the first black nurse to qualify, Cecilia Makiwane (Wilson 1976: 4)), the first black minister trained in Scotland, Rev. Tiyo Soga (Williams 1978) or those who attained a certain notoriety such as Rev. Pambani J. Mzimba who instigated and carried through a secession from the mission (Shepherd 1971: 59, 60). Until recently, the work of Rev. William

Mpamba in establishing congregational work in the Transvaal at Donhill was little known. Manaka (1996: 1, 2, 3, 6, 9, 10) has redeemed this situation in the case of the Transvaal giving us the names of Kamela Raphela, Mokele Raphele, Daniel Moqaba Mamabolo, Timothy and Saul Mamabolo, Jacob Mabija, Timotheus Mamabolo, Daniel Mamabolo, Charles Machaba, Lucas Makoale, Zachias Nyama (cf. Thema 2021: 31) and Revs Yakeni Mbali, Candlish Koti, Arthur Ntuli, Titus Finca and EM Molaba.

Wilson (1976: 8) also acknowledges by name some of those great black missionaries who significantly contributed to the spread of the Gospel among their own people: Jan Tshatshu, Ntsikana, Tiyo Soga, John Knox Bokwe, Elijah Makiwane and Mpambani Mzimba. She also notes that in 1876, thirteen black missionaries offered for foreign service in Malawi, including a William Koyi, Shadrack Mgunana, Isaac Williams Wauchope and Mapassa Ntintili (Thompson 2000: 15–24). Their ability to communicate in their own languages made them especially useful until, and even beyond, the point where the missionaries could speak in the vernacular.

That the missionaries were the focus of mission activity cannot be contradicted in the light of the above. All accounts focus on their activities based on their assumptions and prejudices. That little account is taken of socio-economic factors points to the complicity of the missionaries in the prevailing colonial climate of the time. So they conform to the negative attitude towards blacks, their cultures and civilisations. In the educational sphere the 'Christianity must precede civilisation' (du Plessis 1911: 365) slogan misrepresents the situation where black civilisation was devalued to the degree that it is dismissed because ideologically civilisation is equated with Western civilisation. This is in accord with Dr James Stewart of Lovedale's ambition, echoed by his successor, James Henderson, 'to bring the native people into line with the European occupants of the same land' (du Plessis 1911: 364). The purpose of mission was, therefore, conformity. Even Wilson (1976: 6) identifies sophistication with 'wide-scale relationships, possession and development of a literature, some centralised form of government, and such military power as goes with economic development and centralised authority' compared with 'an isolated people, with limited technology and no writing'.

All this would indicate that mission was perceived as a two-way process between the sending churches in Scotland and the missionaries in the field, little account being taken of the needs and desires of blacks besides what was perceived on their behalf by the missionaries. Scant attention was taken of black experience and there seem to be no available contemporary black assessments of this area of mission work and its implications.

By the 1860s, the impact of the Free Church mission was substantial according to Mackenzie (2007: 199–200):

> In Kaffraria [Eastern Cape] there were thirteen missions and eighty-one Scots missionaries, twenty-eight 'native staff' and seventy-three day

schools with 4,000 pupils ([in] a Christian community of 9,500). In the Transkei, fourteen missions, forty-five Scots missionaries, seventy-one African staff, 202 schools with 10,650 pupils ([in] a community of 17,712). And in Natal, five missions, eighteen Scots missionaries, eighteen African staff, 202 schools and 1,845 (and a community of 10,985).

By any standards this was a considerable achievement. Yet, tension grew between the missionaries' dependence on their black colleagues and their parallel need to dominate them. This tension was resolved by introducing mission councils in 1865 which gave missionaries the upper hand (Duncan 2012b: 217–34) although they were conceived with a different purpose: '. . . the way should be made clear for duly developing the organisation and independence of the native Churches' (Henderson 1902: 4, in *Our Missions in South Africa*, Cory MS 7514n).

African Mission to Nyasaland and Kenya

Lovedale provided an example on intra-African mission. Robert Laws, a young missionary in Nyasaland (Malawi), sought assistance from James Stewart, Principal of Lovedale, in the persons of African missionaries (Macintosh 1993: 45). Four men, Shadrach Mgunana, William Koyi, Isaac Wauchope and Mapasa Ntintili, arrived in Nyasaland in 1877, to be followed by George Williams in 1883. Koyi was to become the longest serving of the four and he represented the essence of African leadership in mission as one who, according to Robert Laws, missionary in charge at Livingstonia:

> can reach their hearts by like habits of thought and speech, in a way which I suspect no European, however great an adept at the language, could ever hope to reach. In the white man there is something at once alien, which, though it may draw attention and, to some extent, respect does not touch the heart as William's presence does. (Laws 1882 cited in Thompson 2000: vi)

Here was the genius of the concept of 'native agency', though it should be named more appropriately as indigenous leadership. Laws and Stewart are to be lauded for this innovative step. Koyi was sensitive to local needs. Regarding commitment to the Ngoni people, themselves a people in migration (Thomson 2000: 150), and a far from cohesive group (Thompson 2000: 152): 'We must get Roots on their country' (Thompson 2000: 109). He was also proficient in communicating with the *Angoni* of Nyasaland, who were a remnant of tribes which survived the wars of King Shaka in Natal. The success of inculturation is demonstrated in the work of the Lovedale missionaries, for example in the transformation of the celebration of the harvest: 'the individuals who first and most happily facilitated this revised ritual were the *Ngoni*-speaking Xhosa missionaries from the Eastern Cape, William Koyi and George Williams' (Thomson 2000: 151).

There was far less unity of understanding and purpose between Scottish and African missionaries (Thompson 2000: 154). One thing becomes clear here – there was no possibility of a complete migration among white missionaries to Africaness.

By 1886, all four had departed and Williams left Nyasaland in 1888, thus ending the relationship between the two missions. Despite their brief tenure, significant advances had been made through a migration of the mind about mission, particularly in the role of the Lovedale missionaries as interlocutors for both the *Ngoni* people and the Scottish missionaries and important facilitators (Thompson 2000: 148–9) of mission: 'The Xhosa presence among the Ngoni and their frequent visits to the villages acted as a mediating force between the Ngoni and the Scots' (Thompson 2000: 203). James Stewart also initiated a later mission at Kikuyu, Kenya, in 1891 but without black evangelists' support. In all his missionary efforts, James Stewart displayed significant vision and innovation by migrating black missionaries to other African mission ventures and transcending the hitherto little acknowledged value of native agents as prime activists in mission history. He was to be less appreciative of local efforts at mission by black people themselves.

Conclusion

A poor profile was accorded to blacks in this area of mission history. Nonetheless, the contribution of the educational establishments especially cannot be denied. Yet, du Plessis (1911: 365) has posed the question of the educational work eclipsing the evangelical purpose. This might be true if evangelism is seen as separate and distinct from education in the unfolding mission and certainly Christian teaching and the expectation of conversion was not absent at places like Lovedale. Saayman (1996: 33) points out that the dual purpose at Lovedale was to 'civilise and christianise' and notes with Stewart's appointment as Principal in 1870 it 'became more strictly Christian rather than secular in the education it offered' (Burchell 1979: 15–18). It might be claimed that the education offered prepared young minds for a future that might not match their expectations given the developing political and economic situation.

We have to acknowledge the efforts and sacrifices made by those missionaries who felt called to serve overseas often at great cost to themselves and their families. However, we may never know the extent to which black missionaries and Christians also suffered for having made the leap of faith, a leap that often led to estrangement from families, friends, lifestyles and cultures. Developing blacks with regard to faith preceding civilisation is answered by the degree of threat they posed which led to the formation of mission councils. This matter would continue to vex the missionaries for years to come. However, a new factor was about to emerge in African leadership.

CHAPTER THREE

Rev. Tiyo Soga (1829–71): A Paragon of Early Indigenous Leadership

Introduction

The narrative of the early Presbyterian mission in South Africa is not just the story of the activities of Scottish missionaries. Nor is it the story of anonymous black South Africans who played a supporting role in the advance of the mission. There were many exceptional characters as we have seen in the mission to Nyasaland. We turn our attention on one remarkable black South African missionary – Rev. Tiyo Soga.

> Tiyo Soga was to be the most famous of all Xhosa converts . . . He was to be the first black ordained minister to be educated overseas, the first black missionary among his own people, and the first translator of an English classic (*Pilgrim's Progress*). (Mostert 1992: 1023)

The name of Tiyo Soga stands out in the mission history of the Eastern Cape province of South Africa. Born a son of the soil and raised in the traditional faith and practice of his people, he became an outstanding example of the transformation/conversion of an African as one who: 'had pride in his church, his race, and in the history and culture of his people' (Switzer 1993: 162).

We may consider Tiyo Soga to be a paradox to better understand him. Otherwise, it would be necessary to conclude that he was a contradiction in terms – neither black not white, neither African nor European, neither a slave nor a master, neither arrogant nor humble, neither British nationalist nor African nationalist, neither an admirer of the British way of life nor a despiser of his own African culture. He stood at a time and place where two cultures collided – the African and the European.

Lineage

Konwana was the nickname of Soga, son Jotelo of the Jwara clan. Konwana was the father of Old Soga (Tiyo's father), and grandfather of Tiyo. He was an adviser of Chief Ngqika (Williams 1978: 1; Hodgson 1980: 20; Brownlee 1896: 184). Old Soga had adopted a form of Christianity and some aspects of modern western agriculture (Millard 1999: 62). Old Soga was Chief Ngqika's, and his son Tyhali's, eyes and ears throughout the eastern frontier region. He had become a Christian before the war of dispossession in 1834 as the result of the prophet Ntsikana's influence and had witnessed the destruction of his people's land. He was a conflicted nominal Christian whose father had been influenced by the prophet, Ntsikana. He instituted family and morning prayer in his household. It was his decision that Tiyo should not be circumcised according to custom: 'he was a man of two worlds, vulnerable in both' (Williams 1978: 7). This decision reflects the influence Christianity had on him. The Soga family were drawn towards mission Christianity and served the missionaries in their search for new sites for mission stations. They interacted in the sensitive area between traditional life and western culture.

Young Tiyo Soga

Tiyo was born into the political arena of dispossession in the Eastern Cape and the expansion of the white settler community with its colonial administrative and missionary resources. His awareness of and response to this material (land) and existential crisis eventually developed into Black Consciousness and protest.

Tiyo was born at Gwali in the Tyumie valley in frontier of the Eastern Cape in 1829. From the age of fifteen, in 1844, he was educated at Lovedale under Rev. William Govan (1841–70). At this time Lovedale was non-racial, non-denominational, gender inclusive, emphasised Christian character, high intellectual standards and equality of opportunity (Duncan 2003c: 102–8). Govan's approach was far more equity driven than the later James Stewart's (1870–1905) paternalistic racist approach to education. This impacted on Tiyo who proved to be an able scholar.

The War of the Axe (1846)

This frontier war caused Lovedale Institution to suspend its educational programme and Lovedale became a military centre and the institution was evacuated; some refugees moved to Fort Armstrong. There a lady, Nosuthu, arrived with her son, Tiyo, who was studying at Lovedale. At the end of the war, which the British won, the *amaXhosa* were removed from their land which was settled with *amaMfengu* who were traditionally loyal to the British and therefore suspect among their black compatriots. The war sealed Tiyo's fate as he committed himself to a new lifestyle. His biographer, Chalmers, wrote that Tiyo's mother told missionary James Laing: 'My son is the property of God; God goes with him: he is the property of God's servants, wherever they lead he must follow' (Chalmers 1877: 38–9).

On the way to Scotland

Just before the outbreak of the war of the axe, William Govan, Principal of Lovedale Institution, had resigned as the result of a dispute which arose between himself and the Free Church of Scotland. He decided to return to Scotland taking four of his pupils with him. Clearly, the young Soga impressed William Govan to the extent that Govan believed he could benefit from an education in Scotland when Lovedale had to close during the War of the Axe (1846), one of the Wars of Dispossession. Following the war, Lovedale was reopened and Govan was invited to return as Principal.

In Scotland Soga was supported throughout his education at school and seminary. He was befriended by Dr William Anderson who baptised him in the John Street UP church in Glasgow on 7 May 1848 and with whom he developed a 'fellow feeling' (Chalmers 1877: 45). This testifies to Soga's ability to understand both those from European and African contexts. The sermon on the day of his baptism was based on the story of the Ethiopian eunuch (Acts 8: 26–39) and presaged the development of black nationalist ideas throughout Africa and particularly in Soga's mind.

Theological Education and Ordination

In June 1851, Soga returned to Scotland (Thompson 2000: 16). Later that year he matriculated as a student at Glasgow University, and after one session moved to the Divinity Hall of the United Presbyterian Church.

Govan's early assessment of Tiyo's ability was correct because he not only completed his education in Scotland but also the requirements for ordination in the United Presbyterian Church of Scotland (UPCoS), one of the Scottish churches which pursued mission in South Africa. He made such an impression that he was well supported by the UPC John Street congregation in Glasgow. During this time he absorbed the values of the middle class in Scotland which offered a counterpoint to his African value system. This has led to charges of betrayal of his African heritage. However, the truth is somewhat more complex than this initial evaluation.

By this time, he was already suffering from tuberculosis. Soga was ordained in Glasgow on 23 December 1856, within two weeks of having been licensed on 10 December. Soon afterwards, on 27 February 1857, Soga married a Scottish woman, Janet Burnside; this was symbolic of his integration into western culture. However, Tiyo longed to return to Africa and the Sogas left Scotland for South Africa on 13 April 1857, never to return.

Return to South Africa

On his return with a Scottish wife, the Sogas were exposed to the full pressure of racism. He commented: 'I would not be surprised if, to some, there was something absurd in the fact of a black man walking side by side with a white lady' (Chalmers 1877: 137). This was the 'curse of colonial prejudice' (Williams 1978: 32). Soga appeared to face this with a certain equanimity and tended to avoid situations where confrontation was possible or inevitable. Yet, this may have caused a tendency towards a sense of black nationalism (Khabela 1996: 21) and later a source of depression.

Uniondale, near Keiskammahoek, was Soga's first teaching post on his return to South Africa where he began his hymn writing career. There he had to endure school boycotts which were a part of the national resistance to colonial and missionary pressures. Under pressure, Soga declared in favour of European culture and values though he later identified with the struggle for black national identity.

In terms of political loyalty, Soga's loyalty to the British crown was demonstrated on the visit of Prince Alfred to South Africa in 1860 (Stapleton 1994: 198) when he exclaimed 'My loyalty knows no bounds now!' (Chalmers 1877: 256). This loyalty was most likely nourished at the mission stations where he was educated, imbued with the Scottish Presbyterian ethic of subservience to the state. For Soga this involved trying to discern the Christian ideal of sanctification in the context of western imperialism and racism.

There can be no doubt that Soga participated in the 'transculturation and transvaluation of the aims and instruments of the civilising mission' (Attwell 1995: 45) which was grounded in the European Enlightenment, which made a significant contribution to Scottish intellectual life. De Kock (1996: 184) describes him as a transitional combative figure. Soga exhibited the 'permanent provocation' of one drawn into power relationships as a voluntary subject, but who shows 'recalcitrance of will' in his own 'free' adoption of the values governing such relationships.

However, a few years later in the 1860s, he had begun his conversion to Black Consciousness and perhaps even nationalism. Yet, he remained a loyal monarchist. In 1864, he foresaw a future with:

> all the natives brought, in God's providence, under the influence of the English government, to smooth all causes of irritation and heart-burnings, and to approve themselves the faithful subjects of the best friend of all men, *Queen Victoria*!' (Chalmers 1877: 307-8)

Soga advocated the consolidation of British control to prevent further disruption in the Eastern Cape. Khabela (1996: 30) claims that alongside these views he was deeply opposed to the British attempt to destroy the power of the chiefs. Yet, he also strongly supported the territorial and moral integrity of blacks and this caused within him a conflict of loyalties. This was the 'untenable ambivalent position' (Saayman 1991: 59) that black and white missionaries had to navigate. Soga gradually became convinced that negritude was acceptable, though it would lead to racial purity and territorial integrity.

Soga's exercised his ministry (1861–71) at two mission stations, Mgwali and Tutura. These stations were considered by the chiefs to be:

> ... symbols of colonial encroachment which had already deprived them of land. Tiyo Soga was sensitive to all this; he was conscious of the necessity of abolishing the grosser practices of traditional Xhosa society while inculcating Christianity with its handmaiden, Western civilisation, under the umbrella of British rule. Yet he strongly believed in traditional Black values and tried to reconcile them with the best aspects of Western civilisation. Traditional society, thus purified, would then have intrinsic and desirable worth. In this Tiyo Soga sought to reconcile his two worlds. (Williams 1983: 3)

Mgwali

Mgwali Mission was founded in 1857 by Soga and the church building was completed and opened on 23 July 1861 (Brownlee 1986: 395). He remained there until 1868. The context was one of resentment and suspicion within the local community. This hampered his work since the missionary task had virtually been subsumed under the colonial project. His ministry began in the aftermath of the cattle-killing tragedy which had a devastating effect on the Mgwali area. It had its source in a prophecy made by the Xhosa prophetess Nonquawuse that led to a millenarian movement that culminated in the Xhosa cattle-killing movement and famine of 1856–8. This 'national suicide' was an attempt to counter the invasion by alien (British) forces. Life was further complicated by Sir George Grey's (Governor of the Cape) settlement of veterans and civilians in the Eastern Cape during the 1850s in an attempt to integrate blacks and whites, thus creating a buffer between the settlers and the indigenous population. Yet, Soga was filled with hope as he established this new missionary outpost in opposition to traditional culture. Those who gathered at mission stations were far from the normal inhabitants of society – they were misfits and displaced peoples and included the *amaMfengu* (Duncan 2003c: 18–26), those accused of being witches, single women, blind women, albinos, lepers, cripples (Khabela: 1996: 12) and lower members of royal families. This raised the question regarding the extent to which native agency rather than missionary initiative was responsible for the advance of the mission?

Then there were Soga's objections to a too facile definition of and approach to civilisation which appeared to betray a distrust of his own indigenous civilisation:

> My faith in civilisation alone, if it does not follow in the wake of Christianity, is gone. The civilisation of civilised men, who care nothing, and do nothing, for the moral, physical, and intellectual improvement of ignorant men in barbarous countries, with whom they come into

contact, is destructive. No man needs to talk about civilisation, apart from Christianity, when I see the native he, only when it is the result of Christianity is rushing to ruin by drunkenness, and other vices of civilised ungodly men. Civilisation is the handmaid of Christianity. (Chalmers 1877: 288)

A crisis arose between Christianity (i.e. Victorian Christian morality) and culture at Mgwali relating to the traditional rite of circumcision which caused Soga much distress. This was expressed by young men in the form of nativism as they challenged any resistance to the traditional rite of passage marked by circumcision. The response of the chiefs has been termed 'nativism': 'rejection of assimilation and the restoration of aspects of traditional African religion and tribal life' (Williams 1978: 83). The challenge of Christianity and colonial aggression, territorial and spiritual dispossession produced the response of Xhosa (Black) nationalism.

Soga left Mgwali for Tutura to the east in the Transkei on 4 June 1868.

Tutura

Tutura mission was founded in 1867. Missionary development had, by this time, been made easier by the continued expansion of colonial authority. Soga deemed it necessary to move into the area of Chief Sarili who had already lost much of his authority over his land as it had been given by the colonial government to the *AmaMfengu* and the *Tambooki* tribes. The assumption in this decision was that the people preferred to be under the influence of missionaries rather than traditional leadership. The threats to the missionary advance were witch-finders and rainmakers, along with the institutions of lobola, polygamy, the levirate and initiation. Williams (1978: 81) correctly states that 'There was little, if any attempt to understand the social significance of these "immoral" features of Xhosa life and their value for society'. In one sense the chiefs were the authors of their own demise regarding missionary relationships for they entertained their presence with mixed motives. However, the missionary motive was clear – 'cultural conversion' (Ashley 1974: 201).

Soga made a sensitive and potentially controversial decision at this time when he sent his sons to Scotland to be educated: 'To bind my boys down permanently to this Institution [Lovedale], admirable as it is, would curb the natural bent or inclination of their minds with reference to the future (Chalmers 1877: 289). Soga's ministry at Tutura was hampered by ill health. Yet, he led a busy life with 'evangelising, church building, Bible translating, hymn writing . . . and was very fruitful, though he did not live to see much of the harvest' (Lennox 1911: 42).

Black Consciousness

Tiyo Soga stands in the forefront of the development of Black Consciousness on the African continent during the nineteenth century (Williams 1978: xix; 2001: 66, 211).

However, his education at a mission institution, in Scotland and his marriage to a white woman were sources of suspicion among his compatriots which caused them to view him with ambivalence. Yet, he was clear regarding his own identity:

> I am one of you – a Kaffir as well as you – One of your own tribe and nation – Why is it that I have not on a painted blanket like you – or have not my ankles & wrists ornamented with those tinkling chains that ornament your own? – Simply because, I have been taught to see the utter uselessness of such things to an mortal being like me – I would not for the world exchange positions with you be[cause] I know that to live like you are now living, is sure and certain future ruin. (*Journal*, 24 July 1862, in Williams 1983: 89)

Here, Soga is referring to the difference brought about by his conversion and subsequent growth in the Christian faith as a Xhosa man. It also implies that he was by this time a 'civilised' man. He later refers to the power of God to redeem: 'even in the bosoms of men accounted savages, God has implanted the noblest instincts of our nature' (*Journal*, 24 July 1860, in Williams 1983: 28). He testifies to the success of his mission:

> The people which sat in darkness saw great light; and to them which sat in the region and shadow of death, *light is sprung up!*' It is this way that the Lord is showing his mercy to this land, that so Ethiopia may soon stretch out her hands to God! (*Journal*, 8 February 1864, in Williams 1983: 102)

Here is a link between God's purpose and Soga's nascent nationalism. The text referred to from Psalm 68:31 was to become the rallying point of the Ethiopian-type churches from the two closing decades of the nineteenth century. Yet, Soga makes an interesting comment about mission: '... the gospel must be introduced into a heathen land by *foreign* agents, it is by native agents that it must be propagated so as to *reach* and *pervade* the *masses of the people*' (*Journal*, 15 August 1864, in Williams 1983: 105). On the subject of land, Soga was clear that there were significant differences in understanding regarding the integrity of property:

> The chief maintains that, as both these stations got even the English government to confirm the grant made by him to them, by appealing to his name and deed, the missionaries should, when they received the lands of those stations from Government, have done so with the understanding that they belong still to him, and that they still consider

themselves as his missionaries, as indeed they were. Instead of this, he says they got the land for themselves, and he was excluded from the stations (*Journal,* 1 October 1867, in Williams 1983: 129).

The truth regarding land is that 'much of it was acquired under false or misleading circumstances as well as different understandings of the ownership of land (Duncan 2015: 92).

Two significant events occurred in 1865 which affected Soga's missionary outreach and presented him with an opportunity to clarify his mission and vision. The first was an article by Rev. J. A. Chalmers on 'What is the destiny of the Kaffir race?' in the *King William's Town Gazette and Kaffrarian Banner* on 3 April. Chalmers argued that black people either had to resist their natural tendency towards indolence to become civilised according to missionary values and participate in the life of the colony or face extinction. Further:

> Imperceptibly, by their disregard to education and its advantages, they are going headlong to ruin, rising only to the unenviable position of wagon-makers and grooms. Neither this generation nor the next may witness this extinction, but it is a law that wherever education is at a low ebb the mass of the people must sink. (Chalmers 1865)

This comment came from Soga's friend and colleague at Mgwali. Clearly, they held widely divergent views on the state of the black population. Chalmers' comment 'when a Kaffir youth has a smattering of knowledge ... his ambition then is to be a gentleman, a sort of peacock bedizened with ornaments of the gaudiest hue' (Chalmers 1865) was a slight on Soga and other black people who aspired to better themselves.

The second event was the declared intention of the colonial government in March of that year to force the *Ngqika* people to cross the Kei River into Gcaleka's land. The chiefs refused to comply after consultation and the *Mfengu* were settled there instead. This occasioned a response from Soga which became the first South African writing on Black Consciousness which promoted the idea of negritude. Soga was furious with the proposal to move his people and wrote to the Editor of the *Gazette*. Here he replied to Chalmers' article under the pseudonym of *Defensor* in an article entitled 'What is the destiny of the Kaffir race?' published on 11 May 1865.

He begins with an interesting observation 'the writer passes over in silence the results of missionary labours among the Kaffirs for the past fifty years' (Williams 1983: 179) and makes an opposite comparison:

> Take a nation – any nation in the exact circumstances of the Kaffirs of South Africa – compare the Kaffirs with that nation (for it is futile and unfair to compare him to a European with the advantage of a civilisation and Christianity of 15 or 20 centuries), give that nation the same number of years – fifty – during which the experiments of civilising and Christianising have been tried ... and he will find that the Kaffirs,

or rather the results of Christian labours among them, will stand nobly the test of the comparison.

This was a direct challenge to the thinking of the likes of Dr James Stewart, Principal of Lovedale Institution (1870–1905) later in the nineteenth century who believed that with regard to industrial training:

> It is not to be expected that a people emerging from barbarism – to many of whom the production of a simple straight line is a difficulty and parallel lines a work of art – should after five years of training turn out remarkably intelligent and efficient mechanics. (quoted in Shepherd 1971: 50)

This exemplified Stewart's negative view, not only of African workmanship but also of his lack of cultural awareness regarding technology in an African context. He was clearly unaware of the enormous contribution made by the ancient Egyptians to the development of technology.

Soga then developed another argument:

> Africa was of God given to the race of Ham. I find the negro from the days of the old Assyrian downwards, keeping his 'individuality' and 'distinctiveness', amid the wreck of empires, and the revolution of ages. I find him keeping his place among the nations, and keeping his home and country. I find him opposed by nation after nation and driven from his home. I find him enslaved – exposed to the vices and the brandy of the white man. I find him in this condition for many a day – in the West Indian Islands, in Northern and Southern America ... I find him exposed to all these disasters, and yet living – multiplying 'and never extinct'. Yea, I find him now as the prevalence of Christian and philanthropic opinions on the right of man obtains among civilised nations, returning unmanacled to the land of his forefathers, taking back with him the civilisation and the Christianity of those nations. (See the Negro Republic of Liberia.) I find the negro in the present struggle in America looking forward – though still and with chains on his feet with chains in his hands – yet looking forward ... I believe firmly that among the Negro races of South Africa events will follow the same law, and therefore neither the indolence of the Kaffirs, nor their aversion to change, nor the vices of civilisation, all of which barriers the gospel must overthrow, shall suffice to exterminate them as a people. (Williams 1983: 180–1)

Soga exemplifies a high view of African civilisation which has been dragged down to the base levels exemplified by the worst aspects of European 'civilisation'. This indicates the existence of a spirit of the Africanist Movement derived from the African Diaspora in the USA. Soga firmly, but with considerable restraint, responded and emphasised that black people occupied land donated by Godself – that it is their right to occupy it. Then he displays

African consciousness (Saayman 1991: 63) by referring to the existence of black people beyond the bounds of the continent. Williams (1978: 97) describes this as a novel contribution to developing black nationalism. This Africa consciousness was a vital component of Black Consciousness and later nationalist thought. This was a continental perspective whose seed lay in southern Africa. This was significant for Africa not only occupied a vast land space and massive numbers but it also had a substantive history as can be evidenced in the history of Egypt, northern Africa and Ethiopia, not to mention the historic academic centres at Alexandria and Timbuktu. Africans can be incorporated only into the wider community based on their distinctiveness, and this indicates to us the development of race consciousness. Their adaptability was stressed as a counter-charge to Chalmers critique of African indolence. For Soga, this involved restructuring the symbolic universe of Africans as they blend their culture with modernity.

Soga's conflicted struggle between two worlds led to the paradox:

> Determined to free his people from the tyranny of obnoxious tribal rites and customs which should crumble with the advance of Christianity and civilisation, he nevertheless saw tribal society as worthy of preservation because it was different from western societies and their mores. And Nationalism, even in diluted form, feeds on the uniqueness of societies. (Williams 1978: 99)

This was evident from Soga's recourse to the history of early African Christianity as recorded by Rev. William Thompson in Cape Town in September 1865, that Soga:

> Suggested to me the names of Cyprian, Tertullian and Augustine, and others of Northern Africa, embalmed in the memory as among the noblest men of the primitive Church, and as the first fruits unto God of the rich harvest this continent has yet to produce. (Chalmers 1877: 215)

This view was shared by other pan-Africanists, Wilmot Edward Blyden and James Africanus Horton. Returning to Soga's article:

> Ethiopia shall soon stretch her hands to God! The total extinction of a people who form a large family of races to whom the promise applies, shall not, surely precede its fulfilment. In this matter, I for one shall adhere to the declaration of the 'old book' before I accept the theories of men. (Williams 1983: 181)

The biblical aspect was vital to Soga's thinking. Here he saw the Ethiopian prophecy as integral to his vision for his people. He resented the negative influences of colonial rule, especially corruption in the form of excessive alcohol consumption whose effect was in the deterioration of morals and loss of their humanity. (Williams 1983: 168). Hence, western influences brought both beneficial and destructive influences. However, faced with these evils Soga stressed the essential nature of black people distinguished by integrity, nobility of nature, dialogue, sense of humour, weakness for exaggeration and hospitality. These characteristics he viewed as composing a purified tribalism (Williams 1978: 101) marked by the Christian values of 'decency and order' (1 Cor. 14: 40). This involved maintaining the authority of the chiefs which was derived from God to provide a structure which guaranteed black confidence. Despite his encouragement of his own people to demonstrate due deference to white people as a mark of respect, he was also influenced by his belief that 'God ha[d] made from creation no race of men mentally and morally superior to other races. They are all equal in these respects; but education, civilisation and the blessings of Christianity have made differences among them' (Chalmers 1877: 421).

By 1870, Soga was a prophet of negritude: 'the refinement of black consciousness to a positive doctrine which saw virtue in black society and sought strength and comfort there' (Williams 1978: 103).

Soga never disparaged black society despite its weaknesses. He became the early icon of Black Consciousness and Pan-Africanism. Saayman (1991: 63; cf. Khabela 1996: 7) presents the view that these sentiments express a form of nascent 'Nationalist militancy'. Soga was considered to be in the vanguard of Africans pressing towards their destiny in which Africans embrace modernity. He was, therefore, a transitional figure in Xhosa history, standing at the confluence or collision point of two universes, Western and African.

Literary Work

Soga's time in Scotland allowed him to develop a love of western culture, literature and history. Bunyan made the deepest impression on him and in 1867 his translation of the first part of Bunyan's *Pilgrim's Progress* was published in isiXhosa, *Uhambo Lomhambi*. It laid the foundations for the rise of Xhosa literature.

He then participated in the translation of the Xhosa Bible. Another project which occupied Soga's attention was the Xhosa hymn book. His inspiration came from his contact with Ntsikana who had written the famous hymn *Olu Thixo omkhuku ngosezulwini* (*Thou Great God in Heaven*). He produced thirty-one hymns for the Presbyterian Hymnbook *Incwadi Amaculo AseRabe* (1929). In addition, we have access to some of his letters written to the Mission Board of the United Presbyterian Church and a selection of sermons. His teachings were revered among his own people (Brownlee 1896: 254). Soga was intellectually acquisitive and this stimulated his desire to reflect his Black Consciousness and black nationalism. Williams (1978: 119) acclaims him as 'an exceptional first of the new Black elite'.

Health

Recurrent family illness was attributed to Soga's eschewing tribal practices. From an early age it was assumed that Tiyo had inherited a predisposition to a 'chest aliment, probably tuberculosis, endemic to his family' (Williams 1978: xv) which would plague his life until his death. At Mgwali:

> He lived in a miserable cottage which had been erected as a temporary building on his first arrival there and it was doubtless because of cold and damp then experienced that the germs of the disease – laryngitis – from which he suffered most acutely during the last two years of his life were laid. But Mr Soga was not the man to complain; he bore his trials patiently and without murmur. (Chalmers 1872: 11)

In addition, this incapacity led to frequent bouts of depression (morbidity, melancholia; De Kock 1996: 175):

> When injured, he repressed his anger but indulged his grief, and was accustomed to conduct himself rather like a person [more] wounded than offended. He possessed that gentleness which shrank with an instinctive recoil from contention. Added to this a tone of sadness which pervaded his whole life; the cause was difficult to find, and only occasionally, when in conversation on questions affecting the native population, he gave utterance to the words 'My poor countrymen', did one get, as it were, to the secret of this depression. Yet, this characteristic sadness was balanced by a deeper sense of happiness and liveliness and mirth, which welled up when in the company of kindred spirits and whilst conversing on subjects congenial to his nature. His merry joyous laugh showed a soul full of inward tranquility, and it was always observable to those who knew him best that the despondency which overclouded his being was owing to something altogether foreign to himself. (Chalmers 1872: 12)

He himself admitted to self-doubt in a letter he wrote in 1862:

> I have sometime great regrets that I ever went to Scotland and entered the ministry – Not alone for its *trials* here but for its solemn responsibilities and yet I had not would I have been a better – less responsible man to Government in another profession? I wish sometimes I could go to some dark spot of earth – live and reside there alone. (Soga to Cumming, 18 September 1862, Cumming papers (Folder 10) SA Library)

But:

> He often took for his text such words as 'I have great heaviness and continual sorrow in my heart. For I could wish that myself were accursed from Christ, for my brethren, my kinsmen according to the

flesh. On such occasions roused to the highest pitch of excitement...'
(Chalmers 1872: 16)

During the last years of his life, he struggled against great physical weakness. '... His own brethren implored him to cease from active work, but he resolutely refused' (Chalmers 1872: 23). This indicates some form of bipolarity in his personality stimulated by his regular periods of physical ill-health. Soga displayed 'solitude amid a crowd' (Chalmers 1872: 7) along with an 'exquisite sensitiveness' (Chalmers 1872: 12).

Conclusion

It is interesting that Tiyo Soga emerged as an indigenous leader early in the life of the Scottish mission. He was the first in a longline of notable black Presbyterians. Soga experienced the pain of the collision of two universes, those of his native African culture and Scottish culture; his marriage was a constant reminder of the commitment he had made to western culture. His traditional loyalty lay with the system of government in which chiefs played the most significant role, yet he loved and admired the British system of administration and justice, and the Royal family. He was a devoted servant of Queen Victoria despite what she stood for and promoted (as the source of the threat of dispossession). He also lived in the Eastern Cape where he could not avoid the 'entanglement between mission and colonialism' and occupied an 'almost untenably ambivalent position' (Saayman 1989: 96). His subsequent life was devoted to mediating between these two competing universes. This gave him the impetus to initiate Black Consciousness and negritude. He was used to conflict, confrontation and compromise in a context of destabilisation.

Soga was also devoted to maintaining the authority of tribal chiefs to whom he was also committed. He was a proponent of justice and its administration in both quarters. His project aimed at adapting Christianity to black society – the process we now know as inculturation, a process by which members of differing cultures engage in 'a constructive dialogue between an original biblical culture, a church tradition and a contemporary culture' (Luka-Mbole 2013: 519). 'He was committed to purifying black culture through the civilising effect of British authority for the salvation and elevation of blacks' which he considered 'a vehicle for civilisation ordained by God' (Williams 1978: 123). Though he remained firmly within the mission, his work was a source of encouragement for developing African Initiated Churches (AICs). Integral to this process was the canon of self-help. He declared to his children:

> As men of colour, live for the elevation of your degraded, despised, down-trodden people. My advice to all coloured people would be: Assist one another; patronise talent in one another, prefer one another's businesses, shops etc., just because it is better to prefer and

elevate kindred and countrymen before all others. (Chalmers 1877: 433–4)

He suffered many indignities at the hand of whites. Yet, he reacted with dignity and a considerable measure of restraint. By the 1860s he was advocating and actually spoke out against racist white behaviour and challenged his people to be proud of their heritage. He himself lived at the point where the universes collided both territorially and psychologically.

Soga's was a lonely, isolated and alienated liminal existence despite the support he received from white missionary colleagues. This was an existence marked more by solitude than solitariness but, nevertheless, the solitariness did overcome him. The only comfort he derived came from the knowledge that his wife was experiencing similar or worse alienation though she bore this with great dignity and devoted herself to raising their family.

Saayman (1991: 62) poses, and seeks to answer, an important question regarding Soga's ultimate allegiance, particularly following his dispatch of his sons to Scotland to be educated. Was he:

> ... a political coward, or a consummate political realist in the context of contemporary colonial society? I think in the light of all that he said and did, we cannot condemn Soga without further ado for his apparent ambivalence. His dedication to the Black cause is too evident, for example, in his view on the place of Blacks in Africa. In this respect he believed that God had given Africa to the descendants of Ham. God himself would therefore establish and maintain Blacks in Africa, also in the southern portion of the continent; *nothing* would break this link between *all* Black people and Africa.

CHAPTER FOUR

The Role of Mission Councils in the Scottish Mission in South Africa, 1864–1923

Introduction – Origin of Mission Councils

The role of Mission Councils in the growth and development of the Scottish Mission in South Africa is confusing and vexatious. Whereas these councils were conceived and established as a means of facilitating mission, they often hindered this by distinguishing between agents of mission, missionaries and indigenous leaders, and delineating spheres of authority through exercise of power, even in opposition to expressed mission policy initiated in Scotland. They were an integral part of the hegemonic missionary worldview which frustrated progress towards the formation of the Bantu Presbyterian Church of South Africa in 1923.

The history of Scottish Presbyterian church policy during the period 1898–1923 was largely influenced by a minute of the Foreign Mission Committee (FMC) of the Free Church of Scotland (FCoS) of October 1864 relating to South Africa, which stated:

> That the ordained European missionaries reared in the colony or sent from this country be constituted into a Missionary Council for the regulation of the affairs of the Mission. (National Library of Scotland [NLS] MS 7801: 80, 81; cf. Brock 1974: 438. Appendix A: 2)

Mission Councils were formed for 'the maintenance, administration or independence of our Mission in South Africa' (*Our Mission in South Africa*, MS 14849, Rhodes University [RU], Cory Library). This minute resulted from Alexander Duff's, Convener of the FMC of the FCoS, visit to Kaffraria in 1864, and the recognition of a need for change in the organisation of the Mission arising out of confusion that emanated from an earlier decision that 'all matters connected with the management of the mission in Kaffraria devolve upon the Presbytery'. This included the affairs of missionaries, which meant that black ministers would have decision-making powers regarding missionaries. The implication of the 1864 minute was that Presbytery should keep to its 'proper functions', i.e. discipline, where relevant, but not those matters relating to missionary conduct or activity. Such matters should be determined solely by whites in the Mission Council. All bodies involved in the mission – Presbyteries, Mission Councils, Financial Board, and Educational Board of the Seminary – should communicate with each other concerning areas of mutual interest that fell within their remits; and that each should relate directly to the FMC on all matters requiring approval or confirmation. From an early stage, some means of conducting the affairs of the Mission would have to be arranged so mission policy could be promoted. This minute was held in abeyance until Dr James Stewart arrived in South Africa in 1870, having been appointed to serve as the second Principal of Lovedale Missionary Institution. Stewart was deeply influenced by the educational ideas of Alexander Duff, who had served in India.

The formation of Mission Councils confirmed that Scottish Presbyterian church policy was not 'the product of an indigenous organisation', but was 'informed certainly by those on the spot' (Brock 1974: 24), who were white, male, ordained missionaries. There was a significant difference between the FCoS mission in South Africa and other missions, which were largely autonomous and made less distinction between black and white ministers. The FCoS was, therefore, less flexible. A further minute of the FMC in 1866 confirmed the FCoS' support of the Three-Self Principle Henry Venn had recently formulated with a view to producing self-governing, self-supporting, self-propagating churches (Schenk 1977). This 'reflected a greater optimism about the abilities of new churches planted by the missions to assume full responsibility for their own affairs in a short time ...' (Reese 2010: 21). The FCoS felt it was appropriate that the mission church should be self-propagating because as soon 'as native congregations are formed, their care ought as speedily as possible to be consigned to the native pastorate' (Brock 1974: 439).

Missionaries were to be pioneers 'for the native congregations were in time to be delivered over to the pastoral care of additional native pastors' (FMC Minute, 27 October 1866). This would entail training an indigenous ministry. Brock (1974: 61) questions the ability of blacks to achieve greater power in the Mission, because between 1881 and 1901 there were no Mission Councils to hamper or even promote their development. There were black ministers in the Mission, but they formed a minority in Presbytery as very few black ministers were ordained during this period: 'Missionary enthusiasm for ordaining African pastors was declining by the 1880s as the arbiters of a segregationist culture began to separate church congregations and limit contact between white and black clergy' (Switzer 1993: 125). Blacks usually supported the appointment of missionaries to charges because of poverty in congregations that could not support black ministers, and the lack of a central stipend fund. They had the support of the missionaries in opposing union with white settler Presbyterian congregations (with their black missions) and presbyteries. Self-support implied growth towards financial independence. This led to a failure of policy. The FMC pressed the issue of self-support in relation to the authority of white missionaries. Rev. John D. Don, Presbytery Clerk of Kaffraria, argued that self-support implied self-government, and he called this 'evil' (Don to Smith, 4 September 1886, NLS, MS7797). The Presbytery opposed the challenge of self-government and, unfortunately, the FMC did not pursue it. FMC policy regarding the union of Presbyterian bodies was consistent in pursuing a three-self church, but whether this issue could best be resolved in the formation of a multi-racial or black church would become a very contentious issue in the 1890s and beyond. Following their formation, Mission Councils were disbanded in 1881, having failed to find a relevant role. They were reintroduced in 1901 (under Act II, 1901 of the General Assembly) with the prospect of forming a black church (Brock 1974: 57; Burchell 1979: 148).

Mission Councils Renewed

However, events moved on apace. In 1897, the Presbyterian Church of South Africa (PCSA) was formed after considerable discussion on the nature of the church in South Africa. Due to a lack of unanimity, particularly among the Scottish missions, union was rejected and the PCSA emerged as a predominantly white church with mission work among the black population. Almost concurrently, in 1898, Rev. Pambani Mzimba seceded from the Free Church of Scotland Mission to form the Presbyterian Church of Africa (PCA). These events necessitated a review of mission policy in South Africa. The forty existing Scottish missions were reconstituted into three mission councils for administrative purposes (Lennox 1911: 43–4).

There were sixteen stations in the Mission Council of Kaffraria, which included the institutions of Lovedale, Blythswood and Emgwali (the latter being directed by the Ladies' Kafrarian Society), four missions under European missionaries (Burnshill, Pirie, Emgwali and Gooldville [in Venda]), six under native pastors and evangelists (Lovedale Native Congregation, Macfarlan, Stuartville, Donhill, Port Elizabeth, and East London), and four colonial congregations with which work was carried on among the natives in their neighbourhood (Tarkastad, Glenthorn, Adelaide and Somerset East).

The Transkei Mission Council area contained nineteen stations – namely, the institution at Blythswood, thirteen stations under European missionaries, Paterson (Mbulu), Cunningham (Toleni), Malan, Main, Columba, Duff (Idutywa), Somerville (Tsolo), Buchanan (Sulenkama), Miller, Gillespie, Ross, Mount Frere and Rainy, and stations at Kidston, Ugie, Matatiele and Incisininde.

In the Natal Mission Council there were five stations (Maritzburg, Impolweni, Kalabasi, Polela and the Gordon Memorial).

At a meeting of the Synod of Kaffraria, held in King William's Town on 17 July 1901, the Clerk read a minute of the FMC:

> The Assembly appoint the following as the Act anent Representation in the Assembly of Mission Councils:–

That a Mission Council shall be appointed in each Mission field where such a Council or Committee does not exist already exist.

That a Mission Council shall consist of:–

(1) All the Missionaries from the Home Church, in the field, ordained and medical.
(2) The Minister and one Representative Elder from each European congregation within the bounds.
(3) Agents and friends of the Missions in the field nominated by the Mission Council and approved by the Foreign Mission Committee. (Minute 14, Synod of Kaffraria, 17 July 1901, UFH, HPAL)

Medical missionaries were now permitted to serve on mission councils, but still no women were appointed. The function of Mission Councils was to act with 'full Presbyterial powers' for the purposes of oversight of missionaries, election of commissioners to the General Assembly of the UFCoS, overturning the General Assembly, giving the European congregations a locus of representation apart from the presbytery, and any other function that the General Assembly might delegate to them. In addition, 'any appeal from the Mission councils shall be to the Foreign Mission Committee in the first instance' (Minute 14, Synod of Kaffraria, 17 July 1901, UFH, HPAL). Further, European congregations were to be represented though there were none in the Mission; yet, there were white Presbyterian congregations in the PCSA. This begs the question why were they not under the supervision of presbyteries dominated by black members? Here, there was a direct conflict with the function of presbyteries, one of whose main functions was the exercise of discipline.

On the following day, Rev. Brownlee J. Ross proposed that a meeting take place with 'missionaries of the former UPCoS to form a Mission Council or Councils, and to report to a special meeting of Synod' (Minute 16, Synod of Kafraria, 18 July 1901, UFH, HPAL). The outcome of the receipt of the Act from Scotland was a decision of the Synod regarding their 'desire to express their readiness to carry out heartily and loyally the policy therein indicated' (Minute 19, Synod of Kaffraria, 18 July 1901, UFH, HPAL). Two councils were then elected for the South Kaffrarian Mission and the North Kaffrarian Mission. The Synod then raised a number of inquiries and statements. One of these was the assumption that 'the intention of the Act is to include only *European* agents and friends of the Mission' (Minute 19, Synod of Kafraria, 18 July 1901, UFH, HPAL).

Regarding the relationship with Presbyteries, and noting the provision 'for a certain section of the Mission Council to have Presbyterial powers', the question was raised of what was meant by the clause 'the constitution and powers of local Presbyteries be left as at present'? (Minute 19, Synod of Kaffraria, 19 July 1901, UFH, HPAL). Was the intention that Presbyteries should only consist of, and be responsible for black ministers and elders, and what was to be the relationship of Presbyteries to the Mission Council and the UFCoS? These questions remained unanswered at that time. There was a further decision that the FMC be requested to establish a General Mission Council to meet annually.

With the move to operate anew through a Mission Council, it is strange that, in a Presbyterian structure, discrimination should extend not only to blacks, but also to the European laity, other than medical missionaries (18 December 1901, First meeting of the Mission Council of Kaffraria, Book 18 December 1901–17 January 1917, Lennox papers, UFH, HPAL). This group included all female missionaries and church members who were good enough to serve the Mission in many ways and were, perhaps, better able to deal with its administration and finance than ordained white ministers. It is also noteworthy that the hierarchical Presbyterian structure characterised by courts of the denomination was bypassed. South African Presbyteries met regularly, as happened following the inclusion of the Presbytery of Kaffraria as a Presbytery of the FCoS in 1857, and the subsequent formation of a Synod and other Presbyteries, i.e. in the Transkei (van der Spuy 1971: 13). Was it not possible for these Presbyteries to carry out the functions delegated to Mission Councils? Had this been the case, blacks would have been eligible contributors in developing mission policy and probably its most able interlocutors. The South African Presbyteries were courts of the UFCoS and to have any real influence it would have been necessary, and not at all impossible, for all members, black and white, ordained and lay, to have had access to the General Assembly meeting annually in Scotland. At this time, only missionaries were members of Mission Councils, though the membership was later widened. However:

> ... to maintain the distinct functions and independence of local Presbyteries and Native Churches it is inexpedient that pastors and office-bearers of Native Churches should be members of Mission Councils unless in exceptional circumstances. (cf. Act I of 1917 in *Rules and Methods of Procedure of the FMC*, 20 February 1923, RPCSA Archives, RU, Cory Library, 4)

This was a direct insult to blacks, who were to be inheritors of a white-devised plan that would form a black church beyond their control. The Councils would be equal in authority to Presbyteries: 'it is desirable that the Mission Councils and the Presbyteries of the Church stand on the same footing' (FMC, 24 August 1908, NLS Minute 1103), but subsequent history would prove the Mission Councils to be more powerful since they exercised, for example, control over grants from Scotland. They would, in theory, have no formal connection with the sending church, other than having been established by it. The only direct contact would be between missionaries and the sending church (Brock 1974: 57).

From this time, whites dominated the advancement of mission policy, in communication with the FMC of the UFCoS. It was their perceptions of the context in which they lived and worked that influenced and determined policy formulation in Scotland. From the beginning of the twentieth century, missionaries' relationships with the UFCoS were regulated by Mission Councils rather than Presbyteries (*Our Missions in South Africa*, 4–5, Henderson Correspondence, MS14849, RU, Cory). Burchell (1977: 51) refers to a meeting of the Synod of Kafraria held in 1900 where a decision had been taken not to exclude white missionaries. This decision relates to a suspicion that had been present before, and was probably exacerbated by the Mzimba Secession from the Free Church mission in 1898, and was taken because of the 'counsel of moderate Africans'. With the advent of 'white Mission Councils suspicion remained and, consequently, a call was made to clarify their functions in the mission field' beyond 'the regulation of the affairs of the Mission' (FMC of the UFCoS, October 1864 in Brock 1974: 438: Appendix A.2).

Mission Councils were, therefore, the result of a clear policy of strengthening the relationship of missionaries and the sending church, and the desire, by some, to prepare for developing an independent black church. A statement of FMC policy arose out of the need to appoint a successor to Rev. J. Lundie at Malan Mission in 1913. When the Kaffrarian Presbytery of the Presbyterian Church of South Africa (PCSA) recommended the appointment of a black minister, Rev. S. W. Njikelana, the Transkei Mission Council sought guidance from the FMC, which stated that the Missionary-in-Charge was equivalent to a Superintendent under the Mission Council, and, as pastor of the congregation, is in 'an interim arrangement' until 'the young growing Native Church finds itself'. If that time has arrived, according to the FMC, let Presbytery approve a call to a pastor whose work will not be related to the Missionary-in-Charge at Malan Mission, who will 'advise and assist him in every possible way'. Referring to General Rules 8 and 9, the FMC states that: 'the missionary is to aim at organising his converts into one or more congregations until a native pastor has been called'. Such congregations are to be formed into a Presbytery or absorbed into an existing one – 'their powers to be carefully respected by Mission Council'. Here is a clear delineation of spheres of influence.

When the Mission Council 'is of the opinion that the time has come in any part of the field for constituting a congregation', Presbytery is responsible for the act, with the Mission Council's approval. Therefore, the relationship of Presbytery to Mission Council is crucial. Thus, a Missionary-in-Charge had to be clear about his relative powers, which were the general supervision of mission work and as assessor on a Kirk Session, of which the pastor is Moderator. While the respective authority is clear, there was considerable potential for misinterpretation and misunderstanding of the regulations, especially when those concerned are both members of a Presbytery and a Mission Council, as with the missionary, but not the black minister, whose only channel of communication was his Presbytery. When a congregation feels able to engage in evangelism itself, and the Mission Council agrees, it should petition the FMC to withdraw the missionary. The powers of decision-making and action were in the hands of missionaries who might disagree on the desirability of removing one of their number, or even themselves. The FMC knew difficulties might arise in applying the principles of the policy (FMC, 29 April 1913, NLS Minute 2681).

The FMC policy was not implemented as speedily and effectively as it might have been for by 1905 Lovedale had produced only ten black ministers (Mission Council, 3 February 1905, File 'Mission Council, 1902–1905', Lennox correspondence, UFH). This was important, because the Mission Council came to rival the Presbytery as an alternative locus of debate and decision-making for all those involved in promoting the aims and objectives of mission. The Mission Councils' Chairpersons and Secretaries were to have powers and duties akin to those of Moderators and Clerks of presbyteries in the UPCoS, and they had powers to decide when new Presbyteries should be established (*Rules and Methods of Procedures of the FMC of the UFCoS*, RPCSA Archives, RU, Cory 4–5). The Mission Councils had the power of Presbyteries regarding missionaries, e.g. discipline. This was necessitated by 'the maintenance of Presbyteries of the Home Church in the mission with churches formed by kindred missions in the same field' (*Our Missions in South Africa*, 1902, MS 14849, Cory Library). While missionaries continued to be members of presbyteries, they also had recourse to the Mission Council while the indigenous church was being established 'providing a strengthened connection for the Scottish missionaries with the Home Church' (Burchell 1977: 42). This occurred when the role of missionaries was declining. The pastoral care of its members was a specific role of the Presbytery, which appeared to be sidelined. Mission Councils adopted a self-perpetuating role, for they favoured the creation of new black parishes while white missionaries would continue to control the mission (Kaffrarian Mission Council, Minute 241, 18 January 1922, 1917–30, Lennox correspondence, UFH, HPAL). This would become a continuing source of tension if Mission Councils existed.

Missionaries were keen to maintain the FCoS connection. Yet the separation of institutions such as Lovedale from Presbytery control aggravated an already tense situation. The institutions were developing rapidly, and were draining financial and personnel resources which could have helped to develop conventional mission and evangelism work. This caused difficult relationships between missionaries, e.g. James Stewart and those 'younger' missionaries, such as Henderson and Lennox; it also caused personality issues. Most problems concerned issues of power and control.

One area in which Mission Councils accumulated considerable power was in the control of property and finance, and in this they were superseding their original remit. In addition, these Councils were expected to play an ever decreasing role in church life; that the opposite happened became problematic for blacks who viewed the Councils becoming the only official channel to the Home Church (Burchell 1979: 174), which saw no need to transfer property to the young church (Burchell 1979: 175). The Secretary of the Churches Act Commission and the law agents of the two churches (FCoS and UPCoS) recommended that 'all grants and lands to Mission properties in Cape Colony are secured to the church or to the Mission, as such, and not to separate congregations' (FMC, 26 June 1906, NLS Minute 560). Earlier, the Transkei Mission Council, in considering a matter of raising funds for mission outbuildings, had affirmed: 'they gladly accepted the principle of the Native Churches taking an increasing part in self-help, but felt that this should rather be for the support and extension of evangelistic work, church buildings' than for the missionary's home. The FMC was asked what kind of self-help was envisaged, but no response is evident. Instead of making separate grants to congregations, the FMC agreed to allocate funds to the Kaffrarian Mission Council, which then reported back to the Committee on monies given and work carried out (FMC, 25 September 1906, NLS Minute 631). This was in accordance with a statement made by Henderson, recorded by Lennox (Lennox to Henderson, 24 May 1901, Letter book of the Presbytery of Kaffraria, Lennox correspondence, UFH, HPAL):

> The purpose of having the Mission Councils apart from Native Presbyteries which can control the entire funds sent out for mission work from the Home Church, and which can appoint assessors to the Native Presbyteries, giving these assessors less or greater powers needed, is nothing new.

Lennox claims that this method had been in operation for two generations, and is well known to the FMC. In addition, titles to property were secured to the General Trustees of the UFCoS. Thus, control could be exercised over black congregations and ministers, especially at such a time when the continued threat of secession was present. Subsequent history (post-1923) shows that Mission Councils accrued power in financial and property matters. In demarcation of congregational boundaries, the Mission Councils superseded the powers of the Presbyteries, e.g. with the Kaffrarian Mission Council determining the boundaries arising out of discussion of incorporating Zoutspansberg into the Mission (FMC, 26 September 1911, NLS Minute 2155: 6). Mission Councils even acted independently of one another, causing confusion in the Mission, as in spheres of interest, as seen above.

In 1910, a report of Deputies of the United Free Church of Scotland, Dr A. Miller and Mr Wildridge, stressed the desirability of joint meetings of the Kaffrarian and Transkeian Mission Councils, but no specific proposal emerged. Their conclusion was that: 'We are satisfied that the main lines of policy and the general forms of enterprise are wisely adapted to the needs of South Africa' (FMC, 24 October 1911, NLS Minute 2164). This is strange considering the need for mutual consultation in the matter of church policy. However, notwithstanding this, joint meetings did occur as reported to the FMC on 25 June 1912 (NLS Minute 2417: 1, 4). Here the matter of transferring Rev. J. Davidson as a Mission Council responsibility is discussed, along with the discussion of the joint issue of a Handbook in co-operation with the PCSA. The FMC responded that they 'cannot denude themselves of the right to initiate proposals of any kind when they seem called for'. This indicates tension between the FMC and the Mission Councils in policy formation. Eventually, the union of Mission Councils became an issue of the transfer of the Mgwali congregation from one presbytery to another. The FMC recommended the union to obviate problems about the lack of unity in policy and organisation. The Transkei Mission Council concurred. The FMC agreed to the transfer, despite the Kaffrarian Mission Council's concerns about the manner in which no account was taken of the Mission Councils' interests in the proposal about the union (FMC, 29 April 1913, Minute 2681). This development, overseen by missionaries was contrary to the policy of the FCoS in Scotland. As long ago as 1866, their policy had been clear:

> [F]inancially strapped parent boards of several mission bodies [including the FCoS] also began urging their missionaries to establish autonomous 'self-supporting, self-governing, self-propagating African churches' opening up to them the most prestigious vocations open to the upwardly mobile elite during the colonial period. (Switzer 1993: 123)

There were reservations concerning this policy change. James Stewart was unwilling to adhere to Scottish mission policy concerning the ordination of blacks. 'In an agitated moment, he *seems* to have claimed that the main cause of Ethiopianism was to be found in the interfering European mission boards in the matter of the ordination of Africans' (Sundkler 1961: 39). Further, Dr Lindsay, Convener of the FMC, claimed in 1901 that missionaries 'do not seem to have grasped the idea of a Native Presbyterian Church' (Brock 1974: 49). This demonstrates this idea was already present in FMC thinking, and that the missionaries were obstructing its implementation. The new approach of forming three-self churches was introduced in Mission Councils (Duncan 1997: 120). However, missionaries continued to subvert this noble aim:

> The projected ideal was that of a three-self church where extension work would be done by missionaries and consolidation of existing work by blacks. The missionaries turned this round, sending blacks to do the extension work while they busied themselves with consolidation. (Duncan 1997: 120)

The General Interests Committee of the FCoS determined that mission policy was the responsibility of the Mission Councils, and according to the Rev. George Robson, Convener of the FMC (letter to missionaries in SA, 15 January 1908, MS 10711, RU, Cory), the FMC stated:

The courts entrusted with the direction of the South African Mission in the Cape Colony are the Mission Councils of Kaffraria and the Transkei, which include all the missionaries and act in co-operation with and under the authority of the Foreign Mission Committee ... It is obvious that within the Mission there are divergent views as well as important and varied interests to be treated with the utmost consideration, and the Mission Councils must have a careful regard to these in advising on the policy of the Mission of our church. But it is to them that this function belongs.

Robson continued by clarifying the position regarding presbyteries from the time of union in 1900: 'The Presbyteries ceased to be courts representing the Home Church, and their place in that respect was taken by the Mission Councils.'

The continued existence of the two mission councils in Transkei and Kaffraria caused concern. Rev. Frank Ashcroft, Secretary of the FMC, inquired about the possibility of forming one council because 'this will be as great [a] help as the one Native Church' (Ashcroft to Lennox, 22 September 1909, file 'Synod', UFH, HPAL). The Transkei Mission Council was reticent and the FMC delayed any action. Transkei instead favoured the formation of sub-councils attached to presbyteries. Its position was essentially conservative, as seen from its attitude to the place of women in the church, which is 'neither practicable nor greatly desired' (FMC, 21 December 1915, NLS Minute 3642: 4).

The FMC approved the union of the two mission councils, to be named the Kaffraria Mission Council (FMC, 17 July 1917, NLS Minute 4151: 5). But there was also a need to clarify the position of the Natal Mission Council, which was prepared to unite with the Kaffrarian Mission Council, despite its concern about being swamped by the greater number of missionaries and black elders in the Cape. The Kaffrarian Mission Council had twenty-four missionaries with 15,379 members, while the Natal Mission Council had just four missionaries and 6,490 members (FMC, 20 September 1921, NLS Minute 5669). After some discussion regarding the possibility of proportional representation, the Natal Council agreed. However, because of issues raised about the attitude towards polygamy by the Natal Council, the place of the Natal Mission Council was not resolved until after the formation of the Bantu Presbyterian Church of South Africa in 1923.

Meanwhile, discussions had also been in process regarding the union of the two FMCs of the former denominations, the UFCoS and the UPCoS in 1900. It was proposed that male and female members should be members of mission councils with equal rights, as it was perceived that there was no longer any need to separate the work. Mission Councils had been dealing with proposals dealt with by two committees 'differing in their point of view when one committee consists mainly of men and the other mainly of women' (FMC, 16 January 1923, NLS, Appendix: Report of Special committee on 'Assembly's Remit on Amalgamation').

By this time, another major advance had taken place with the decision of the Kaffrarian Mission Council 'that the time has now come in South Africa to invite certain outstanding natives to sit as members of the Mission Council' (FMC, 16 July 1918, NLS Minute 4397: 1). It is assumed that the missionaries would decide who qualified to be designated as 'outstanding'. By this time, formal discussions were well underway to form an autonomous Native church, so the Kaffrarian Mission Council proposed adding one member of the soon-to-be-established church to represent each presbytery on the Mission Council 'and that it be the concern of the Council, as sanctioned by the Foreign Mission Committee, to devolve progressively upon the highest court of the Native Church the duties heretofore belonging to the Council' (FMC, 17 April 1923, NLS Minute 6407: 8). Discussion on this matter was delayed by the Commission on Union as they thought this could best be dealt with after the formation of the BPCSA.

In 1920, two Deputies from the FMC of the UFCoS, Rev. Frank Ashcroft and Mr Andrew Houston, visited South Africa with a view to resolving the future of their mission work by attending a conference at Blythswood Institution. They concluded and recommended in their report that 'control of the future must be with the Native church and not with the Mission Council' (FMC, 15 February 1920, NLS Minute 5386, Appendix 1: 3–4). The deputies highlighted the problem that the Mission Council would be the unifying bond of their South African missions 'proved unequal to the task, torn as it was, by controversies over the question of our union'. They also commented on the 'highly unsatisfactory state of affairs in Natal where overlapping was much in evidence'. The conference resulted in a proposal to unite the Synod of Kaffraria with the Presbytery of Kaffraria in a body that would take over much of the work of the Mission Council, including arrangements whereby the appointment of missionaries would be considered jointly by the Synod and Mission Council; evangelism would be allocated as a responsibility of the new body, and the reduction of missionaries would begin. This would facilitate the formation of an independent, self-supporting church. The same policy was to be adopted in Natal. The proposal was accepted and a Commission on Union was formed. Among several issues remitted to the Commission was that Mission Councils should cease to exist or have greater black representation (Duncan 1997: 146).

A special meeting of the Mission Council was held on 30 March 1921 to consider a response to the proposal of devolution to black UFCoS Presbyterians (cf. FMC, 23 March 1921, NLS, Minute 5518). The Council aimed to challenge the process, which would culminate in blacks assuming complete power over their own affairs, despite reservations about the timing. The missionaries felt this step taken by the FMC was a reaction to the failure of the attempt to unite the missions with the PCSA (Duncan 1997: 149). The power of Mission Councils is revealed clearly, even in the period preceding the formation of the Bantu Presbyterian Church of South Africa (BPCSA) when, in January 1921, James Henderson, Principal of Lovedale, submitted a detailed statement to the Mission Council for approval about the state of property, the use of land, and the extent of the boundaries of mission territories (2 February 1923, Mission Council, 1917–1930, Minute 309, RPCSA Archives, RU, Cory). It would have been reasonable to assume that the Mission Councils would be disbanded when the Bantu Presbyterian Church was formed in 1923. This represented the end of a process of granting autonomy to the UFCoS mission in South Africa. However, it was not to be so. At a convocation called with the Union of Presbyterian Missions in South Africa (BPCSA) on 4 July 1923 to constitute the Bantu Presbyterian Church of South Africa, the Mission Council of Natal was represented (BPCSA Minutes of General Assembly, 1923 [GA]: 6), but it had not met to decide whether or not to become part of the new church. An early item of business concerned relations with the Mission Council of Kaffraria which had also not yet become part of the BPCSA (BPCSA, GA 1923, Minute 60: 32). It was agreed to appoint a committee to engage in a joint consultation regarding the relationship between the Council and the General Assembly of the BPCSA. A regular feature of the continuing influence of the Mission Councils was evident in the transaction of certain items of business in which the regular decision was 'to send a copy of this minute to the Mission Council for transmission to the Foreign Mission Committee' (BPCSA, GA 1925, Minute 225, Pirie, 45). It was a matter of concern that an autonomous black church could not communicate directly with another church, but had to go through a white council. This situation remained until the dissolution of the Mission Council in 1981.

Conclusion

The role of mission councils was problematic as they were meant to be bodies that would facilitate the growth of the Mission towards the formation of an independent church. They were self-perpetuating exclusive clubs, which prevented blacks, women, and certain members of the white male laity having a voice in the formulation of policy, and in being prepared to take over the organisation and administration of their own church. They operated more like mission societies funded from overseas than an authentic part of a growing church.

UFCoS Mission Councils were even independent of one another. Following the union of 1900, which produced the UFCoS, the powers of presbyteries were reduced as Mission Councils were reintroduced. This created a potential problem area, as one body was dominated by whites, and the other by blacks. Beyond the area of personnel, mission councils had considerable authority in dealing with property and finance, another potential minefield for racial misunderstanding. Mission councils were essentially conservative bodies that could easily obstruct progressive ideas and policies. Because they were relatively autonomous, they were not compelled to consult those who would be affected by the consequences of the decisions they made. Their comprehensive control of all matters related to missionaries enabled the same missionaries to avoid being responsible to the presbyteries within whose bounds they served. One of the purposes of mission councils was to develop fellowship amongst missionaries, and this made them even more exclusive. It is important to consider whether or not mission councils were necessary in the first place. Early in their history they fell into disuse and were reintroduced specifically to facilitate the development of an independent black church, besides dealing with conditions of service relating to missionaries. It is doubtful if the mission councils performed any better than presbyteries had done *vis-a-vis* the decision to establish them, to make up for any deficit in presbytery supervision. Mission Councils had created a 'them' and 'us' mentality between black and white ministers, and this was evidently supported by FMC policy. The BPCSA that grew out of the Scottish Mission actually became subordinate to the Mission Council after 1923 as the result of its control of finance and missionary personnel. Its independence was restricted by the control exercised by the UFCoS through the Mission Council. Because mission councils were exclusive, they were able to exist without taking any great account of the views of blacks. These views were possibly not expressed in presbytery as the result of 'intimidation' by missionaries who 'knew better', but understood less. The position was worse with women, who were not represented in the courts of the church. However, Mission Councils survived, in various forms, until 1981 in South Africa.

In the meantime other forms of church life were being explored beyond the Missions of the churches of European origin (CEO).

CHAPTER FIVE

The Rev. Edward Tsewu's Dispute with the Free Church of Scotland Mission

Introduction

Within South African Presbyterianism, the Mzimba Secession is relatively well known. What is far less well known is that in 1896, two years before Mzimba's secession, there was another disruption within Presbyterian church life in Johannesburg led by Rev. Edward Tsewu. This occurred within the context of the growing phenomenon of Ethiopianism as part of the African Initiated Church (AIC) movement. To understand the broader context of this movement it is necessary to take a brief detour into the circumstances which led to this development.

The African Initiated Church Movement

The origin and development of AICs were '... a part of the broad and long term process of national politico-economic emancipation' (Lamola 1988: 6; Claasen 1995: 15) which was based on 'self-reliance and refusal of foreign financial support' (Pretorius & Jafta 1997: 211). This was a period which witnessed mass migration to cities for work (Christian Express [CE] May 1895: 1): 'AICs arose in the context of growing industrialisation as blacks from all race groups met in the workplace, talked, interacted and developed a "National Spirit" which was susceptible to being transferred into the ecclesiastical realm as a protest against this form of colonialism – capitalism' (Duncan 1997: 75). This 'resulted from being tied to the political economy of dominant capitalism' (Duncan 1997: 76). But there were other factors at work which affected the economic situation.

In 1894 alone the country suffered from drought with the consequent great loss of cattle, horses and grain for 'natives'. This was followed by the rinderpest pandemic in 1896–7 (Comaroff & Comaroff 1997: 209). The credit system was a contributing factor which led to impoverishment (CE May 1895: 1). The primary issue was 'Africans dispossession from the land, the dispersal of groups from their homelands, the lack of legal resources, unemployment, starvation wages, poor education, poor urban housing, and police mistreatment of Africans' (Pretorius & Jafta 1997: 213). These were predominantly economic matters. This provided an economic context for the formation of AICs.

> The Witwatersrand was the key industrial centre and also that part of the country experienced the most secessions from white churches. It was unacceptable for them to find that simultaneously the church was an agent of the process of dehumanisation and exploitation in the religious realm. It was not strange then that blacks began to think of establishing their own church, where they could rediscover their humanity together. (Balia 1994: 25–6)

This had a ripple effect far beyond the Witwatersrand because many living in the rural areas depended financially on relatives working in urban areas. Living in the squalor of 'native reserves, in an underworld of misery where, like dark phantoms, they were ceaselessly reminded of their sub-humanity', it was not unnatural for black labourers to experience the extinction of their character and culture.

The church was aligned to the dominant power structures and English-speaking churches or churches of European origin at this time were no exception (Cochrane 1987). 'Missionaries thus tended to behave like the other settlers. However, there were positive aspects to the establishment of independent churches'. Pretorius & Jafta (cf. Etherington 1979: 2) claim 'that some African Christians were pushed over the edge into independency in the last decades of the nineteenth century, as a prospering black peasantry saw its secular opportunities for leadership and material advance crushed by growing economic and political oppression'. These were '. . . a clear religious response to domination and conquest. This elite consisted of the black landed gentry in the rural areas whose land was derived from the traditional system of land tenure, and the "new elite"' (Ntantala 1992: 213), i.e. those who had received a '"liberal" education in missionary institutions and were, mostly, professionals' (Duncan 1997: 74). But, more directly related to the church context:

> AICs have the potential of embodying a type of Christian spirituality and faith that does not merely contextualize some superficial elements of a Western interpretation of Christianity but rather represents a legitimate version of Christian faith, a non-Western religion, that has taken root in the distinctive heritage of that continent. (Kärkäinen 2002: 195)

Whether successful or not, 'Independent Churches have ... attempted to creatively synthesise traditional and Christian beliefs, ... they represent radical indigenisation and Africanisation of Christianity' (Motlhabi in Mosala & Tlhagale [eds] 1986: 80). This was their genius. The AIC movement accommodated Christian beliefs to the realities of black people's lives; they related Christianity with black history and identity and were, therefore, 'Ethiopian'; and they wished the organisation of churches to be under the control of blacks.

Ethiopianism

Sundkler (1961: 13, 33) claims that 'Ethiopian- type' churches 'originated as a result of secession from white churches on political and racial grounds'. While an early secession from the Paris Evangelical Missionary Society occurred in 1872 in Lesotho, in a situation of political instability, it displayed three features of later secessions: 'the resentment of white control, the possible political implications, and the resistance to disciplinary regulations' (Hinchliffe 1968: 90).

The first Ethiopian-type secessions in South Africa mainly involved defections from the Methodist Church. Ethiopianism altered the means of black political protest and challenged 'those who believed in evolutionary change through constitutional means' as they 'were impatient with white control and pessimistic about protest for evolutionary change' (Odendaal 1984: 23). It was based on blacks' having a right to self-determination through 'self-pride, self-reliance and service to humanity' (Lamola 1988: 9), rejection of the accommodation approach favoured by J. T. Jabavu's newspaper *Imvo Zabantsundu*, and the recognition of a need for economic power. So it was not just a spiritual or ecclesiastical movement as confirmed by Alexander Roberts of Lovedale's deprecatory assessment at the General Missionary Conference (1904): 'First, it is a race movement; second, it is political; third, it is a church' (Kuzwayo 1979: 17 in Lamola 1988: 9).

The 'native problem' was *the* issue of the day and Ethiopianism was part of it being the sole national religio-political body. The Native Affairs Commission (1903–5) met 'under the cloud of Ethiopianism' and resulted in 'a consequent obligation to give some recognition to the increasing number of educated, civilised Africans' (Brock 1974: 335) but with little concern for the remainder who constituted the vast majority of the people. It had enabled several regional organisations to form the South African Natives' National Congress (SANNC, renamed the ANC in 1923) in 1912. Lamola (1988: 11) argues that the years 1910–30 witnessed a 'new convergence of black political opinion' stemming from black alienation arising out of the Treaty of Union (1910) which 'sealed their inferior political position'. And this fell within 'the classical period of Ethiopianism', 1882–1928 (Bridgman in Brock 1974: 409).

Ethiopians saw a convergence of the political and the religious motives and methods. However, in conceiving the reason for the founding of the Black Church as being primarily missiological even to the extent of visualising the principle of the ecumenical dimension of Christian mission, they were the formulators of the concept of Pan-Africanism. They preached that the church in colonial South Africa and the entire African population should be so developed, freed and equipped that it can go out and serve other people, – 'Africa for Humanity' (Lamola 1988: 12). This appealed to people such as Rev. Edward Tsewu.

The Development of Ethiopianism

Ethiopianism received its inspiration from and was symbolic of independence in church life as the nation of Ethiopia was symbolic of an independent Africa. Ethiopia was also a centre of historic Christianity hardly touched by westernisation, and was based on the Old Testament text Psalm 68: 31 – 'Ethiopia shall soon stretch out her hands to God'. Kalu's (2005: 259) view of this novel phenomenon was significant: 'Ethiopians were ahead of their times and had started a process of reflection that perceived Christianity as a non-western religion, asserted African contribution in the Jesus movement and sought to fashion an authentic African response to the gospel's good news.'

The contrary view was that:

> Whatever of religion and education exists among all the different tribes of South Africa is due to the expenditure of money by the great Missionary Societies of the home country and to the labours of the present and past generation of missionaries. These missionaries and Societies naturally wish to consolidate their work, and if possible bring those churches they have fostered, to a position where they can be left as self-sustaining congregations in connection with the denominations which have created them. (CE 1989: 45)

But the secessionists were only doing what the home mission bodies had been advocating for years! The problem was with missionary reluctance to transfer authority and assets. But they were dishonest brokers:

> A large amount of freedom is given to self-supporting native churches, and the day must come when they will also be self-governing churches. The question is whether in the present attempt, as in all premature movements, it may not be that raw haste is but half-sister to delay. It would relieve the funds of the Home Societies, and set free their men for work in regions where the gospel is as yet entirely unknown. (CE 1989: 97)

Within weeks of Mzimba's secession, the Ethiopian churches were condemned before they had an opportunity to prove themselves, and what was the nature of this freedom which they were 'given' and by whom? As the result of their philanthropic and evangelistic work, the missionaries were caught between the Scylla of having taught their converts to think better of themselves and the Charybdis of failing to make fellowship efficacious in the church (Comaroff & Comaroff: 105). This was a spiritual quest controlled with material elements. The changes they wanted did not affect the essence of their ecclesiastical identity for, unlike other forms of AICs, they maintained significant continuity in doctrine, liturgy, polity and ecclesiastical dress. The leaders of the Ethiopian-type churches:

... sought a share in the power structure as decision-makers – in allocating funds, controlling and administering property ... In short, the ordained African clergy wanted to become equal partners with the missionaries in the ongoing life of the mission and church. When they were denied this role, they felt they had no choice but to separate. (Switzer: 187)

Ecclesiastically, the formation of Ethiopian-type churches took place in the shadow of the formation of the Presbyterian Church of South Africa (PCSA) (1897) and strong missionary reaction against this union. In a report on the General Assembly of the PCSA (1898), the motivation for the formation of independent churches was questioned particularly relating to 'attempting to seize their (missions') property' (CE October 1898, 156). This was the church whose birth may have been a contributing factor to the formation of the Presbyterian Church of Africa by Mzimba and his colleagues. The claim might be related to losing potential property in the union which brought the PCSA into being.

Rev. Edward Tsewu

Edward Tsewu was born in Grahamstown in 1856. He claimed to be 'an *Amaxosa*, a *Gaika*' (SANAC IV, 43,754: 803). He was the son of a deacon of the Lovedale congregation of the Free Church of Scotland and attended school at Gqumahashe village near Lovedale (Millard 1999: 73). At the age of fifteen, he began to train as a teacher at Lovedale Institution from 1872–5, (Lovedale Missionary Institution [LMI] reports 1872: 16 [where he is described as coming from Buchanan, a mission situated north of Mthatha], 1873: 17, 1874: 1717, 1875: 18) gaining the Elementary Teacher's Certificate. Moir (1898: 2) describes him in retrospect as having made 'creditable efforts to help himself and suffered somewhat from the worldliness of others'. Tsewu then taught at Adelaide. Following the receipt of a call to the ministry, Tsewu returned to Lovedale to study Theology (LMI 1880: 27; 1881: 25; 1882: 20; 1883: 35). Despite 'a slight feeling, even then, of uncertainty about him' (Moir 1898: 2), he was licensed a probationer of the Free Church and sent to Cunningham mission, Toleni, in the Transkei in 1884. In 1886, he was transferred to Idutywa (Millard 1999: 73) and Main but 'Nowhere did he do well', according to Moir, and: 'when a proposal was made to promote him to a more independent sphere at Johannesburg ... and when the question of his ordination to the full status of a minister was raised in connection with this proposal, the Presbytery did not feel justified in declining, though again some members hesitated' (Moir 1898: 2). This 'hesitation' was to have a subsequent problematic outcome for the Presbytery.

Another reason for ordaining Tsewu may have been that, between 1856 and 1910, 'only about twenty-two African Presbyterians were ordained'

(Switzer 1993: 125, 126). This was the heavy price paid for maintaining high educational standards and an unwillingness to ordain black men to equal status in ministry (Switzer 1993: 123, 125). Switzer (1993: 187) argues that '[t]he mission's subordination of the ordained clergy, in particular, was a major factor in the schisms'. Stewart must bear some responsibility for this state of affairs for his segregationist views and policies had caused anxiety among black church leaders by the 1880s to the extent that they 'could no longer trust Lovedale and Stewart to act or speak in their best interests' (Brock 1974: 344, 345). He and others, Moir included, had produced men who:

> ... sought a share in the power structure as decision makers – in allocating funds, controlling and administering property, choosing suitable candidates for the ministry and promoting them to positions of authority. In short, the ordained African clergy wanted to become equal partners with the missionaries in the ongoing life of mission and church. When they were denied this role, they felt they had no choice but to separate. (Switzer 1993: 187)

For instance, Rev. P. J. Mzimba was one of the first graduates in theology (1874) under the system introduced by the new Principal of Lovedale Institution, James Stewart. This was a significant development and change of policy which allowed black ministers trained in South Africa to join the ranks of the Free Church of Scotland Mission. African clergy wanted to upgrade their status through ordination. '[F]inancially strapped parent boards of several mission bodies [including the FCoS] also began urging their missionaries to establish autonomous "self-supporting, self-governing, self-propagating" African churches' opening up to them the 'most prestigious vocations open to the upwardly mobile elite during the colonial period' (Switzer 1993: 123). However, there were reservations concerning this policy change. Stewart was unwilling to adhere to Scottish mission policy concerning the ordination of blacks 'In an agitated moment he *seems* to have claimed that the main cause of Ethiopianism was to be found in the interfering European mission boards in the matter of the ordination of Africans' (Sundkler 1961: 39).

The Johannesburg Congregation of the Presbytery of Kaffraria

In 1890, Rev. P. J. Mzimba, minister of the Presbytery of Kaffraria of the Free Church of Scotland [FCoS] at Lovedale, was sent to Johannesburg to evaluate the work in the Free Church of Scotland congregation there which was mainly composed of young men from the Eastern Province who were migrant labourers. This led to Rev. Edward Tsewu being called as minister to the Johannesburg congregation in 1891 (Tsewu to Smith, 31 January 1891, NLS 7797). The Foreign Mission Committee (FMC) of the FCoS refused to take responsibility for this congregation and the Transvaal

Presbytery did not want to be involved in this placement, and denied Tsewu a seat in presbytery and financial support. So the Presbytery of Kaffraria retained responsibility though it was almost impossible to exercise authority from such a great distance. Tsewu was transferred to Johannesburg where his work went well until a group in his congregation accused him of unspecified 'irregularities' (Millard 1999: 73).

The Tsewu Secession

By 1896, Tsewu was alleged to have become involved in the Ethiopian movement and Mzimba was sent by the Presbytery of Kaffraria to assist in dealing with the problems in the Free Church Mission in Johannesburg led by Tsewu. This resulted from charges of mismanagement of the congregation's affairs 'with a view to worldly gain' (UFH, HPAL, Proceedings of the Synod of Kaffraria of the Free Church of Scotland, July 1897: 7). However, Tsewu denied that he was a member of the Ethiopian Church. He informed the South African Native Affairs Commission [SANAC] on 14 October 1904: 'I do not belong to the Ethiopian Church, except the word Ethiopian may mean black. I am a Presbyterian . . .' (SANAC IV, 43,618: 793). He claimed that often the Ethiopian term is used 'by others saying "This is an Ethiopian" as if they were doing something quite apart from other Christian brethren'. He made a critical comment regarding the missionaries who were, he claimed, stirring up emotive responses: 'I do not blame the Government so much as the missionaries, who go to the Government and say, 'Look at these people who are rebelling against you" (SANAC IV, 43,618: 793). He employed the metaphor of a tree: 'pull up a good tree and push it outside' (SANAC, 43,621: 793). He regarded this as a great mistake 'without investigating the thing fully, or they might spoil a work which was intended to do good in the hearts of man'.

A congregation of four hundred members, by this time reduced to one hundred due to an inter-tribal dispute in Tsewu's congregation, led Mzimba to the conclusion: 'They have joined the Independent or Ethiopian churches' (Mzimba to Stewart, 12/8/1896. UCTL, Stewart Papers, BC106: C167.8). At this time, Mzimba favoured following the procedures of the church. As a result, he gained experience and became aware of the different circumstances of blacks in the Transvaal who enjoyed less legal protection than those in the Cape. On the issue of land, for instance, Tsewu believed 'that the Natives ought to be allowed to buy land in their own names, and have title deeds in their own names' (SANAC IV, 43,552: 787). Mzimba concluded that 'uniting the native has increased the Ethiopian Church' (Mzimba to Stewart, 1/9/1896. UCTL SP BC106.C167). However, Brock's (1974: 362) critique was, in a retrospective sense, prophetic: 'In the immediate past, as has been seen, the record of the mission in opposing discriminatory legislation had been fair, but they [i.e. the missionaries] could not positively stand for equality within their own ecclesiastical domain'.

Subsequent events were to prove how little they learned from the incident.

The inter-tribal dispute had resulted in the *amaZulu* withdrawing from the congregation leaving a majority of *amaXhosa*. This was followed by a dispute about a church building which Tsewu had erected. At its meeting at Burnshill on 14 November 1895, the Presbytery of Kaffraria received a report that led them to conclude that 'a change seemed desirable both for the sake of the mission and for the sake of Rev. Tsewu' (Synod of Kaffraria, July 1897). On 16 July 1896, the Presbytery of Kaffraria decided that Tsewu should be replaced by Rev. Elijah Makiwane of Macfarlan Mission (Presbytery of Kaffraria, 16 July 1896; Synod of Kaffraria, July 1897: 5). Tsewu refused and on 21 July 1896 sent a letter from a different group of his congregants to affirm that they were happy with his work (Millard 1999: 73). Presbytery was rather sceptical about the source of the letter stating that it was 'purporting to be from his congregation' (Synod of Kaffraria, July 1897: 5).

Revs Pambani Mzimba and James Stewart were sent as a commission to Johannesburg to investigate. Mzimba was to conduct services and provide pastoral care in Tsewu's congregation. This was probably the first direct contact Mzimba had with the secessionary movement. In a letter to Stewart (12 August 1896. UCTL, Stewart Papers, BC106: C167.8) he stated:

> I have now been three days my impression is that these men (the office-bearers) are going to separate themselves from the Free Church and that the congregation practically does not exist ... They have closed the door against services being held by me in the location Church which was built by Tsewu and the new one is not opened yet though completed ... Ever since the Burnshill [Presbytery] meeting the work of separating has been going on ... Practically the work must be started afresh. All this is in the supposition that Mr Tsewu is removed or changed to another sphere of labour whether he should be removed or allowed to remain that will be the result of the investigation. The idea here is that he is already removed as he is practically suspended.

However, at least Mzimba operated in the town congregation of the Free Church:

> The place open for me to preach is the town church because the stand belongs to the Free Church. There is a church at the location, a few of Mr Tsewu's supporters have closed the church. It is plain they are leaving the Free Church where they are going to I do not know ... A good many of these are strangers and others had left the Church, some have not returned they have gone to the Wesleyans, Ethiopian Church and Congregationalists.

This appears to be largely supposition on Mzimba's part, though it is probably true. There were financial issues relating to the payment of Tsewu's stipend as there appeared to be, at least, a boycott on congregational liberality. It also seemed that Tsweu also held some congregational funds.

> I understand Mr Tsewu has consulted lawyers and threatens to go to court... Church work especially finances is blocked that is endeavouring to have everything stopped that is if the seceding party succeeds. I think they will fail. They are not strong enough.

As was often the case in disputed situations, money became an issue and this hampered the work of mission and caused suspicion. It is not clear why Bilbrough consulted the Deacons' Court about whether to pay Tsewu if there were no funds available to do so. Whatever monies Tsewu held, they were never returned. 'It is noteworthy that Tsewu's actions, namely, his refusal to return church money, correspond closely to those later adopted by Mzimba himself' (Burchell 1979: 121–2).

When Mr Tsewu went to the King William's Town Presbytery in July (1896) the Deacons' Court here (Johannesburg) had opened the new church finished on 9 August. Mzimba reported that he had been unable to conduct services in a church building purportedly owned by Tsewu (Mzimba to Stewart, 12 September 1896. UCTL, Stewart Papers, BC106: C167.9). Some of the members wanted him to preach while others objected.

It is clear from this that not all of Tsewu's location congregation was opposed to Mzimba carrying out the functions assigned to him. Ownership was also contentious as apparently, Rev. Tsewu had not funded the building since it was sanctioned by the Presbytery of Kaffraria and they would not have agreed to the erection of a building owned by an individual. The building would be owned by the General Trustees of the church. Using the building would also have been an issue because in Free Church law, the minister has almost total control of the building use except 'for any purpose not connected with the congregation, without the acquiescence both of the Session and the Deacons' Court' (BPCSA 1958: 8, 17–18). The Bantu Presbyterian Church of South Africa (BPCSA) adopted Free Church law on its formation in 1923.

The commission sat during the latter part of September into October 1896. Tsewu accused James Stewart of undermining his work by dividing the congregation as the result of not hearing the witnesses in his defence. 'The evidence produced was very full' (Deposition 1897: 1). A report was submitted to the Presbytery meeting at Lovedale on 9 December 1896. Tsewu was cited to appear before the Presbytery on 22 January 1897 having been paid until the end of December 1896. Tsewu did not appear on the date cited but sent a telegram stating that he would arrive late. He did not arrive. On 16 April, Presbytery instituted a case of libel against Tsewu and he was cited to appear on 5 May 1897. Again, he did not appear. Neither did he appear on 21 May and 2 June when he was again cited to appear (Synod of Kafraria 1897: 6). The Presbytery referred the matter to the Synod for action. The charges were included in a slightly expanded form (Synod of Kafraria 1897: 6) but still without details. Despite this, the Presbytery decided there was substance to the accusations, and Tsewu was accused of making false reports, not calling banns for marriages and charging unreasonable fees for performing marriages during the week. In addition he was accused of not acting according to church law and procedure in the election of elders and forcing members to pay church dues (Millard 1999: 74). The Synod of Kafraria noted in 1897 that 'for some time past the condition of the congregation under his care has been in an unsatisfactory state' (Deposition 1897: 1) and that the charges were of a serious nature. The charges were '*wilful deception, abuse of ministerial functions, as well as dubious conduct* in connection with various matters about church property' (Deposition 1897: 2). These were very non-specific charges. Under these heads various comments were made but these were also non-specific though it is noted that 'A fuller statement will be found in another column containing the report of the meeting of Synod' (Deposition 1897: 2). Sadly for Tsewu 'No counter evidence of any value against the many serious charges of very non-ministerial conduct was ever produced' (Deposition 1897: 3). This was the first case of so serious a nature in the history of the Scottish Missions of the Free Church of Scotland in South Africa. The reason given for such a strong judgment was:

> But for the credit of mission work and that of the native ministry as well as in justice to his unfortunate congregation . . . and prevent him doing further mischief. If any error has been committed it is that of leniency, and of considerable delay in the hope that such a sentence might have been avoided. (Deposition 1897: 3)

Non-appearance, according to church law constituted an admission of guilt. So, due to Tsewu's non-appearance, the Synod decided to:

> hold him as having confessed and to deal with him according to his offences – therefore the Synod did by their vote depose the said Edward Tsewu, like as they hereby do in the name of the Lord Jesus Christ, the alone King and Head of the Church, and in virtue of the power and authority committed by Him to them, depose the said Edward Tsewu, from the Office of the Holy Ministry; prohibiting and discharging him to exercise the same or any part thereof. (Synod of Kaffraria 1897: 7)

This decision was transmitted to the General Assembly of the Free Church of Scotland. Tsewu had allowed himself to be isolated by the vagaries of church law by not appearing when requested to do so. Yet, it is strange that so harsh a sentence was meted out to him for a first offence by any legal standards. Perhaps this was a signal to like-minded ministers to warn them against similar action in the prevailing and growing secessionary movement.

The *Christian Express* (August 1897) article, following the outcome of the Synod case ends with an apologia for the training of ministers: 'In the Presbyterian Church every precaution is taken by long training and moral supervision to prevent unsuitable men entering the work of the ministry. The moral failures have been comparatively few...' (Deposition 1897: 4). This constitutes a damning indictment of Edward Tsewu. He had refused to attend Presbytery meetings giving various excuses including the death of his child and his brother-in-law which prevented him from leaving Johannesburg. These were considered inadequate reasons: 'Courts cannot postpone grave business for such a cause as Mr Tsewu pleads' (Moir 1898: 4). However, Tsewu's bereavements were substantial enough reasons according to African custom and culture. He was required again to appear before the presbytery; he refused and resigned from the ministry.

The Rev. W. B. J. Moir of Blythswood Institution and Moderator of Presbytery, wrote a negative review in a letter quoting directly from a document entitled 'Defence of the Rev. Edward Tsewu of Johannesburg, on Dispute in Church Matters', This letter was also reprinted in the Synod minutes from the *Christian Express* (Synod of Kaffraria, 1898). Moir had taught Tsewu at Lovedale and claimed to 'know most of his people' ('Defence', Synod of Kaffraria, 1898). Tsewu had claimed that he was not heard in his own defence. This was true. He had not had or taken the opportunity to defend himself. Moir (1898: 2) challenged this by explaining that the Presbytery had devoted five days in February 1897 to hearing Tsewu's defence in a preliminary enquiry in an informal setting, according to church law, to avoid a formal hearing. Moir (1898: 2–3) is correct in his assertion that this was a hearing and not a trial, but with such patience 'that native auditors remarked to us we were having far too much patience with him'. This could not, however, be considered exoneration of the Courts of the church since they had well established procedures to follow. Then he tried to subvert the process by challenging the jurisdiction of the court and then resigning. He was the victim of deposition by default. Tsewu claimed that the problems which arose in his congregation were 'purposely and largely planned' (Moir 1898: 3) to which Moir replied that it would be incomprehensible for the FCoS Mission to destroy its own missionary efforts or one of its ministers. Tsewu also claimed that his membership roll was greater than it was and Moir (1898: 3) gave downwardly revised figures drawn from the Communion Roll.

To the charge that Dr Stewart had maliciously attacked Tsewu, Moir (1898: 3) responded by saying that the charges were 'nearly all, brought by church-members and office-bearers. The words were the words of the Presbytery, but the facts were the facts of church-members and office-bearers'. Tsewu's charge was 'The very point that caused a split in my church' was 'the refusal of Dr Stewart to have the witnesses of the accused (myself) heard fairly' (Moir 1898: 304). But the division was evident before Stewart became involved and that was why Stewart was sent to Johannesburg on the basis of his assumed neutrality.

Regarding the congregation's petition in favour of Tsewu, Moir (1898: 5) reveals that it was not only Tsewu who was disciplined but also his office-bearers after colluding with him. He even admitted to the Presbytery that 'some came to him, and withdrew their names, when they heard the nature of the petition, and one or more of the names he erased with his own hand'.

The Aftermath

In response to his deposition, Tsewu established the Independent Native Presbyterian Church (SANAC IV, 43,774: 787) Open for Reunion and, led the first secession from the FCoS. However, Tsewu did not regard it as a secession or schism. He made it quite clear to the South African Native Affairs Commission (14 October 1904, IV, 43,561: 787; cf. 43,562, 43772): 'The Independent Presbyterian Church is the separation [not secession] of our church from the Free Church on a church dispute at present, but we are open for re-union'. This constituted a prelude to the Mzimba Secession but had little long term effect. In all this, Tsewu then took his story to the press (Millard 1999: 74), probably to expose the matter and solicit support for his cause. The sad situation arising out of Tsewu's discipline was exacerbated by his replacement by a white missionary, Rev. C. B. Hamilton, as requested by the Presbytery of Kaffraria, supported by the Synod of Kaffraria, to the FMC. This decision of the Synod of Kafraria in 1899 worsened the situation. Rev. John Lennox, writing to Dr Stewart commented:

> Affairs in the Johannesburg congregation are at a deadlock. The office-bearers refuse to collect contributions even from those who are ready to give. It was felt by all in the Presbytery and Synod that a deputation should go there without delay, and Erskine and I were thought of. Stuart [of Burnshill] cannot leave his two stations and there is no one else who can go from this side, or who knows the circumstances fully. (5 August 1899, UCTL Stewart Papers [SP] BC106: 167. 31)

Not surprisingly, such problems arose considering the great distance between the Presbytery in the Eastern Cape and Johannesburg. It was even difficult to be apprised of the intricacies of the situation.

Reverends P. J. Mzimba and E. Makiwane raised the race issue by commenting on the Presbytery's or white missionaries' view that 'The Free Church Native Congregation at Johannesburg is fit only for a white missionary' (15/4/1898–16/4/1898, Minutes of the Presbytery of Kaffraria, 14/4/1894–27/1/1900, Lennox Papers, UFH). Rev. J. D. Don, Clerk to the Presbytery of Kaffraria, in a letter to Dr Lindsay, Secretary of the FMC of the FCoS, emphasised the inequality of whites and blacks, 'We cannot afford to act upon the assumption that the native is equal to the European' (24/1/1898, NLS: 7798). Yet, Don did not see this as a factor in

Tsewu's dispute, according to Tsewu: 'Before the late Mr Don died in King William's Town we spoke on that point, and he said to me, "So far as you are personally concerned, I know it is not a matter of white *versus* black". It was a church dispute' (SANAC IV, 43,621: 793). This led Mzimba to conclude that black ministers would always be allocated subsidiary roles and never attain full equality with their white counterparts and there was little hope of developing a self-supporting, self-governing and self- propagating church. This became one of the main causes of the subsequent Mzimba Secession in 1898. In addition, the Tsewu Secession demonstrated that 'it was possible to disagree with the Presbyterian church authorities' (Millard 1995: 215) and survive.

By 1903, the Johannesburg congregation was transferred to the care of the Transvaal Presbytery. Tsewu remained in Johannesburg and subsequently joined the American Methodist Episcopal Church (AMEC) contrary to his protestations about being a Presbyterian. Perhaps he had concluded that re-union was no longer a possibility after his replacement with a white minister. Millard (1999: 74) notes that in 1905, Tsewu along with other AMEC members, Marshall Maxeke, John Mtshula and James Tantsi challenged the refusal of the Register of Deeds which would not register land on the name of an African by bypassing the official channels of the provincial administration and achieved his wish. This was significant for African Initiated Churches as it gave them the right to purchase land in urban areas. Millard (1999: 74) affirms 'His desire for religious freedom became channelled into a struggle for political freedom'.

However, there were other localised secessions from the Free Church Mission in Qumbu, Port Elizabeth and Mafeking, all predating Mzimba's secession, perhaps demonstrating the potential of the Ethiopian movement as a national political, and a religious, movement. In this context the better known Mzimba Secession occurred.

Conclusion

One question that arises regarding Edward Tsewu is: should he have been ordained in the first place given the misgivings about him, despite the pressures emanating from the policy to ordain black ministers? That he became a problem to the Synod and Presbytery of Kaffraria must be attributed in some measure to these courts of the FCoS. It also appears from the evidence available that Tsewu had a disruptive personality. There is no evidence he tried to heal the rifts in his congregation. He was also defiant in the face of the Presbytery's attempts to bring him to justice, but clearly the parties were operating with differing concepts of what constituted justice. As in the case of other secessions, money became a confusing and complicating factor. Despite accusations to the contrary, Tsewu was not against European practice and influence. For instance, regarding marriage, he took the view that he should 'encourage the Christian native in the way of marrying according to European custom' (SANAC IV, 43,579: 789). As in other secessions, when a decision is made to separate from a parent body, there is no going back. Perhaps it would go beyond the evidence in this case to conclude this was a matter of 'Pull up a good tree and push it outside'.

CHAPTER SIX

The Mzimba Secession, 1898: A South African 'Disruption'

Introduction

A significant stimulus to the formation of an autonomous church whose roots were in the Scottish mission was the rise of resistance to mission domination in the latter part of the nineteenth century. This was an African continental phenomenon and took the form of Ethiopian-type churches whose origin and development were a paradoxical phenomenon in the history of Christianity in South Africa. They expressed the success of missionary work which had prepared African leadership through providing a thorough education which resulted in the twin, but opposing responses, of conformity and resistance. The organisers of what became Ethiopian-type churches were resisters, although some appeared to be conformists. On the other hand, the missionaries lamented their rise because they undermined their power and authority and suggested that they had outgrown their missionary purpose with the developing maturity of their scions. The missionaries had seriously underestimated the option of rejection of their mentorship in whole, or in part as they reached spiritual and other forms of maturity. Missionaries believed that their subjects were not yet fully equipped for the responsibility some were taking upon themselves, but could give no reasonable estimate regarding when that state of 'readiness' would occur. History has not been kind to this interpretation as several such churches arose and many have survived the dismal prediction that they would not stand the test of time.

Prelude to Secession

One such example is the Presbyterian Church of Africa which came into being when Rev. Pambani J. Mzimba, an experienced minister and one of the first blacks to be ordained by the Free Church of Scotland Mission in South Africa, seceded from the mission in 1898. Mzimba had been minister of the Free Church of Scotland Mission at Lovedale adjacent to the historic Lovedale Missionary Institution since his ordination in 1875. He had received his education and had worked at Lovedale, before his ordination. In 1893, he was sent to Scotland to attend the jubilee celebrations of the Free Church of Scotland as a representative of the Mission. While there,

Mzimba raised a large sum of money for a building fund in his congregation supported by Dr James Stewart, his mentor and Principal of Lovedale Missionary Institution (Burchell 1979: 120). He later claimed that he had the right to use the money as he himself saw fit, although this idea was refuted by the missionaries in the Presbytery of Kaffraria. Shepherd (1971: 59) links this conflict directly to the subsequent secession. According to Brock (1974: 354) 'money and property were the precipitating factors in the quarrel between the Free Church mission and Mzimba'. Shepherd (1971: 59) relates that Mzimba was given substantial amounts 'he claimed he had the power to allocate to such objects as he saw desirable' (Mzimba 1893). The secession occurred in response to demands of the Presbytery of Kaffraria that he hand over the money raised. 'Mzimba was angered by the fact that congregations built and maintained their churches and paid a high proportion of the expenses but had no rights when it came to ownership or control of church property' (Switzer 1993: 186).

The founders of Ethiopian-type churches had discovered to their cost that money is a material representation of power and control, an issue 'that defines personal self-awareness' and a challenge to what it means 'to be human' (Farrell 2011: 70). Creating a dependency syndrome was part of the missionary approach. It was an error 'to regard local people as uniformly in need of benevolence instead of drawing on the resources they held for mission' (Reese 2010: 30). It was in this situation that the Ethiopian-type churches wrested the self-government from the missionaries' control. In the global context: '[i]t is the self-support principle that created self-respect, self-reliance and independent spirit which are necessary for any successful movement' (Park in Reese 2010: 31).

Hence, '... money was an issue in terms of stipend, living conditions and funds raised overseas' (Duncan 2003b: 187). The mission-initiated stipend system led to a discriminatory approach in the treatment of local black ministers compared with their missionary brethren. The missionaries controlled the money and disbursed it in a manner which lacked transparency and accountability. Inevitably, this led to rivalry regarding the control of finance between missionaries and the emerging black leadership. The missionaries were responsible for dealing with the spiritual development and maturity of their missions. This would naturally lead to the ordination of a formed and qualified native ministry, and to grant ordination would be 'to signal their ecclesiastical and financial equality with the white missionaries' (Switzer 1993: 123) for '[t]he ordained ministry would be among the best paid' (Switzer 1993: 123). Yet, the missions failed 'to produce more pastors' (Switzer 1993: 125). The South African context was one where '... the standards set by the Presbyterians ... virtually eliminated prospective candidates for ten years' (Switzer 1993: 125). They could, however, 'raise funds on behalf of their congregations' (Switzer 1993: 123).

The Mzimba Secession

Mzimba's letter of resignation (University of Fort Hare [UFH], Lennox correspondence, Minute book of the Presbytery of Kaffraria) states *inter alia* clear financial reasons:

> 8. The words of ministers were not acceptable to me and to my elders, when they said, 'that church was not suitable for blacks, it is beautiful and they must not be allowed to ask for overseas assistance' and the money that was raised by me must not be given to my congregation and me.
> 9. The money I collected years ago is still not with the congregation it was asked for, and I also did not receive it. I was told when it arrived, but there are people who insisted that it must not be given to us. It is for the second time, first it was mentioned that the money must be sent to Pondoland to build ministers' houses.
> 10. Dr Ross sympathised with us and asked you to let us build the church this year (1898) and the Presbytery decided that let us fundraise four hundred pounds first.
> 11. We did fundraise with difficulties and the Presbytery agreed to build the church and destroy the old one.

In November 1898, Mzimba stated his intention of forming a new church and in the following month published its Constitution because:

> You have done well in leaving, and, try to stand alone; all we missionaries have come to train you for that, we have come to leave you by yourselves and unrelying [sic] on the white man. If it be so then, what may cause fear to the native Christian in standing alone. (Mzimba 'To the Christian Public of the Free Church', Cory Library, Stormont papers, MS 7492)

The Presbyterian Church of Africa came into being at a synod meeting held at Seshegu, near Lovedale on 27 December 1898. In the midst of this there were further secessions from the FCoS mission (Duncan 1997: 99–100).

During the ensuing crisis, it emerged that the presenting cause of Mzimba's resignation was a dispute between himself and the missionaries Stewart and Lennox regarding the new church for the Lovedale district congregation and the fact that the money had taken four years to reach Lovedale: 'With fuller and franker interchange of views, the thing might have been prevented altogether' (UFH, Lennox correspondence, Minute book of the Presbytery of Kaffraria, Commission of Enquiry, 20 April 1898).

There is no direct evidence that Mzimba was influenced by the three-self formula although he was a convert to the concept of self-reliance:

> I am looking forward to the time, which I hope will come, when, while we control our own Church matters separately . . . (Rev. P. J. Mzimba,

SANAC 1904, vol II, 10,907, 793) . . . the idea that we are working for ourselves and that we are responsible for what we are doing stimulates us in making self-sacrifice in our work. (Rev. P. J. Mzimba, SANAC 1904, vol II, 10.910, 794)

This was an alternative to remaining under the control of both Presbyteries. Also 'suspicion of the role of the White Mission councils remained' (Burchell 1977: 51).

In the event, Presbytery refused Mzimba's resignation because:

On his ordination as minister of the Lovedale congregation, certain properties belonging, some to the congregation, others to the Free Church of Scotland, were practically placed in his hands. It was his duty on tendering his resignation to have handed over these funds and properties. This, however, he has persistently refused to do . . . Had Mr Mzimba rendered a full and final account of his stewardship, and plunged into the darkness of this land, there to tell the story of the Cross, after leaving home and friends, the brethren, Native and European, would have been only too glad to see him do so, and would have wished him God-speed. (Rev. W. Stuart, Burnshill in Editorial, *CE*, XXIX, 344, 2 February 1899,17)

These properties consisted of: 'six buildings, the sum of £1,361, the regular books and documents of the Church, including baptism and marriage registers, six title-deeds to garden lots, and other assets . . .' (Rev. W. Stuart, Burnshill in Editorial, CEXXIX, 345, 7 March 1899, 33). They 'were assigned to their legal owners, the Deacons' Court of the Lovedale Native Congregation' by the Supreme Court of the Cape Colony (Rev. W. Stuart, Burnshill in Editorial, CEXXIX, 345, 7 March 1899, 33). In that court action, the Chief Justice stated:

And there is evidence to show that from time to time sums of money which had been obtained from Scotland were paid to Mzimba as part of his stipend. His allegation, therefore that the whole of the funds from which these buildings were erected came from the natives from the different congregations, is not borne out by the facts proved in the present case . . . the fact that there has been no transfer to and no title deeds in the Free Church, ought not to affect the present case. (CEXXIX, 345, 7 March 1899, 33)

It is helpful to consider the case of The Lovedale Native Congregation versus Mzimba and others in the first of three cases referred to the Supreme Court of the Cape Colony. The declaration of the plaintiffs stated that:

5. Prior to the said month of June, 1898, a certain sum of money, amounting to the sum of £1,361, or thereabouts, which was vested in and under the control of the Deacons' Court for the time being, was placed by the said Court placed in possession of the defendants Mzimba, Kala,

and Mabeqa, as a committee, to be by them held for the purpose of a building fund, with a view to the erection of a new church for the use of the said congregation. (*CE*, XXIX, 345, 7 March 1899, Supplement, 49)

The source of these funds was not specified but their purpose was clear. However, the defendants' plea was equally clear. They had never received the money and that the funds raised, about £950, had come from the members of the congregation. It was administered by a building committee under Mzimba's chairmanship. The Treasurer was John Knox Bokwe (*CE*, XXIX, 345, 7 March 1899, Supplement, 50). An amount of about £1,076, raised by Mzimba, remained with the congregation (*CE*, XXIX, 345, 7 March 1899, Supplement, 50). The source of the funds Mzimba collected is not clear and Mzimba did not secede with the money.

Rev. J. D. Don (Treasurer to the Presbytery of Kaffraria) giving evidence for the plaintiffs stated that the FCoS had given £1,400 for the new church at Lovedale and that Mr Mzimba informed the Presbytery that £400 had been donated by the congregation between October and December 1897. This money should have been handed over when he resigned. Mr Mzimba had been instructed to account to the Presbytery but had refused (*CE*, XXIX, 345, 7 March 1899, Supplement, 51). This conflicts with the plea of the defendants. Rev. D. D. Stormont (*CE*, XXIX, 345, 7 March 1899, Supplement, 51) reported that 'All the books, documents, rolls and the outstations title-deeds were missing' but did not claim that Mzimba had refused to release them.

In his defence, Mzimba claimed:

> ... making up my mind that I would leave the congregation, all the congregational monies that were in my hand I transferred to Kala ... The only monies that I did not touch were the monies that came from Scotland. I left them in the fixed deposits, and the congregational money was kept separate from the monies from Scotland.

He was prepared to hand over £275 (*CE*, XXIX, 345, Supplement, 7 March 1899, 53). On 28 February 1899, Mr J. M. Kala (Building Fund Treasurer) was questioned. He acknowledged that he had £973 in his possession and that he 'put it on the table' at a meeting of the congregation (*CE*, XXIX, 345, Supplement, 7 March 1899, 54). He later said '. . . when I was going to hand it over to the Missionaries, the congregation stopped me from doing so' (CE, XXIX, 345, Supplement, 7 March 1899, 55). In further testimony, witness Mabeqa said: 'the books were handed over to him by Mr Mzimba, and that he handed the books to Sihawu'.

> Sihawu said he received the books from the last witness [Kala], and he then handed them over to the seceders. He did not know what had become of them. He did not hand the books over to the Presbytery because the seceders stopped him. (*CE*, XXIX, 345, Supplement, 7 March 1899, 55)

The judgment of the Supreme Court was that:

> ... the plaintiffs, as members of the Deacons' Court, are entitled to obtain possession of, and to control, all moneys, books, documents, and all assets belonging to the congregation (*CE*, XXIX, 345, Supplement, 7 March 1899, 55).
>
> It is this Deacons' Court, which has control of the assets of the congregation, which has brought the present action. The plaintiffs are entitled to succeed on the first ground. (*CE*, XXIX, 345, Supplement, 7 March 1899, 56)

The following report was given:

> 1. Mr Mzimba and others were instructed by the Supreme Court to make delivery of the keys of the Outstation Churches to the rightful owners.
> 2. Mr Mzimba has to restore £388, received from Scotland, traced into his possession and belonging to the Lovedale Native Congregation.
> 3. The late Treasurer Kala is instructed to deliver up the £973 for which he alone is responsible.
> 4. Delivery is to be made of all documents, books and title deeds in the hands of the defendants.
> 5. An account is to be rendered and payment made of all other Congregational assets and property, which are held by the seceders and belong to the Native Congregation.
> 6. Costs are to be paid by Mr Mzimba and others;
>   a. on case *re* interdict on buildings;
>   b. on case *re* documents and monies:
>   c. on rule *nisi* granted in the case of Messrs. Myimbane, Mbema, Gwabeni and Marawu.
>
> We understand that the keys have been delivered and that Mr Mzimba has paid in a cheque of £388. So far as the other matters are concerned, Mr Mzimba and the seceders have to date done nothing to fulfil the instructions of the Supreme Court. (*CE*, XXIX, 348, 1 June 1899, 82)

This became the accepted missionary version of what happened. When A. W. Roberts, Acting Principal of Lovedale, was asked about the circumstances of the secession at the South African Native Affairs Commission (SANAC), he said:

> It is alleged that it was a matter of funds; certain funds which the Free Church of Scotland claimed, were also claimed by Mr Mzimba and others, and the matter was brought before the Supreme Court; it was decided by the Supreme Court, as far as my memory serves me, that the funds did not belong to Mr Mzimba and others, and he was accordingly instructed to hand them back to us. These funds have not been

handed back to this day, but we have taken no further legal steps in the matter. (SANAC, 1904, vol II, 11.025: 803)

Despite this, confusion remained on several issues. Clearly different understandings were at play regarding the 'facts' of the dispute, amounts in question, who held the funds and questions of ownership. Money raised by seceders was involved but for what purpose? If it was for a new church at Lovedale district, then it could be argued that is what it ought to have been used for. Hence, since they were members of Lovedale until the secession from Lovedale, they had no claim on the funds from the moment of secession. But was there a different understanding at play – that money raised by seceders was to be disposed of in a manner decided by the seceders? Also, there was no clarity regarding the actual proportion of the funds raised by the seceders.

Following this Supreme Court action, the Foreign Mission Committee of the Free Church of Scotland thanked the missionaries 'for the care they have taken to secure funds and property which belong to the church and the Mission, and approve of all the legal proceedings taken for the end' (*CE*, XXIX, 349, 1 September 1899, 131). The security of funds and property seem to have been more important than the care and cure of souls at Lovedale.

The matter was resolved to an extent when 'Mr Lennox reported that Mr Mzimba had paid over the £388 for which the Supreme Court held him responsible, and the costs. All efforts to secure the remaining money, books and documents adjudged to be the property of the Lovedale Native congregation had failed' (*CE*, XXIX, 354 1 December 1899, 189). 'On resigning his position he [Mzimba] persisted in retaining properties which had been entrusted to his custody. These included buildings, title deeds to land, the sum of £1,361, with the records and documents of the Church (Bridgman in *CE*, XXXIII, 1 October 1903, 151). Outstanding financial issues remained, so the matter was unresolved. In addition, account needed to be taken of the negative effect on morale which resulted from the dispute:

> That effort . . . has cost the Presbyterian Mission a clear loss of £1600 in actual money, not merely in estimated expenditure. To this has to be added the breaking up of one of its oldest and best stations, though the work of reconstruction has now begun. (*CE*, XXIX, 375 1 December 1901, Editorial)

> In many cases the congregations that they have created have been completely broken up through internal jealousy or financial difficulties. Many of the men, who have been enticed to embark on the venture of the ecclesiastical agitator with dreams of power and riches before them, are much to be pitied, for today they realise in their poverty and obscurity the nature of their mistakes. (*CE*, XXX, 354, 1 January 1900, 2)

Doubtless there were substantial difficulties but these were, for the most part, not serious enough to bring those who had struck out for freedom back to the mission fold. In northern Natal the Free Church of Scotland experienced serious problems:

> The purchase by natives of thousands of acres in open competition with Europeans, thus perhaps giving a sense of superiority, the exemption of many from native law, tribal politics, questions of discipline, and consequent friction with missionaries, were all contributing factors to this schism ... In neighbouring districts the Gordon Memorial [Free Church of Scotland] Mission and the Wesleyans have also suffered by split-off parties. (Bridgman in *CE*, XXXIII, 1 October 1903, 51)

By April 1900, after taking advice from the Synod of Kaffraria It was agreed 'to take no further action in the Mzimba case, and that this recommendation be forwarded to the Foreign Missions Committee for their information and advice' (UFH, HPAL, Minutes of the Synod of Kaffraria of the FCoS, 1894–1906, 6 April 1900). It seemed to be an appropriate time for closure:

> Read minute of the presbytery of Kaffraria dated 27 January 1900 anent the Mzimba Case. Mr Young proposed and Mr Matheson seconded that the Synod confirm the action of the Presbytery of Kaffraria; and that the Synod now declare PJ Mzimba to be no longer a minister and a member of the Free Church of Scotland. This was agreed to unanimously. (UFH, HPAL, Minutes of the Synod of Kaffraria of the FCoS, 1894–1906, 20 July 1900)

The subsequent work of the South African Native Affairs Commission (SANAC, 1903–5) took up the matter of the new church movement. David Hunter, a lay missionary at Lovedale, giving evidence from reading about the African Methodist Episcopal Church (AMEC) in the *Voice of Missions* (USA) stated that: 'mission work as carried out by the European missions in South Africa is a failure, and that the European missions ought to hand over their money, and their missions to the African Methodist Episcopal Church, and let them run the whole concern' (SANAC, 1904, vol II, 9251, 675). Referring to Mzimba he had claimed that he is not associated with the Ethiopian movement 'well, not the original Ethiopian Church, but the term has come to be used as applying to Native Separatist movements generally' (SANAC, 1904, vol II, 9299, 679). Mzimba was questioned at the SANAC: 'Have you been associated in any way with the movement popularly known as the "Ethiopian movement" – NO ... ours is purely a religious matter, and arose out of religious difficulties' (Rev. P. J. Mzimba, SANAC 1904, vol II, 10,9000, 10.901, 793). Rev. David Stormont, 'regarded Ethiopianism as more than merely a threat to missionary hegemony – it was a political counter-culture aimed at redressing the loss of African independence to colonial regimes' (Cuthbertson, 1991: 59). Hence there was no agreed definition of or view of this new movement. Added to this 'Stormont also reported that the [ministers] were poorly paid, which further exacerbated dissatisfaction' (Cuthbertson 1991: 61).

On being questioned about the reasons for Mzimba's 'unilateral declaration of independence, Hunter claimed that:

> ... he went home as a delegate of the mission to be present at the Jubilee Assembly of the Free Church of Scotland, and he was treated there very much as a European, and when he came back he did not see why he should not have the same position and salary as a European missionary. I think that is the bottom of it. (SANAC 1904, vol II, 9299, 679)

To leave a secure financial establishment for the wilderness was quite a leap of faith for Mzimba's Presbyterian Church of Africa. It did not restrict its work to ecclesiastical matters having a clear educational agenda which cost money. Mzimba admitted that the PCA sponsored schools and that they were supported 'By the parents of the children, attending, paying school fees ... and there are special fees [unspecified]' (SANAC 1904, vol II, 9299, 679). The school committee collects the fees, hands it to the minister who pays the teacher. In Alice, the government contribution is paid to the Native Location Inspector who pays the teacher (Rev. P. J. Mzimba, SANAC, 1904, vol II, 10.922, 10,932, 10,924, 794). This involved a high degree of trust regarding the disposition of money. But this was tied to a higher cause related to the desire to manage their own affairs: 'I think it is just a desire to work by themselves. They become incited, when they work by themselves, to do better' (Rev. P. J. Mzimba, SANAC, 1904, vol II, 10.956, 796).

The Chairman [SANAC] asked 'From what sources do you derive the money which supports your church? – From the contributions of the church members and adherents. Entirely from that? – Entirely from that.' (Rev. P. J. Mzimba, SANAC, 1904, vol II, 10.963, 10,964, 797). Here was a significant example of self-reliance. Yet, this was open to misinterpretation. Roberts, Acting Principal of Lovedale, was asked by SANAC whether he regarded:

> the desire on the part of the Native ministers to control their own church affairs as a wrong one or not?

> – Their own individual churches, as a right one; but that they should entirely control the future of the whole body, I think would be a wrong idea, because they are not capable yet of dealing with such issues as the future of their church. I think that they would be better guided if they had a body of Europeans with them to help them. (Roberts, SANAC, 1904, vol II, 11.092, 807–8)

He considered that 'Those Native ministers who are in charge of mission stations have exactly the same status as a white minister' (Roberts, Lovedale, SANAC, 1904, vol II, 11.095, 80). Even Stewart, Principal of Lovedale, contributed to the view of Mzimba's desire for self-reliance. Regarding the Ethiopian mission, he said 'It has arisen solely from a desire to have control of their own ecclesiastical affairs' (Stewart, SANAC, 1904, vol IV, 44,949, 90). This was a problem since he appeared to equate the visible effects of the secession, 'equality' and 'anti-white' (Stewart, SANAC, 1904, vol IV, 44,9509, 906) for '[t]here exists a strong desire for independence . . .' (Stewart, SANAC, 1904, vol IV, 44,952, 906).

This independent approach, as has been noted, was not restricted to purely church affairs. Stewart grudgingly acknowledged Mzimba's action in taking students to the USA (Balia 1991: 75):

> It is contributed in various ways, I think the Ethiopian Church here helps, and the parents also help. In the case of Mzimba, who took the lads over, I have no doubt he got funds from his congregations – probably not from one source, but several. (Stewart, SANAC, 1904, vol IV, 44,967, 909)

But Mzimba and his followers had a more localised vision for which funds were required:

> One of the efforts of the Ethiopian Church was to found a New South African College, . . . They wanted a large sum of money, and if they had not fallen out with Dwane, this new effort would be existing today as the New South African College planned for the Fort Beaufort area and close to both Lovedale and Healdtown (Methodist) Missionary Institutions. (Stewart, SANAC, 1904, vol IV, 44,976, 910)

Stewart was far more caustic when it came to the actual secession claiming that Mzimba:

> . . . ran amok ecclesiastically and caused us the loss of £1,600. Before we had done with him we had two cases in the Supreme Court, the rebuilding of a church, and there was also the disappearance of 700 sovereigns which were placed in a bag on a table and never seen again. The Mzimba ecclesiastical movement commenced thus. (Stewart, SANAC, 1904, vol IV, 44,976, 910)

It had become clear to Mzimba that '. . . there was little hope of developing a self-supporting, self-governing and self-propagating church within the mission context in the foreseeable future. This became one of the main causes of the Mzimba Secession' (Duncan 1997: 84). Secession came to be seen as a 'particular assertion of black independence' (Brock 1974: 367). 'Perhaps money and property played too great a role compared with the resolution of broken relationships which are not healed through court cases. The same might be said of Mzimba's followers' reaction though they acted out of a position of comparative poverty of resources' (Duncan 1997: 101).

However, an interesting situation arose in connection with the court cases relating to the secession. The Free Church of Scotland Mission was the only mission to revert to legal proceedings against a secessionary group. This was contrary to the Free Church tradition which eschewed any involvement of the state in matters spiritual. The Constitution of the Bantu Presbyterian Church of South Africa, derived from the FCoS (1843) constitution stated:

> This church has the inherent right free from interference from civil authority (BPCSA 1958: 115); that the Church derives from Him [Christ] a government distinct from civil government; and that civil rulers possess no jurisdiction in her spiritual affairs. (BPCSA 1958: 124)

Further, it is strange that, within a church context, no evidence of informal approaches had been made to resolve the matter out of court. Rather, the missionaries exercised a high-handed hegemonic approach to dealing with their former colleagues. This was an application of Ashley's (1980: 49–58) 'universes in collision' paradigm. One factor in this collision was competence in financial management.

Financial and Administrative Competence

The Rev. Donald Fraser, missionary in Venda, raised the matter of black people's competence to organise and administer their own affairs with Henderson on 12 June 1922 (Cory, Henderson correspondence): '... the committee is fairly sound on the general principle that the African is not ready to manage his own affairs, and that his executive gifts have got distinct limitations'. If this was so, then how does Fraser know this if the Africans referred to have been given no opportunity to develop these gifts? This was a common assumption.

Writing in 1926, Lea stressed the incapacity of black people to handle finance on the basis of an assumed lack of competence in this area. This was an assumption which was promoted by missionaries:

> So often the trouble arises in administration over financial matters and it is not so much a question of bad intention and evil misuse of money by the Native officer, as it is just incapacity to manage money matters. There has been no sufficiently developed financial capacity and can we wonder? It is so recent that the Bantu first handled our coinage. (Lea 1926: 58)

He developed this further with a suggestion:

> One of the most urgent matters requiring attention is the training of Native Church officers in the proper handling of trust money. The lack of this has brought the Church into disrepute. It will be a long and painful process – this education and development of capacity to deal with Church finance. Many a Native Minister has gone to pieces here and made a shipwreck of faith, as, indeed, have some Europeans. (Lea 1926: 78)

Lea's somewhat sympathetic view was penned seventy years after the ordination of Rev. Tiyo Soga (Saayman 1991: 59), the first black minister to be ordained, and more than 100 years after the Glasgow Missionary Society, precursor of the Free Church of Scotland Mission, arrived in South Africa (in 1821) (Shepherd 1971: 1). It can hardly be argued that black ministers and members had such recent acquaintance with currency, particularly in a missionary context marked by '"canny Scots" with their reputation for thrift, prudence and caution especially in money matters' (Devine 2011: 241). In addition, it may be someone who is highly skilled in finance who misappropriates funds. The problem is more likely to be moral carelessness than financial ineptitude. It is also important to note this was not a racially defined problem.

Evaluation

Ethiopian-type churches are 'the outcome of a desire on the part of the Natives for ecclesiastical self-support and self-control . . .' (SANAC Report, 1905, 321, 64). They resulted from a conscious choice to adopt a self-imposed moratorium with all its consequences. To infer that leaders of Ethiopian-type churches 'were inspired by a lust for power or wealth in their endeavours would be misleading' (Balia 1991: 80). Great financial sacrifices were made where previously dependent churches now had to become immediately self-supporting. Even if they began with some financial reserves these were soon used up and they were reduced to soliciting funds for further building projects (Sundkler 1961: 82ff). All these issues related to independence and self-reliance, even at great cost. Kamphausen (1995: 90) refers to a call from Ethiopian church leaders to their followers:

> . . . let your men cease to stretch out an imploring hand for pity and for help, and begin to claim as a right which is your heaven given inheritance, declaring unorthodox all churches and all Christians who refuse to adopt and put into the fullest possible practice the teaching of the Universal Brotherhood.

It is interesting to note there was no overt criticism of missionaries. Mzimba was reticent when talking about the secession when he testified to the South African Native Affairs Commission of 1903. He was more preoccupied with issues and not personalities. His reticence may have been due to a desire not to alienate the authorities whose support was needed, e.g. when applying for land on which to build their churches.

Money was certainly a significant issue and all money issues related to power and control, i.e. deeper issues of humanity and humanisation. In terms of humanisation, it was a missionary who said:

> Let us first recognise the ground for hope underlying the restlessness of which Ethiopianism is but the manifestation. This hope is that born

of life, a life not superimposed but imbued by Him who came that they might have life and have it abundantly. The primary expression of this life may be crude. It is shown in the desire to be somebody, to do something, to initiate, to enjoy the sense of proprietorship in homestead, business, school and Church ...' (Bridgman in *CE*, XXXIII, 1 November 1903, 166)

Specifically regarding the Mzimba secession, money came to occupy a central role. The Free Church of Scotland Mission was the only church body to go to law. Not only that, but it repeatedly did so to prove its point.

Conclusion

Money, amongst other matters, was an issue in the formation of Ethiopian-type churches in a direct and indirect manner. The politico-economic situation was a contributing factor so it cannot only be said this was solely a religious matter. It was rather a religio-economic expression of the times. Money was employed as a representation of power and a hindrance which led to arresting of the development of managerial and spiritual maturity in the black membership of churches until black members grasped control of their own destiny. However, there were direct internal causes which were derived from all not being well within the structures of the missions themselves. Mzimba and others realised money was a source of power and control concentrated in the hands of the missionaries. They altered that perception by transferring that power from the missionaries to themselves to achieve a self-reliant independent future in which they themselves could be active participants. There was missionaries' unwillingness to recognise that the results of mission education were having the paradoxical effect of conformity and resistance. This brought about a clamour for independence through developing self-reliance. Lovedale, in particular, was not ready or prepared to loosen the ties that bound the black communities to them. It thrived on dependency which had become its *raison d'être*. It had not taken account of the powerful commitment of those who yearned for a free independent future. Had the missionaries heeded the call of their sending bodies and acted accordingly, they might have mitigated some of the impact of the secessionary movement. It is a pity that Stewart, who had pioneered innovative educational methods at Lovedale, was insensitive to the contemporary needs of the situation and did not make appropriate concessions. This led to a situation which had to be remedied by the next generation of missionaries and led to the formation of the Bantu Presbyterian Church of South Africa.

But more than that, had there been a recognition of the progress made by Africans, along with the need for power to be transferred, and had a timescale been negotiated regarding the formation of an autonomous church, perhaps such extreme measures as secession could have been avoided.

Perhaps the focus on money is a diversion from the main issue. Pobee and Ositelo (1998: 55–6) draw on Nussbaum's (1994: 7–8) thinking which points historically defined mission churches towards a re-evaluation of their role:

> The African Independent Churches have exposed the limits of the old three-self formula by achieving it without being complete models of mature churches. Their pioneering experiences after achieving it are experiments at the cutting edge of mission which point us towards a restatement of the three-self formula: self-motivating, self-contextualising and self-critical.

CHAPTER SEVEN

Presbyterianism in South Africa, 1897–1923: To Unite or Not to Unite?

Introduction

Racism is a pervasive and perennial problem in South Africa. This chapter will examine how opportunities aiming to build a better more inclusive South Africa at the close of the nineteenth and beginning of the twentieth centuries were squandered through racism. Racism has its roots in the economic, political and social relations between people. Biological and other theories were developed later to justify the domination of one racial group by another. Studies and research carried out in recent years have demonstrated clearly the links between colonial and economic domination and institutional domination. The racist regime of South Africa is the most extreme example of this (Sjollema 1982: 100) as it was a culturally constructed evolutionary attitude of mind based on power with tragic consequences when enacted. This developed in South Africa from the time of the settlement of Europeans, particularly the 1820s, and was manifested in the century-long wars of dispossession from late in the eighteenth century against the 'Other', the indigenous peoples. Exercising crude, and often violent, power was symptomatic of the hegemony of empire.

Richard Elphick makes the central claim that:

> ... the struggle over racial equalisation ... was pivotal to South African history; that this concept was rooted in the missionaries' proclamation of God's love to all people, as manifested in the birth, crucifixion and resurrection of Jesus; that the ideal of equality was nurtured in large part by missionary institutions, even though missionaries themselves repeatedly sought to limit, deflect or retard its achievements. (Elphick 2012: 7–8)

This was related to two main assumptions:

> ... that networks linking members of South Africa's disparate racial and cultural groups are not of recent origin, but go far back in South African history; and that, in seeking to understand the religious origins of apartheid historians should ... see the Dutch Reformed Church as a predominantly evangelical church, closely akin to British and American Protestant churches, which was determined to shape

its policies in constant dialogue with the English-speaking world. (Elphick 2012: 9)

Martin Meredith (2011: xiv) asserts that scientists have uncovered the origins of human life in Africa seven million years ago before a mass migration around 60,000 years ago which populated the rest of the world. Therefore the debate about who came first, white or black, is outdated. The relationship with the Dutch Reformed Church (DRC) community was not that of a separate church. Many of the early missionaries were of similar origin and the DRC called many Scottish ministers to serve its congregations; so it is to be expected there would be contact of various kinds.

With regard to the formation of the Bantu Presbyterian church of South Africa Vuyani Vellem (2013: 148) ably discusses this in the context of:

> Ambivalence in black faith, *ipso facto*, a faith distinguished by blacks in their struggle against the ubiquitous defects of white faith and dominance right through into the post 1994 South Africa.

Referring to earlier attempts at union among the Presbyterian communities, he 'suggests only one reason for such a dissonant model of union: racism' (Vellem 2013: 150).

A Historical Disclaimer

It is not at all easy to locate written sources for history which are coherent in a context of racism. There are several reasons for this. First, in South Africa there has always been considerable denial which is difficult to access and assess. Second, during the period under study the concepts of 'paternalism' and 'trusteeship' were dominant discourses. Third, racism operates in a covert and subliminal manner in many people and their responses to situations in which they are unsure of how to express their feelings demonstrate their attitudes towards the 'Other'. Writing about events in the 1960s and 1970s, Rev. Rob Robertson (1997: 2), writing from the margins of the PCSA could write: 'In these days when few people will own up to having supported apartheid, the Church needs to be reminded how much its own membership either approved or connived with the system, and the reasons given for so doing'. Referring specifically to the 1960s, but acknowledging its historical existence, he commented: 'That is what it was like in almost all local congregations or parishes of all South African denominations' (Robertson 1997: 4). 'At national level, many of these churches took high-sounding resolutions on race relations, but the reality on the ground was segregation' (Robertson 1997: 4; cf. Bax 1997: 22). Fourth, this is further complicated in an ecclesiastical context where biblical hermeneutics plays an important role: 'All history is interpretation and interpretations change as time passes and new hermeneutics develop, and also when new sources become available' (Duncan 2005: 189). Fifth, who decides what is racist –

the victim or the perpetrator – and on what basis? Are what are perceived to be racist comments always racist? These were issues and questions current in the years preceding the formation of the PCSA and the BPCSA. They remain contemporaneously relevant.

The Move Towards Union

In South Africa, the path to union for Presbyterians was to be lengthy and complex. The possibility of union was, at least in part, determined by the social and political context of racism towards the close of the nineteenth century. According to Vale (2014: 3–4) this was a time of 'the development of a mining economy, the rise of grinding poverty, the accumulation of fabulous wealth and the gradual legislation of institutionalized racism ...' It was also during the early years of the twentieth century when the outcome of the South African War (1899–1902) was the alienation of black people in the settlement which helped to form the Union of South Africa (1910) and the notorious Land Act (1913). Part of the ideological support for this was derived from the views of liberalism espoused by white ministers, politicians and academics more in tune with the needs and aspirations of white people than the majority of black people. Their reaction to white racial superiority was central to the race issue and was 'largely an expression of assumed cultural superiority ... Given the tenacity of South African racial assumptions, it is reasonable to assume these forms of liberalism are peculiarly local expressions of prejudice' (Friedman 2014: 41). Translated into the ecclesiastical context in muted form:

> ... there was a general tendency to depreciate liberal principles in the political life of the country between 1880 and 1930. Similarly, there was growth of colour consciousness in both Church and State. Stewart's belief that whites would separate from blacks in a predominantly native church was as true then, as it is in the present day. (van der Spuy 1971: 29)

James Stewart, missionary statesman and Principal of Lovedale Missionary Institution, drawing on the contemporary thinking of Benjamin Kidd (1894) on social evolution, was not immune from racist thinking:

> Under the influence of some of the forms of natural religion – it may be that of fetishism, or that of any other name or kind, the African is a very slightly evolved man, especially as compared with men of many other races. This black believer in his own natural religion of fear and grotesque faith, of dread of witchcraft, and strange practices to protect himself from its influence, is in consequence and at times rather an incomprehensible creature ... the spiritual man was sleeping, the new religion took him by the hand and led him out of a land of thick darkness, gloom, and horror – filled with malevolent shades and

dreaded spectral powers – and brought him into the clear, sweet light of a simple belief in a God of goodness and love, such as Christianity reveals. (Stewart 1894: 42–3)

Throughout the nineteenth century, the distinction between settled indigenous peoples and settlers was emphasised as the result of the frontier wars of dispossession, the collapse of traditional society through the destruction of the authority of tribal chiefs and the social, cultural, religious and economic structures they represented and upheld. Again, this had an ecclesiastical impact:

> The relentless expansion of 'settler' attitudes and the hardening of political and social attitudes had a definite effect on the churches whose members represented both racial groups. Missionary credibility and optimism shrank in their wake and the complex problem of interracial relations was left to individual churches to work out. (van der Spuy 1971: 26)

Even in church black ministers 'met with white men who refused to worship with them' (van der Spuy 1971: 27). This was the context in which union discussions took place.

R. H. W. Shepherd, Principal Lovedale Missionary Institution and Director of Lovedale Press, writing prior to 1940, distinguished two views regarding union. Some believed that:

> African congregations should be an integral part of the Presbyterian Church of South Africa, even though that body was a predominantly European one. Others felt that such a union between peoples at very different stages of Christian experience and development [read civilisation], separated by language and tradition, lacked real unity. Not that this need mean dissension, but it was felt that the African Christian needed to be in circumstances where he could best develop his own Christian manhood, so that he might be free to engage in the tasks that were peculiarly his. (Shepherd 1971: 88; cf. Duncan 1997: 125–32)

It is interesting to note how Shepherd's former view was against an autonomous black church as seen from his reaction to the Mzimba Secession (1971: 59–60) and the formation of the BPCSA (1971: 88–9). Shepherd exemplified the paradox of commitment and service in exercising his vocation. He served as a UFCoS missionary from 1920 and a minister of the BPCSA from 1923 until his retirement in 1955. Thereafter he moved to the PCSA (Bax 1997: 21) where he served until 1968 and remained a member until his death in 1971. He moved from a lifetime of missionary service among black people to membership of a white congregation not 2 kilometres away, while there was a vacancy in Adelaide in his own BPCSA (1956: 2) Presbytery of the Ciskei. He remained a minister of the Church of Scotland throughout (Oosthuizen 1970: 119). His commitment to the black church was ambiguous, if not covertly racist.

The Context for Union

> Racial inequality was ... a factor in the formation of the Bantu Presbyterian Church. (Thema 2021: 23)

It is important to set the formation of the Bantu Presbyterian Church of South Africa (BPCSA) in the broader context of encroaching racism. From 1850–1900; '... missionaries relinquished their original intent to establish "native churches" quickly and became convinced that tight control must be maintained over indigenous evangelists' (Elphick 2012: 34). The missionary principles of Henry Venn (1796–1873) ... and of Rufus Anderson (1796–1880) stated clearly that the main aim of missions was a 'native church' under 'a native pastorate', where missionaries should surrender control of the churches they founded, and not take ownership of the 'native church'. But the missionaries' approach was far from the policy of their masters in Scotland and from the advocates of the Three-Self Principle:

> The home boards of several English-speaking missions, notably the ... Scots Presbyterians ..., were convinced that missionaries should rapidly work themselves out of a job and move on to unevangelised areas; they accordingly pressed their missionaries in South Africa to ordain more Africans ... (Elphick 2012: 85)

The Convener of the FMC, Dr Lindsay, claimed in 1901 that the South African missionaries 'do not seem to have grasped the idea of a Native Presbyterian Church' (Brock 1974: 49) because, he argued, that was the aim of missionaries like himself, to form a black church 'in harmony with the church's avowed policy' (Lennox to Henderson 24/5/1901, UFH). This indicates that it was missionaries themselves who were obstructing development. They were living in a period of rising imperialism which was itself 'a religion – a religion remarkably like Christianity in its emphasis on morality and character; in its call for dedication, sacrifice and duty' (Elphick 2012: 62). During this period, it was 'black Christians, who most clearly drew out the implications of the gospel's insistence on the equality of all souls before God, and the equality of all languages and of all ministers as bearers of the word of God' (Elphick 2012: 64). 'As blacks themselves increasingly assumed responsibility for evangelism of the "heathen", many missionaries came to see their work as a contribution to what Henderson called "world utility", that is, South Africa's future' (Elphick 2012: 65). This gave the lie to the idea that the missionaries themselves were the prime agents of conversion.

But the missionaries claimed that they knew best how to develop the mission; they, were the people on the ground in touch with the local context. They protested, in the words of Scottish missionary J. Davidson Don that the home board's policy was:

> based on a radical misunderstanding of the conditions existing in this country ... A native is not made fit to occupy the position of a missionary in charge of an old station with its schools, its finances and manifold relations to the European community and to the government by passing through the educational mill. (Brock 1974: 49)

The local missionaries occupied a dichotomous position: some had little faith in Africans who were to administer organisations, manage money, rebuke sin, or maintain high standards of doctrine and morality. Yet, many hoped that ordained black ministers would assist them in their war against laxness and vice and prove to the world that missions were successful.

The black candidates were in a similarly dichotomous position. While they were without doubt motivated, as their European colleagues were, by a sense of God's calling, they also were, no doubt, related to that calling, aspirants to leadership positions. In addition, during 'the 1890s, Africans' opportunities in cash-crop agriculture were shrinking, and they were barred from most professions; the ministry offered almost the only route to wealth and eminence outside the traditional economy (Elphick 2012: 86; cf. Beinart 1994: 20–25). The one area missionaries were prepared to delegate was supervision of the perceived materialism and laziness of black members; and when the 'native agents' failed to deliver missionaries reasserted their control. For many black ministers 'who had sacrificed a great deal to gain professional equality with whites, this was intolerable' (Elphick 2012: 62).

Union

The first move towards union occurred in 1880 when the Free Church and United Presbyterian Presbyteries of Kaffraria prepared a preliminary report on the possibilities of union (Report of Committee on Union between the Free Church and United Presbyterian Presbyteries of Kaffraria, 1884, William Cullen Library [WCL], University of the Witwatersrand [Wits], Ac1971/Ag2). Nothing came of this attempt.

In 1891 a further movement was initiated to establish 'a union of all the Churches and Congregations in South Africa holding the Presbyterian form of Church Government' (PCSA, Federal Council 1895: Prefatory Note). A Federal Council was established. It is not clear who was invited to participate besides references to 'the Churches concerned' and 'brethren from all parts of South Africa'. By the time of the fourth meeting in 1895, a draft constitution was presented having been scrutinised by sessions, congregations and presbyteries. It was then sent to participating 'Churches and Presbyteries' which included the Presbyteries of Kaffraria, Transkei (Free Church of Scotland), Transkei (UPCoS), Transvaal, Adelaide (UPCoS),

Cape Town, Natal and Port Elizabeth. The Colonial Committee of the FCoS expressed its support particularly in terms of 'the christianisation of the native races, and the consolidation of the Christian communities in South Africa' (PCSA, Rae to Federal Council, Minutes 16 July 1895, 19 March 1895). At this stage the UPCoS missions decided to participate in the union although a number of ministers and congregations were uncomfortable with the arrangement as were many in the FCoS tradition; yet, the UFCoS missions voted to remain separate as the Synod of Kafraria. It clearly 'feared that the predominantly white PCSA would allow racial discrimination to determine its life and work, including its mission policy' (Hunter 1983: 1).

The union was consummated on 27 September 1897. The Presbyterian Church of South Africa (often called the South African Presbyterian Church, e.g. Lennox 1911: 81, and what was 'termed the colonial Presbyterian Church' [Shepherd 1971: 88]) had four presbyteries along with the congregation of Port Elizabeth. Three presbyteries were predominantly white (Cape Town – four congregations [yet mission work had been established as early as 1838] (Quinn & Cuthbertson 1979: 15); Natal – eleven white congregations and two 'Native' congregations; Transvaal – seven white congregations and one 'Native' congregation; the fourth was the UPCoS Presbytery of Kaffraria with nine mission congregations. While the Presbyteries of Kafraria (FCoS), Transkei (FCoS) and Adelaide (UPCoS) approved the union, they refused to participate in it at that time (Bax 1997: 10–11). The following year, the Presbytery of Adelaide – six white UPCoS congregations and one 'Native' congregation, the Presbytery of King William's Town – five white FCoS congregations and one 'Native' congregation and the Presbytery of the Orange Free State – four white congregations (to be joined later that year by the congregation at Bulawayo), joined the PCSA.

The PCSA now had twenty-four 'European' and ten 'Native' congregations, 110 mission stations, 2,961 'European' and 3,778 'Native' members, 3,046 'European' adherents and 1,394 'Native' candidates and 101 'European' and 100 'Native' elders (Bax 1997:11; see also note 21: 32–3).

The Presbyteries of Kaffraria (FCoS), Transkei (FCoS) and Adelaide (UPCoS) all approved the union but felt:

> unable to enter into the proposed union at present in consequence of the want of acquiescence on the part of native congregations in two presbyteries, and in view of discussions which have arisen among Europeans on the subject of the native vote in Church courts . . . [which required] First, that some method be devised of adjusting the balance between Colonial and Mission Churches, which shall be satisfactory to both races; e.g. that a majority of white and a majority of black, separately and conjointly, be necessary to pass a proposed measure into law; or that, in view of future eventualities, the proportion of votes in both races in the General Assembly be strictly defined and preserved.

Second, that there be a final Court of Appeal in certain questions be carefully defined. (Proceedings of the First General Assembly, PCSA [1897], WCL, Ac1971/Ah1.1: 6–7)

So from the beginning issues of race and distrust were evident while they were clear to those who opposed the union they were seen differently by white proponents of the venture. The General Assembly was not convinced of these arguments which were:

not deemed sufficient to prevent the consummation of the union . . . 1) that the application of Presbyterian principles will obviate difficulties as to the balance between Colonial and Mission churches; and 2) that the matter of a final court of appeal has been adequately dealt with . . . in the draft constitution, and which has now been adopted by the General Assembly as part of the constitution of the Presbyterian Church of South Africa. (Proceedings of the First General Assembly, PCSA [1897], WCL, Ac1971/Ah1.1: 26–7)

This view was adopted unanimously. The result was clear. 'Presbyterian principles' can be manipulated to support racism as happened in the separation of mission into white and black categories. Black people were rightly suspicious of the union because, alongside the missionaries they had certain rights in decision making. The issue is that black people would form a majority in the union and white people could not tolerate majority black decisions and possibly also the scope black members would have to express their gifts.

From the inception of the PCSA, mission work among the indigenous peoples became the responsibility of the Mission Committee, while mission work among whites was the preserve of the Colonial Committee – soon to become the Church Extension Committee. As a result those whose expressed fears regarding union on the grounds of race were justified (Cory, MS Ac1971/Ag 2: 8):

Initially the PCSA failed to perceive that mission to Africans and Whites were part of the same process . . . This dual mission policy was further complicated by the PCSA's failure to formulate a clear and consistent policy whereby African mission congregations could achieve full status. (Hunter 1983: 3)

This problem was that 'the church as a whole failed to forge this new relationship' (Hunter 1983: 20) partly because 'the link between the white churches and the mission congregations tended to be tenuous and limited to financial aid rather than personal contact' (Hunter 1983: 20). Such attitudes 'effectively postponed the forging of this new relationship for more than sixty years' (Hunter 1983: 20).

Rev. D. V. Sikhutshwa (1946: 4) of the Bantu Presbyterian Church commented:

> ... at a time when the two sections of the population were at different stages of development – religiously, educationally and socially – it would have been quite inopportune to run European and African congregations exactly on the same lines; and the attempt to do so would have been disadvantageous to both sections of the population.

This is confusing because the 1897 PCSA General Assembly had affirmed it was working according to 'Presbyterian principles [which] will obviate difficulties'. The threat to white domination would be that they would not always get their own way (*Christian Express [CE]*, XXVII, July 1897: 99). However, meanwhile a threat arose from a different quarter which came as 'a judgment on missionary attitudes' (Brock 1974: 50) – the Mzimba Secession.

Progress Towards a Realistic Resolution

Further to all this, on the grounds of race, the combination of the formation of the Presbyterian Church of South Africa in 1897 and the Mzimba Secession in 1898 left the missionaries in a vulnerable position realising that African demands for autonomy could not be resisted for long. The younger generation of missionaries, including James Henderson and John Lennox, realised that by 'adopting a more consultative and cooperative stance, they might continue to influence a religious movement they had initiated but could not hope to dominate much longer' (Elphick 2012: 94). This was not to be the case.

In 1901 and 1909, the FMC of the UFCoS supported the principle of a multi-racial united church. Although James Stewart was opposed to joining the union, he was not yet ready to espouse the idea of an independent black church because of the lack of readiness among those black Presbyterians who may be:

> a hanger on to the wealthier white section – abject, inert, and lifeless and without any of the spirit necessary for its right vocation, the extension of missionary work when it has reached the position of self-support. (James Stewart to FMC [1904], *BPCSA Souvenir Programme*)

Here Stewart's inherent paternalistic form of racism was expressed from within the black mission church context. Regarding a native church, Stewart believed this could be a natural development as whites left the PCSA and as blacks assumed a majority position. He appears to have been unaware of the deteriorating racial attitudes (Wells 1909: 209) within South Africa. Yet, he was content to maintain the *status quo* in the medium to long term, i.e. 'the foreseeable future'. Congregations were consulted and the Burnshill Kirk Session declared:

> If the Foreign Mission Committee cannot see their way to establish a Native Church, they wish, as a Session and congregation to remain

under the care of the Home Church through the Committee. (FMC, 25 October 1904, Min.113; cf. Don to Young, 1 March 1897, NLS 7798)

The Synod of Kafraria struggled with the racial issues which delayed union as expressed in the pages of the *Christian Express* (XXXIII, April 1903: 49):

> If the attitude of the rank and file of white church members could be changed to meet the African in the same spirit as the missionary met him, a real union might be practicable; 'but so long as the Native minister or elder is only a "boy" to the white elder – a "boy" with whom it is not "good form" to shake hands or to invite into your pew in church, there may be a legal bond but there can hardly be a true union'.

The Synod of Kafraria stood firm on three matters; equal representation in all courts, free access for all at the Lord's table and interpretation into African languages in the courts of the church (*CE,* XXXIII, April 1903: 50).

Stewart died in 1905. In 1906, James Henderson, his successor at Lovedale, expressed a desire to pursue the matter of a black church and the Synod of Kafraria agreed in 1907. Rev. G. Robson, Convener of the General Interests Committee of the UFCoS, stated that in terms of its resolution to unite with the PCSA, it was:

> recognised that it must be left to the brethren in South Africa [presumably white missionaries?], who were conversant with the local circumstances, to decide for themselves as to the time and manner of carrying out the resolution. (Robson to Lennox, 15 January 1908, Cory MS 10711)

Arising out of a joint consultation between the Synod of Kafraria and the PCSA held in 1914, the following events occurred. The Kaffraria Mission Council came into being in 1917 on the union of the Kaffrarian and Transkeian Mission Councils (FMC, 21 March 1916, Min.3746). The Natal Mission Council joined in 1922 (FMC, 16 October 1922, Min.6166, 21 November 1922, Min 6194).

An early step forward was taken when it was agreed to 'invite certain outstanding natives' to join the mission council' (FMC, 16 July 1917, Min.4397: 1). This was a discriminatory move on the part of white missionaries. Who would do the selection? However, John Lennox stated the racial positions of the respective ecclesiastical bodies with some clarity:

> It was easy to fail here, easy for the individual missionary to forget the temporary character of his mission office and to fail to shape his work in preparation for a day when the mission will be withdrawn and be replaced by the permanent native church; easy for the church through a high sense of its Christian duty and a noble scorn of racial distinctions in the church, when we are one in Jesus Christ, to place black and white in a juxtaposition and professed equality of standing in the sight of God, in which the native Christians quite unintentionally but

really shall be overshadowed and dwarfed by their European brethren. (Lennox to PCSA General Assembly, 20 September 1915, Lennox correspondence, File Synod 1914–16, UFH; cf. Burchell 1977: 53)

At this point, Lennox and Henderson were in a minority among the missionaries. Yet, they realised that whatever resolution was adopted, it would not accommodate everyone:

> You [i.e. the PCSA and its missionaries] have stood for the visible unity of all in one church. We have stood for the liberty of the development of the Native Christian community which we believe was not sufficiently secured by your method. Each side had, I believe, been conscious that it lacked something and had not reached finality. (Lennox to PCSA General Assembly [PCSA GA], 20 September 1915, Lennox correspondence, File Synod 1914–16; cf. Burchell 1977: 53)

Potential white domination and intimidation of blacks was still evident despite General Assembly motions which indicated a more inclusive attitude. In 1911, following the establishment of the Union of South Africa in 1910, the PCSA General Assembly passed a resolution which 'views with apprehension the serious inequality in the administration of justice as between Europeans and Natives . . .' (PCSA GA, 335, WCL Ac1971/Ah1.:1). However, as Bax (1997: 22) has pointed out relating to a later period but relevant to the period under study: '. . . the Church's opposition to apartheid was for long limited to words, without any thought of what action could be taken'. Even in terms of representation at General Assembly black participation was minimal, at least in the first twenty-five years of the PCSA, partly due to the lack of full status of African congregations.

The Presbytery of Mankazana was established in 1915 to allow black people an arena for the 'mutual discussion of matters peculiar to the Native portion of the Church' (PCSA GA, 1915: 31). This, however, only exacerbated the racial divisions. The PCSA still hoped for a union and made attempts in 1915 and, in 1916, instructed its Native Mission Committee to promote another approach regarding union (PCSA General Assembly Minutes 1916, WCL Ac 1971/Ah1.3–1.4: 30; PCSA GA 1917: 77). The PCSA General Assembly presumed that because the Synod of Kafraria 'offered no constructive criticism' of the basis of union, the planned union was still 'impracticable'. In 1919, it was reported to the PCSA General Assembly that 'an approximation towards it [union] has been attained' (PCSA GA 1917: 180). This perception was manifestly incorrect. By 1920 nothing had changed substantially except that having been a denomination for over twenty years the PCSA had much more experience, of being a church than the black mission (T. B. Soga to Lennox, 15 November 1920, File 'Commission on Union' HPAL, cf. Burchell 1977: 54).

By the 1920s, after Protestants had been conducting intensive missions in parts of South Africa for more than a century, the fulfilment of the implication of their gospel was – the equality of believers before God entailed equality (Elphick 2012: 81). It is noteworthy that it was only in 1920 that the Scottish church considered the future of black Presbyterian worthy of its serious concern. A conference called by the UFCoS focused on a way forward for Presbyterianism rooted in the Scottish tradition in South Africa. At a church meeting in Johannesburg on Sunday 19 September 1920, the United Free Church of Scotland (UFCoS) Deputies' view was confirmed that the General Assembly of the PCSA:

> was not a suitable supreme court for the Kafir congregations, nor a useful Assembly for the Kafir ministers, who would be much more at home in a united synod of their own; and for permission to secure the change the deputies pleaded earnestly and successfully with the Assembly. (Ashcroft & Houston 1920: 8)

They had noted the 'anti-white racism' among black ministers and recommended that the solution was greater consultation and independence. This would result in a reduction in the number of missionaries as greater autonomy was granted to black ministers (Ashcroft & Houston 1920: Appendix I: 8). They recommended what has been described as the 'Native church' (FCoS Synod of Kafraria) option and the 'United church' (UPCoS Presbytery of Kaffraria) option (Ashcroft & Houston 1920: 9; cf. Duncan 1997: 125–32). The FMC of the UFCoS preferred the 'United church' option and voted to this effect in 1901 and 1909. Ashcroft and Houston did not agree. They argued that such anticipated benefits had not accrued to the Presbytery of Kaffraria (1920: 9). While they regarded the situation concerning the Synod of Kafraria as little better. They had the wisdom to recognise at a meeting of the General Assembly of the PCSA that:

> it was not a suitable supreme court for native matters. The differences of language and social condition are too considerable, and they sympathised with the irritation of the native ministers in being there at the consideration of business wholly connected with the colonial church. An authoritative supreme court of their own is needed, aware of the real needs of the Native Church, and in which the Native ministers and elders would have a real voice. (Ashcroft & Houston 1920: 9)

It is difficult to avoid the conclusion that even with the 'interests' of black people at heart, there was a lack of consideration on the part of the elders and ministers of the PCSA for their black colleagues, and that racist motives were operative.

The UFCoS deputies, Ashcroft and Houston, recommended that the two black bodies unite to resolve duplication and improve organisation and oversight. The Presbytery of Kaffraria and Synod of Kafraria were liberated in the sense of being permitted to discuss union. The matter of their future relationship with the PCSA was subordinated to the prime aim of union. Union was consummated on July 1923 and the Bantu Presbyterian Church of South Africa came into being (BPCSA 1923: 6–9). Brock (1974: 60) adopted a rather cynical view that this was a not very 'inspiring' example of ecclesiastical 'separate development'. But this was the first black independent church to be established through a process of delicate negotiation and '... despite reservations about the ability of blacks to handle their own church affairs, the birth of the BPCSA was a triumph of realism in the South African context' (Duncan 1997: 167).

Conclusion

All the discussions, and movements towards union of Scottish Presbyterian presbyteries, congregations and missions were plagued by a variety of problems, but the issue of racism was ubiquitous. It was the unspoken agenda of every meeting and the source of many problems. The church was not immune from the problems of society in which white people possessed an increasing amount of power and having power led them to see no particular issue with 'separate development' even within the church. For them this was normative. It was the consequent resentment, suspicion, distrust and frustration among black Christians which led to the Mzimba Secession in 1898 and the formation of the independent Bantu Presbyterian Church of South Africa twenty-five years later in 1923. The period 1910–48 has been dubbed the 'Age of Segregation' leading to a 'moderate African nationalism' (Elphick 2012: 4). This was already an ecclesiastical issue as has been seen in the formation of The Presbyterian Church of South Africa (PCSA) as a separate white dominated church with an African mission in 1897 and in the Mzimba Secession from the Free Church of Scotland Mission in 1898 – one of several secessions from mission churches in the last decades of the nineteenth century. Despite all this, by the 1920s, even beyond the confines of the church, 'the missionary influence in politics reached its peak' (Elphick 2012: 5).

Racism resulted in the Presbyterian body presenting a divided witness to the South African nation and 'if a kingdom is divided against itself, that kingdom cannot stand; if a household is divided against itself, that house cannot stand' (Mark 3: 24–5).

CHAPTER EIGHT

Preparations for the Formation of the Bantu Presbyterian Church of South Africa, 1897–1919

Introduction

It took 100 years for an autonomous black church to be established by the Scottish Presbyterian Mission in South Africa. The process gained momentum after 1898, and moved inexorably towards the formation of the Bantu Presbyterian Church of South Africa in 1923. The context was the developing policy of the Foreign Mission Committee (FMC) of the Free Church of Scotland (FCoS) which aimed to transfer leadership to autonomous black churches in the face of opposition from missionaries who were ensconced in positions of authority and who felt strongly that black people were not yet capable of assuming authority. A younger generation of missionaries facilitated the process.

An overarching vision on the part of the Scottish Presbyterian church prefigured the formation of an independent church. As the nineteenth century progressed, that aim seemed to recede as generations of missionaries faithfully carried out their mission in the way they considered best for the advancement of Christ's Kingdom among black South Africans. However, in the process, they brought all their western values and presuppositions about the superiority of Christian culture to bear on what they considered a primitive context. Yet, as missionaries' work both in evangelism and education resulted in the emergence of a group of educated black people, there was a reluctance to entrust and share responsibility with them. Missionaries' power was exercised through non-indigenous Mission Councils (Duncan 2012b: 217–34). It was imposed without consultation with blacks and was self-perpetuating. In this way the role of the courts of the church were subverted and the views of blacks were suppressed until they took courage in a time of protest and resistance to express their views cogently, and request that their views be taken seriously and acted upon that they might play their full role in the journey towards the Kingdom of God.

By the close of the nineteenth century, the time had arrived when various options had to be seriously considered seriously for the sake of the future of the Mission. One option was rather drastic – secession, manifested in the Presbyterian mission through the Tsewu and Mzimba secessions. This was a stark challenge to the missionaries that their power and authority was no longer absolute. Yet, this alone does not tell the complete story as other factors were at work including United Free Church of Scotland policy which was itself evolving as events developed.

The one sphere in which blacks asserted their determination was in their church lives. During this time two policy options evolved within the settler and mission church communities.

The Two-option Policy:

The 'United Church' option

The Foreign Mission Committee (FMC) of the United Free Church of Scotland (UFCoS) was keen to promote its ideal of one church where black and white would co-exist happily on an equal basis. James Henderson (1902: 1–2), a missionary of a younger generation, was probably largely correct when he commented that 'It is admitted by all that this is the Christian ideal'. This, however, failed to take adequate account of the developing racial situation in South Africa: 'there is largely prevalent among the colonists a sentiment adverse to association with the African *native*' (Henderson 1902: 9). It was anticipated that the Presbyterian Church of South Africa, established in 1897, would build up an independent 'native' church in South Africa. It would seem this was an unrealistic view as a result of the racist attitude of white people towards blacks, the colonialist ethos of the church, the desire to maintain white power and authority and the early desire to unite with the Dutch Reformed Church. While it may have been 'the Christian ideal. It attempts to overcome racial differences by following the mind of Christ' (Henderson 1902: 9–10):

> The Committee . . . has no reason to anticipate that any detriment would ensue to the cause of Christ from the whole of the Native Church formed by our Mission uniting on an acceptable basis, as part of it has already done, with the Presbyterian Church of South Africa. While fully alive to the serious difficulties which always attend the mingling in one Church of those with antecedents so diverse as European colonists and the Native South African peoples, the Foreign Mission Committee believes that all such difficulties will be most happily overcome by being left, as far as possible, to be dealt with by the brethren in each of our Mission fields, trusting them to act in a spirit of loyalty to the one Lord and Head of the Church, and of kindly consideration and forbearance one towards another for His name's sake. (FMC 1904; Henderson 1902: 12)

This minute was agreed following representations by South African missionaries to the African sub-committee of the FMC in 1904. It moved against the sentiments expressed by James Stewart (see below), Lennox, and others, who opposed the concept of the 'incorporating union' of the white and black sections of Scottish Presbyterianism. While this might appear more democratic, it does not, necessarily, lead to freedom of expression and the opportunity for development and leadership (Sundkler 1961: 31–2). The formation of the Presbyterian Church of Africa (PCA) had made Lennox realise the inadequacies of colonial mission policy and also critical of it. In 1909 he could say:

> ... we offer the native church the finest product of our thinking and experience, while at the same time we remove from them the discipline of thinking out these questions in relation to their own traditional life ... We could do no greater disservice than to do all their thinking for them. They must take their responsibilities on their own shoulders ... They must cast themselves on the future in faith and must garner and use the lessons of their own experience ... They are not ..., to be reckoned failures. (Shepherd 1937: 223)

These rather innovative views were encapsulated in the only other option available for consideration.

The 'Native Experiment' option

In 1902, the paper *Our Missions in South Africa*, probably written by James Henderson of Lovedale, claimed that 'The Mission begins in order to create a native Church; the Mission naturally ends when the native Church has become self-supporting, self-governing, and self-propagating', not to mention self-reflecting and theologising. The term 'Native' 'meant a church proper to the country in which it was planted. Such a church might be inclusive of different races dwelling in that country' (Henderson 1902: 1). This interpretation was formulated by the General Assembly of the United Free Church of Scotland. This comment was significant in the light of later criticisms made of an autonomous 'native' church. But, beyond this, the aim followed the contemporary view of Protestant missions enunciated by Henry Venn, Rufus Anderson and Gustav Warneck who were the originators of the concept of the 'Native Church' and who 'understood that local pastors should be trusted and trained to assume the government of new churches' (Reese 2012: 27).

From 1900, the FMC pressed for the formation of a native church in correspondence with missionaries, the word 'native' being synonymous with 'indigenous'. Theoretically, it might consist of people of all races though this was not clear. Rev. John Lennox, a fairly recent addition to the missionary body in South Africa, interpreted this to mean a 'black church'. This confirms that this idea was already in the minds of the FMC as Lennox refers to this being the policy of three successive conveners (Lennox to Henderson, 24 May 1901, NLS 7799) so the policy was not a new development. The three conveners' policy supported the development of self-supporting, self-governing and self-propagating churches. Yet, a new method of achieving this had been introduced in the form of Mission Councils. While accepting Lennox's integrity, it is not clear that all missionaries shared his view on this matter. This would raise the question of the indigenous nature of the PCSA when the term 'colonial' more clearly expressed its ethos. Earlier, the *Kaffir Express* in June 1871 had stated there had been little success in creating a 'three-self' church and optimistically projected a time:

> when all Native Churches in our colony and on our borders must be largely, if not altogether, supplied with pastors from themselves. The native churches must be stirred up more and more to realise and even to desire this coming state of things . . . They cannot remain forever in the leading strings of the European church, and must endeavour to maintain and perpetuate themselves. And the sooner they begin to aim at this consummation the better.

This was an ideal explication of the 'three-self' theory but the question arises about who is to do the stirring up? The FMC would see this as the role of its missionaries. Clearly, joining the PCSA would not achieve the end of severing 'the leading strings of the European church'. The FMC policy before 1867 and maintained by Dr George Smith, its Secretary, was that vacant charges should be filled by black probationers although there was little active interest in this policy for in 1905 there were only ten black ministers in the entire Mission. FCoS missionaries worked through the Synod of Kafraria and remained outside the 1897 union, four members having voted in favour while ten, including Lennox and Mzirnba, voted against. Yet, the views of blacks were not clear by 1904 from the black vote in the PCSA (Lennox to Stewart 28 February 1904, D65/48,23A [ix], JW Jagger Library, University of Cape Town: 32).

James Stewart of Lovedale and William Stuart of Burnshill favoured a black Presbyterian church, which could be inclusive of blacks and whites, distinguishable from the Presbyterian Church of South Africa, and took the view that:

> a Church constructed on the basis of uniting colonists and natives in one ecclesiastical fellowship must at some future time encounter difficulties occasioned by racial antagonisms which will prove disastrous to it. (Henderson 1902: 10)

In addition, Stewart considered that the new PCSA would struggle to support itself for some time, lacking sufficient personnel, finance and church management experience, not to mention an inclination for missionary work in its early days. As has been noted, this confirms that Stewart normally took the long view of progress in mission. He had support in Scotland from Sir William Dunn and Lord Overtoun, among others, who felt that Scotland was not in a position to formulate policies opposed by missionaries (Burchell 1977: 39–58, n. 23, n.48). Van der Spuy (1971: 29) affirms Stewart as a 'realist' who 'knew the racial attitudes which existed in the South African situation'. This led to the conclusion that a black church was the only viable alternative. Yet, Stewart was not so liberal that he derived any positive benefits from the vision of an independent church such as the opportunity for blacks to develop their own gifts in a situation where they had total responsibility for their actions and consequences. Nor was he keen to ordain black ministers as per the wishes of the FMC concerning 'the elimination of the European and the handing over of all these older as well as new stations to native guidance and care' (Sundkler 1961: 30). Stewart viewed this prospect with great foreboding: 'We know what will happen if this takes place' (Stewart to Roberts 26/12/1902, in Burchell 1977: 44).

Despite his support for a black church, Stewart did not regard this as an imminent prospect for 'the African would need the Anglo-Saxon alongside of him for the next 50 or 100 years' (SANAC, II, 44980: 911). David Stormont of Blythswood shared Stewart's attitude claiming that the older generation of missionaries encouraged the belief among black ministers that the missions were their inheritance, and objected to missionaries doing pioneering work: 'they [black people] want routine work and a fixed salary' (Stormont to Auld, 18 March 1910. MS 7352, Stormont papers). It is fair to say this from the position of being in receipt of a regular guaranteed stipend while black people did not, and what stipends they did have were substantially lower than their white colleagues (Millard, 1995: 222).

The opposite argument was presented by Henderson and Lennox who believed that missionaries had to occupy a continually decreasing role. This indicated a potential change in policy. Brock (1974: 430) comments that: 'There were few who managed to rise above . . ., natural handicaps [i.e. imposed by Victorian imperialist society], few whose imagination could so overcome contemporary prejudice and mores as to commend to their followers the adoption of alternatives'. They were 'typical of that younger generation of missionaries at the beginning of the twentieth century who were "filled with the ideals of a self-governing church"'. Their emergence coincided with the worst period of secessions. Burchell (1977: 45) believed 'Henderson and Lennox had confidence in the ability of the African to reshape Christianity in an original and meaningful way'. This came to be especially true of the Women's Christian Association (*uManyano*), formed in 1893, and the Young Men's Christian Guild (*amaDodana*). They based their case on the *status quo* where:

> The mission fields are passing into the hands of Native converts as pastors and officebearers. Christianity is beginning to take on a South African garb and adapt itself to the genius of the African people.
> (Henderson to Smith, 7 January 1908, in Burchell 1977: 45)

This follows the view of Bredekamp and Ross (1995: 1) that the process of Christianisation 'could only be carried to completion by men and women from the African communities themselves', i.e. gender-inclusive mission. Elphick (1995: 17) contends that from the beginning of the Christian mission African converts embraced some form of gospel with enthusiasm and carried it, with or without missionary approval, to their families and villages, often to new regions altogether, citing the examples of Ntsikana and Cupido Kakkerkal.

Mission boarding schools initiated the growth of a feminine elite (Donaldson 1985: 5) – many married ministers and church officials and this led to the domination of the *uManyano* by ministers' wives who were excluded by gender from other forms of church leadership. In relation to male evangelical activity, Hastings (1979: 265–6) asserted that *manyanos* offered a greater 'dynamic core' than male evangelists could.

Henderson and Lennox exercised a strong influence on the Synod of Kafraria, the superior court of the FCoS Mission. They believed that the autonomy of the Synod was vital in the progress towards the evolution of an independent mission church. In 1920, Lennox described it as a 'true native court' (Lennox to Soga, 27 November 1920, Commission on Union, Lennox correspondence NAHECS, UFH). For Henderson, it was virtually an independent organisation whose business was dealt with in good spirit. Lennox was convinced there was a possibility that 'the material of Native Christianity is ... still so sufficiently plastic it may initially set into a mould different from the recognised European patterns' (Report of the Proceedings of the Third General Missionary Conference of South Africa [GMCSA], July 1909: 84 in Burchell: 45). Time would tell that this assessment was a little too optimistic in the light of some of the more conservative developments, e.g. in worship, polity, discipline, doctrine and ecclesiastical dress. For him, white control stifled indigenous development. Missionaries would still be required in a distinctive church but in the role of 'advisers, not the devisers of policy' (in Burchell 1977: 45). This was a vain hope because of the continued existence of Mission Councils in the post-1923 period and the strong views of the personnel involved. Lennox preferred a more grassroots democratic approach:

> The whole system of Church government, all the regulations for worship, everything in fact which gives outward expression to the belief and permanent form to the Church is imposed from above on that which is below. (Burchell 1977: 46)

He would never have agreed to a federal arrangement with the PCSA.

The Ongoing Effects of the Mzimba Secession

Shepherd's (1971: 59–60) assessment that the Mzimba Secession had no significant impact on the African church nor on Scottish missions is inaccurate for it had an ongoing psychological effect on Scottish missionaries, especially James Stewart for it had 'caused him great anxiety and taken greatly from his strength' (Lindsay to Stormont, 20 October 1898, MS 14303, Stormont papers, Cory). Burchell (1977: 47) is probably correct in saying it 'contributed much to the turmoil, uncertainty and anxiety in the Scottish mission field particularly in the first decades of the twentieth century'. While it is difficult to assess how much Mzimba affected thinking regarding future mission policy, he did do this having adopted a conservative view of the future of the PCA, envisaging a time when it might enter an arrangement with another church, presumably the PCSA, after he failed to secure recognition by the FCoS: 'a time when, while we control our own church matters, there will be incorporation or federation with the Colonial Presbyterian Body' (SANAC, vol. II, 10907, 793).

The threat of secession did not disappear once the Mzimba Secession had occurred. Referring especially to the missions at Macfarlan and Rainy, Lennox wrote to Lindsay of the FMC that 'Mzimba is unceasingly active in trying to increase his following by breaking up existing missions' (23 June 1898, Letterbook of the Presbytery of Kaffraria, 28 July 1898–4 April 1904, Lennox correspondence, HPAL, UFH). This was confirmed in 1909 in a *communique* on the FC mission:

> Since 1898 ... certain of the native converts have been unsettled by movements which have affected other missions in South Africa. In a very few of the outstations week-day and Sabbath schools work has been temporarily arrested, chiefly, it is understood, through the unsettlement of the population among which the schools are situated. (Cowan & Dalmahoy to Simpson & Marwick, 3/6/1909 in file 'Synod 1909', Lennox correspondence)

The Native Affairs Commission Report of 1925, reported that anti-white feeling was attracting seceders who had been loyal to the missions of the sending churches until that time. Some of this had its source in black ministers meeting together in fraternals (Sundkler 1961: 63).

In 1909, Henderson had sought an accommodation with Mzimba as the result of problems relating to land tenure, overlapping congregational boundaries and disputes about secession, but not, it seems, from a genuine desire for rapprochement. Henderson was correct in his estimation of the time and energy wasted in fighting one another compared with what could have been achieved in trying to further the mission of the Kingdom, i.e. in proselytising rather than evangelising, for this created a bad public image of mission. Mzimba appeared to agree and promised to end 'this time of dissension and strife' (Henderson to Lennox 7/4/1909, in file 'Synod 1909', Lennox correspondence). Mzimba viewed the missionaries as directly responsible for the secession because 'we generally see things in different ways which introduces bad feeling and distrust' (Minutes of Presbytery of Kaffraria, 15 April 1898, HPAL, UFH). There were 'religious difficulties' plus a desire 'to work independently thinking that it might work better that way' (SANAC, vol.II, 10893, 10901, 793). So foresight might have prevented secession along with a willingness to hand over authority gradually as Henderson and Lennox desired. Mzimba could say, with justification, that 'Our experience is that the missionaries of the United Free Church are at present unable to understand the South African native or work with them. The minds of the Natives have been occupied with secessions and attempts at union' (Marks 1970: 179).

The impact of secession on the Mission was such that Lennox (to JH Oldham, 11 December 1922 in file 'Personal 1919–1922', Lennox correspondence) could comment on the years 1910–22 as 'a period of no outstanding spiritual movement'. He claimed this on behalf of black people but missionary energy had been depleted by matters related to both secession and union. However, he did feel that advances had been made in race relations although no settlement with the secessionists was achieved. Early in 1923, as the formation of the Bantu Presbyterian Church of South Africa (BPCSA) approached, an attempt was made by Rev. S. W. Njikelana to initiate a union consisting of all the black presbyterian bodies. This was judged by the missionaries to be too late (Lennox to Henderson 29 September 1922, Henderson correspondence, Cory Library in Burchell 1977: 49). This would support the assertion that genuine rapprochement was not the real desire of the missionaries because this would seem to be consistent with their aims. In addition, it may be wondered if it is ever too late to proceed with Christ's aim that all should be one (John 17: 21), even had such moves been delayed until after the birth of the BPCSA, with a clear commitment to talk further on the matter.

It is necessary to consider the extent to which the Mzimba Secession directly contributed to the formation of the BPCSA. In 1937, a memorandum was prepared which stated that it was 'better to have formed a Bantu church' than to 'let a new sect rupture the work without let or hindrance' (compiled from notes from members of the SA Mission Council of the Church of Scotland [CoS] in terms of Mission Council minute no. 312 of April 1936 and of Mission Council Executive Minute no. 10 of 10 October 1936. Document dated 14 February 1937, BPC Office, Umtata in Burchell 1977: 49).

Burchell (1977: 49ff.), in an attempt to be objective, considers influences other than the Mzimba Secession for the problems that attended the years between 1898 and 1923. One was the desire of the FMC for a union between the mission churches and the PCSA. By 1907, this was causing dissension among black ministers and officebearers who favoured pursuing the spirit of the 'Basis of Union' (May 1900), i.e. developing a 'Native' church predominantly governed by black people themselves. Rev. R. Mure, in 1908, argued that: 'The discussion of alternative solutions of the present difficulty in the presence of natives is calculated to bring about the very split we desire to avoid' (Burchell 1977: 50). Secession had made the discussion about union sensitive especially at missions like Pirie where it was felt the issue was being forced while other issues were being evaded.

There had been no presbytery visitations for some time, finances were in a very poor state and no records had been kept for twenty years. Interference was likely to produce suspicion which might lead to further secession and the main purpose of achieving the growth of a black church could be defeated. Mure was concerned about missionaries' anxieties in the light of 'divisions between some of the missionaries and some of the Bantu ministers, and between the former United Presbyterian side and the former Free Church side of the Mission' ('Union', attached to Mission Council minutes 5 August 1908 on Mission Council minute, 1908–1915, BPC Office, Umtata in Burchell 1977: 50). This had an unsettling effect on ordinary church members.

When the views of black ministers and officebearers were canvassed, it became clear that no change would be welcome if it altered relations with the Home Church, and that included union with the PCSA. They were proud of their Free Church heritage in building up work amongst blacks during the nineteenth century and in virtually constituting it an 'Order' in the FC with blacks 'being trained to conduct business and to accept responsibility both in maintaining ordinances, and in sending the Gospel to the heathen' (Memorandum of Native Ministers and Officebearers, UFCoS Missions, SA, 26 September 1908, file 'Synod', Lennox correspondence). This policy had been ruptured by the Mzimba Secession. UFCoS ministers (mainly white) and elders (mainly black) were not prepared to support union with the PCSA and those who were motivated by their concern to maintain unity in their congregations. Rev. Elijah Makiwane, spoke out at a Presbytery meeting at Lovedale, claiming that if members were coerced into joining the PCSA 'they would lose them to the last man' (Report of Makiwane, 29 April 1908, file 'Synod', Lennox correspondence). Probably the only benefactor would be Mzimba if the FMC pushed its policy to its logical conclusion. It was perceived that:

> wisdom lay in allowing in the meantime that each section should continue to strengthen and consolidate all its efforts and forces just as they would have done if there was no question of Union being discussed, rather than allow any side to stand paralysed by the hope or proposal of Union. (Memorandum of Native Ministers and Officebearers, 26 September 1908, file Presbytery Synod of Kafraria, Sundry correspondence 1/4, Lennox correspondence)

We may wonder at how much missionary voices were suppressed in reaching this conclusion.

A Change of Plan

When John Lennox spoke to the General Assembly of the PCSA in 1913, he proposed a plan which came to fruition in 1914. Along with Revs James Henderson, Elijah Makiwane, John Knox Bokwe and Holfort Mama,

Lennox was appointed by the Synod of Kafraria to a joint consultation along with representatives of the PCSA. Their remit was to consider the possibility of formulating an agreement on ways of co-operating in the mission field 'so as to maintain the unity of the Church and at the same time admit of the native section of the Christian community assuming duties and responsibilities that are properly theirs' (Conference Report, 14 May 1914, BPC Office, Umtata in Burchell 1977: 52).

This was in line with the need to take a pragmatic approach in which mission and unity were integrated. Theological issues were not a prime concern. This may have been partly due to the fact that these discussions were taking place in the wake of the World Missionary Conference, held in Edinburgh in 1910, where:

> The growing ecumenical impulse from the 'mission fields', though, inevitably brought these missions to an encounter with the Church, as being *the* theological context in which the interrelationship between unity and mission could – and must – be expressed. (Saayman 1984: 9)

The Edinburgh conference had taken a prior decision that theological issues would be eschewed for the main aim of the conference was to garner the missionary forces of a united Christianity to evangelise of the world in that generation. Further to that, the ideal to be promoted was the establishment of 'one undivided Church of Christ' in every country (Rouse & Neill 1967: 359).

Lennox's plan was achieved in theory, but the *status quo* remained because:

> In the opinion of the conference the organisation of native Presbyteries and Synod would meet the existing situation ... The relationship of the Synod to the General Assembly should include the right of appeal, submission to the Assembly of reports of work, and consideration of questions arising from the relationship of the Synod with non-synodical areas of mission work. (FMC, 15 September 1914, minute 3155, NLS)

Within this proposed federal arrangement, there was to be mutual representation in each other's highest courts. The FMC approved the outcome of the report. However, the position of the Presbytery of Kaffraria became anomalous resulting from the union of the UPCoS and FCoS missions, since missionaries in the Kaffrarian Mission Council were unhappy about Synod having property vested in its name rather than in the Trustees of the UFCoS. This arose out of fear of further secessions, fear of black control of property and an attempt to limit its power. A further anomaly continued to be the existence of two Mission Councils in Transkei and Kaffraria. On behalf of the FMC, its Secretary, Rev. Frank Ashcroft, questioned the possibility of 'the formation of one General Council' because 'this will be *as* great [a] help as the one Native Church' (Ashcroft to Lennox, 29 September

1914, file 'Synod' 1914-16, Lennox papers, Box F76-83). However, because there was no initial enthusiasm in the Transkei Mission Council, the FMC hesitated to approve the union (FMC, 20 July 1915, minute 3514, NLS) though it advocated the desirability of devolving responsibility for specified areas to native pastors and of having one general Mission Council meeting annually with three sub-councils (FMC, 29 April 1913, Minute 2682, Ashcroft to Lennox, Box10, F76-83, NAHECS, UFH). The Transkei Mission Council considered the proposal inappropriate and favoured the formation of sub-councils attached to Presbyteries (FMC, 16 November 1915, minute 3614:4, NLS). Its conservatism at this time may be noted from its attitude to the place of women in the church, which 'idea is neither practicable nor greatly desired' (FMC, 21 December 1915, minute 3642:4, NLS).

The FMC approved the union of the two Mission Councils which became the Kaffraria Mission Council (21 March 1916, Minute 3746, HPAL, UFH) in 1917 despite opposition from some Transkei missionaries, e.g. Rev. W. Auld (FMC, 17/7/1917, minute 4151:5, NLS). Clarification of the position of the Natal Mission Council about union was also considered necessary. It was prepared to unite with the Kaffrarian Mission Council but it complained about being swamped by the greater number of missionaries and black members in the Cape. It argued for proportional representation and for the same in representative bodies. The Kaffrarian Mission Council had twenty-four missionaries and its area contained 15,379 members, while the Natal Mission Council had four missionaries and 6,490 members respectively (FMC, 20 September 1921, minute 5669, NLS). The FMC (21 March 1922 Minute 5904:1, NLS) asked them to reconsider the point of proportional representation. The Natal Mission Council agreed on the conditions as stated (Lennox to Standing committee, 4 September 1922, NAHECS, UFH; FMC, 16 October 1922, Minute 6166; 21 November 1922, minute 6194, NLS). The Kaffrarian Mission Council was pleased with the prospect and 'sees no insuperable barrier to union' (FMC, 17 April 923, Minute 6407, NLS). This referred to differences of attitude in the Natal Mission Council to polygamy which was more liberal and more accepting though it did not approve the practice. The place of the Natal Mission Council was not to be resolved until after the formation of the BPCSA.

As discussions advanced in Scotland about the union of the two FMC's of the former FCoS and UPCoS, it was proposed that male and female members should be members of Mission Councils with equal rights as it was perceived there was no need to separate work for the existence of two committees in Scotland had necessitated a separation of business in South Africa. Mission Councils had been dealing with proposals dealt with by two committees 'differing in their point of view as is inevitable when one committee consists mainly of men and the other mainly of women' (FMC,16 January 1923, Appendix: Report of Special Committee on *Assembly's Remit on Amalgamation*, NL).

A further advance was achieved when the newly formed Kaffrarian Mission Council agreed that 'the time has now come in South Africa to invite certain outstanding natives to sit as members of the Mission Council (FMC, 1617/1918, Minute 4397: 1, NLS). This was a significant move though it smacked of paternalism and the basis of how a person is deemed outstanding is not defined though, while not stated, it is obvious that missionaries as members of the Mission Council will do the choosing. Thus 'outstanding' might be equivalent to 'acceptable' and 'quiescent'. The Kaffrarian Mission Council proposed adding one member of the about-to-be-formed Native Church to represent each Presbytery on the Mission Council 'and that it be the concern of the Council, as sanctioned by the Foreign Mission Committee, to devolve progressively upon the highest court of the Native Church the duties heretofore belonging to the Council'. This was remitted to the Africa sub-committee of the FMC to consult with other Mission Councils and report (FMC, 17 April 1923, Minute 6407: 8, NLS). The Commission on Union (draft resolutions of *Committee on Relations with Other Churches*, Lennox correspondence) refused to recommend this feeling that it was a matter that could be discussed after the birth of the new church.

Arising out of the 1914 conference, Lennox had sought to address the problem of the relationship between the white and black sections of the Christian community. The situation required sensitivity for:

> It was easy to fail here, easy for the individual missionary to forget the temporary character of his mission office and to fail to shape his work in preparation for a day when the mission will be withdrawn and replaced by the permanent native church; easy for the church through a high sense of its Christian duty and a noble scorn of racial distinctions in the church, when we are one in Jesus Christ, to place black and white in a juxtaposition and professed equality of standing in the sight of God, in which the native Christians quite unintentionally but really shall be overshadowed and dwarfed by their European brethren. (Lennox to PCSA General Assembly, 20 September 1915, 'Synod 1914–1916', Lennox correspondence)

In this, Lennox was being farsighted. Besides Henderson, few missionaries shared his vision. Neither union with the PCSA nor the formation of a native church would satisfy everyone as Lennox was well aware:

> You [i.e. the PCSA and its missionaries] have stood for the visible unity of all in one church. We have stood for the liberty of development of the Native Christian community which we believe was not sufficiently secured by your method. Each side had, I believe, been conscious that it lacked something and had not reached finality. (Lennox to PCSA General Assembly, 20 September 1915, 'Synod 1914–1916', Lennox correspondence)

Lennox was moving towards the 1914 solution of a synthesis of an independent synod with mutual representation where blacks would be free to work out their future and where contact would be maintained between black and white, allowing for consultation between Presbyteries and congregations. However, this would not alleviate the possible problem of white (PCSA) ministers dominating proceedings of Synod and intimidating black members. The PCSA, by this time had had twenty years of experience as a church plus considerable business, commercial and legal expertise at its disposal compared with black presbyterians who had none (T. B. Soga to Lennox, 15 November 1920, 'Commission on Union', Lennox correspondence). Soga preferred union with other black churches, a point also mooted by Henderson (Draft of Committee on Relations with Other Churches', Henderson correspondence, in Burchell 1977: 157). The Congregational Church was already talking to African Presbyterians and to the PCSA.

The PCSA continued to hope that union might be effected. As early as 1915, it had expressed a desire for closer relationships with the Synod of Kafraria and in 1916 approved a Draft Basis of Union adopted by the Synod. On 18 September 1916, the General Assembly of the PCSA resolved to:

> instruct the Native Mission Committee to forward in every way possible the movement towards union of the Missions of the United Free Church of Scotland in Kafraria and Natal with our Church. (PCSA General Assembly Minutes, Ac 1971/Ahl.3.–1.4., William Cullen Library [WCL], University of the Witwatersrand)

The Presbytery of Kaffraria declared such a step 'impracticable' and by 1919 there was still no agreement on union despite the view that 'an approximation to it has been attained' (PCSA General Assembly Minutes Ac 1971/Ahl.3.- 1.4., WCL); yet, there was still a hope that agreement might be achieved by May 1920.

Conclusion

This was not to be, probably as it was realised that it was a futile exercise at that point in the history of the missions' development because of opposition which existed on the side of black ministers and elders in the missions. This was the situation Ashcroft and Houston of the FMC came to South Africa to try to resolve in 1920. Their mission was to lead to the foundation of the Bantu Presbyterian Church.

CHAPTER NINE

The Formation of the Bantu Presbyterian Church of South Africa, 1920–3

Preparations for a New Birth

In 1920, two United Free Church of Scotland FMC deputies, Rev. Frank Ashcroft and Mr Andrew Houston, were sent to South Africa to deal with the issue of bringing together the two branches of the Scottish Mission in South Africa. Burchell (1977: 55) points out one innovation in the approach adopted by the Deputies: 'they came prepared to listen to the demands of these [black] ministers' and this may have been the actual catalyst for the resulting change of policy with regard to establishing a black church. During his visit, Ashcroft addressed the 1920 General Assembly of the PCSA in support of uniting the missions. As a result, Rev. J. Pollock of the PCSA proposed that:

> This Assembly in view of the strong desire of the United Free Church of Scotland, . . . to have the congregations connected with their missions in Kaffraria and the Transkei united under one ecclesiastical authority, agrees to give the Presbyteries of Kaffraria and Mankazana full power to decide on the question of union with the Synod of Kafraria, leaving for future consideration the relationship to be established between the enlarged body thus formed, and this Presbyterian Church of South Africa. (PCSA General Assembly Minutes 20/9/1920, Ac 1971/Ah1.3.–1.4., William Cullen library [WCL], Wits University, 225)

The PCSA unanimously agreed to this proposal and appointed members to attend a Conference at Blythswood Institution on 20 October 1920. It is unclear why they were there as they were not part of the negotiations (Vellem 2013: 151–2). Also present were representatives from the Mission Synod of Kafraria, the Presbyteries of Kaffraria, Mankazana and Natal, and the Mission Council of Natal. This Conference was called to resolve the anomalous situation which had arisen over the existence of the two separate branches of the UFCoS mission and the deputies urged accordingly. They had come to the conclusion that the relationship with the PCSA could be dealt with at a later stage because it was no longer considered a vital part of having one mission entity to deal with. The Commission on union was well balanced in terms of black and white, ministers and elders with the preponderance of elders being white.

In their Report of 21 December 1920 to the FMC (15 February 1921, minute 5386, referring to minute 5298, Appendix 1:4, National Library of Scotland [NLS]) the deputies stated that their views were 'evidently in parts not quite welcome to all the missionaries'. They reported there were 15,000 members in the mission church and that the period of expansion was over. This must mean geographical expansion and not numerical expansion. The deputies felt that the areas evangelised could have seen greater success had they been 'more homogeneous and more limited in extent'. Too much development had been carried out at the whim of individual missionaries without sufficient control and the formation of a strategy (Appendix 1: 3). They considered that the Mission Council had failed because of 'lack of union in the Mission between the missionaries formerly belonging to the Free Church and the United Presbyterian Church'. In their view the situation had improved, but they also believed that 'control in the future must be with the Native Church speaking through its Ecclesiastical Courts and not with the Mission Council'. They thought this resulted from the development of competence in the black ministry and eldership (Appendix 1: 4).

They highlighted the problem – the Mission Council which they had hoped would be the unifying bond of their South African missions 'proved unequal to the task, torn as it was, by controversies over the question of our union'. They also commented on the 'highly unsatisfactory state of affairs in Natal where overlapping was much in evidence'. Union with the PCSA had not achieved significant benefits, e.g. blacks were not happy with the discussion of colonial church business being forced on them. The Deputies reported that the General Assembly of the PCSA was:

> evidently mainly concerned with the work of the colonial congregations ... not a suitable supreme court for the Kafir congregations, nor a useful Assembly for the Kafir ministers, who would be much more at home in a united synod of their own. (Report of Deputies, 21 December 1920, PR 3983, Cory, 8)

There was also the memory of recently failed negotiations. But separation from the Synod of Kafraria had produced great problems. The Conference resulted in a 'new and bolder' proposal to unite the Synod of Kafraria and the Presbytery of Kaffraria which would take over much of the work carried out by the Mission Council. The place of missionaries was an issue and it was felt that the FMC should express its mind on the appointment of missionaries with the Mission Council and new appointments should be made jointly between the Synod and the Mission Council, with the ultimate aim of reducing the number of missionaries in parish appointments. However, the Deputies recommended that missionaries be full members of the enlarged Synod. The new body should be responsible for evangelism and the withdrawal of missionaries should begin. The strength of anti-white feeling was acknowledged along with the lack of unity among missionaries which was impeding the growth of the Mission. The Deputies considered their proposal to be proactive: 'to meet the desire for more independence by such a scheme as we suggest seems to us to be true Christian statesmanship' (Report of Deputies, 21 December 1920, PR3983, appendix 1: 5, Cory). Their aim was 'to give increasing responsibility to the Synod with a view to forming, as early as possible, an independent, self-supporting Church' and 'the Mission Council should entrust as much business to it contenting itself with confirming arrangements made by it unless they seem so detrimental as to compel interference', i.e. the missionaries' *modus operandi*. The problem was that the Mission Council was largely ineffective as an administrative unit. Here, an elevated position and role for the Synod was envisaged, including the establishment of central funds, training evangelists, the supply of students and the production of a simplified creed. For the first time, account was taken of the suspicion black members had for the Synod due to not being represented on it. This was an early example of positive discrimination. The same policy was to be applied in Natal which was not strong enough to replace the Mission. The Presbytery was not well developed and was too small to sustain withdrawal. It was acknowledged that such withdrawal would simply benefit the Ethiopian-type churches.

It is interesting to note that in their report the Deputies seemed to have little knowledge or understanding of the implications of the Mzimba Seccession on their arrival in South Africa:

> It is disappointing to hear that a large proportion of the Lovedale congregation seceded under Mzimba about twenty years ago . . . which should never have occurred. The tendency to divide over comparatively small matters has been the curse of our missions in South Africa. (Report of Deputies, PR3983: 2, Cory)

The same lack of understanding is revealed later in the same report when the Deputies commented on the riot at Lovedale in 1920. They could not understand the connection between the 'strength of racial antagonism, . . . traces of which were evident to them even within the Christian Church' and what they described as 'largely a domestic matter . . . no doubt inspired by the new political feelings so prominent in the native press' to which they were susceptible' (Appendix 1, Riot 1: 10). By the time they wrote their recommendations, they had become much more aware of the situation arguing that too rapid withdrawal of the mission in Natal would lead to much of the work done disappearing and 'the bulk of our converts would pass into the Ethiopian Church, with its strong anti-white feeling' (Report of Deputies, PR3983, Appendix 1,12: 9, Cory). The missionaries divided over the deputies' proposals about the formation of an independent black church. Revs J. Lundie, W. Stirling and the Aulds believed the establishment of a black church reflected a racial attitude (Blythswood Conference, file 'Commission on Union', Lennox correspondence). Rev. J. Auld was nominated and declined the office of Moderator of the General Assembly of the BPCSA. Rev. T. B. Soga favoured a black church for black people. Shepherd (1972: 676–7) claimed:

> It became manifest in the conference that union was desired by the whole Synod and by the Native ministers and elders of the Presbytery of Kaffraria, forming a large majority of that body, but that some of the older members of the Presbytery were unwilling to abandon an ideal to which they had clung during many years, with the approval of the Home Church.

The views of the majority prevailed and a Commission on Union was established with Rev. James Henderson as Chairperson and Rev. John Lennox as Senior Clerk. In working towards the union of the two strands of the mission, the Commission considered:

- the name of the proposed new church, which was to be the United Presbyterian Church of South Africa;
- membership of the superior courts, especially the place of missionaries;
- the relationship between the new church and the PCSA, which was to be one of federation with each being represented on the General Assembly of the other by six members;
- the date of the union, which was set as 4 July 1923;
- Mission Councils should cease to exist or should have black representation on them.

An important issue was the relationship of the Scottish missionaries and black ministers 'who have not been a spiritual force in the Church nor excelled in any way in administrative work' (Henderson to Ashcroft, 28 August 1922, Henderson correspondence, Cory) yet wanted unrestricted freedom. W. M. Eiselen (in Schapera [ed.] 1934: 73 in Sundkler 1961: 36) argued that 'contact with a population of White Christians has raised the quality and lowered the quality of Bantu Christians'. It was agreed that missionaries would have an equal place in the black church 'for the present', but that their contribution would decrease in time and that their envisaged role will become purely advisory' until 'they will no longer be required' (Lennox to Oldham, 11 December 1922, 'Personal 1919–1922', Lennox Correspondence). In a multi-racial church there would be no guarantee that blacks would enjoy equal rights and status in reality, whereas in a black church none would be specifically excluded, and where the question of control would be uppermost, especially in relation to the role of missionaries. While there was parity between Scottish missionaries and ministers in Scotland this was not the case with black ministers.

Hinchliffe (1974: 31) has suggested that 'there is a direct connection between this insistence on standards and the decision to create an independent Bantu Presbyterian Church in this century'. This was a significant factor, but only one amongst others. If the problem was that of differentials in levels of training and attainment, these would also exist in the PCSA for in neither solution was there parity, e.g. in stipends. Ordination would lead to parity in the Mission, i.e. black ministers would, in theory at least, be eligible to be called to charges in Scotland. But, the tradition was that black missionaries should not have all the rights and privileges of their white colleagues. Black clergymen who might sometimes be young and inexperienced would remain, for the whole of their working lives, subject to white domination. Education might be regarded as the source of long term solutions. In the short term it seemed only to increase the tensions and frustrations. One can imagine how secessions to form AICs occurred for such approaches 'provided so little scope for the emergence of a really indigenous Christianity' (Hinchliffe 1974: 36, 37).

This problem was caused and exacerbated by the social and political circumstances of the country: 'granting full autonomy to a Native Church was something completely new in South African society' (van der Spuy 1971: 41). This occurred in a situation of unease where the development of the Scottish mission in the period 1898–1923 could be destabilised. FMC policy had aggravated this situation though it did respond to the developing situation despite its intended policy of promoting union with the PCSA stated in 1901 and 1909, and in spite of the reaction of black ministers in 1908 against a multi-racial church (Burchell 1977: 55). Listening to the views of black ministers and elders was a priority of the 1920 deputation for the blacks concerned were educated people of some standing in the community and they had remained faithful to the Mission during, and in the aftermath of, the Mzimba Secession. Perhaps the formation of a black church was considered a form of appeasement or of thanks for faithful service?

In 1921, the FMC supported its Deputies and their resolutions and reversed its previous policy of forming a multi-racial church. The Deputies' opinions originated in the realisation that the two mission organisations had to be united to present a united front for mission and bring about unity amongst missionaries themselves. The Deputies argued, in line with Stewart's view, that the issue was a practical one to be resolved in the field and not a theoretical matter to be dealt with in Scotland. Separation from the Synod of Kafraria caused problems in a homogeneous area where two organisations were operating. There was a need for 'An authoritative supreme court of their own . . . in which the African ministers would have a real voice' (BPCSA 1971). A united church is necessary for evangelisation of the entire area with suitable regional divisions and one practice and procedure. It was agreed that the General Assembly of the UFCoS and of the PCSA were not appropriate bodies in which black people could relate easily.

The Deputies' resolutions included a note on the growth and development of the black church with a well-trained ministry and eldership 'anxious' to undertake evangelism which, until this time, had been under the control of the Mission Council. The location of missionaries was still to be arranged by the Mission Council. Was there a contradiction here between the agent and the appointee in terms of who would be likely to be appointed if there were to be both a suitable black and a white missionary available for appointment? They further advocated a reduction of missionary powers as the natural result of the above, of only appointing new missionaries in exceptional circumstances, and also reducing numbers of missionaries as suitable blacks became available (Sikutshwa 1946: 60). This represented a novel move towards the formation of a 'Native' church and a greater sharing of responsibility with black people (FMC, 15 February 1921, Minute 5386, 'South Africa – Report of Deputies', PR3983: 2, Cory).

A special meeting of the Mission Council was called on 30 March 1921 to consider a response to the proposal of devolution of power to black members (FMC, 23 March 1921, Minute 5518, NLS). It challenged this process which would culminate in black people assuming complete power of their own church affairs, despite reservations about the timing (Rev. D. Frazer to Henderson, 12 May 1922, unclassified Henderson correspondence, Burchell 1977: 56). The view of missionaries was that, resulting from failing to promote the union of the missions with the PCSA, the FMC adopted a reactive, rather than a proactive, role. The work of the Deputies, according to some missionaries, enabled the FMC to begin financial retrenchment (reply to FMC minute of 18 February 1921 in Burchell 1977: 56). However, certain matters had to be taken on board. The Mzimba Secession had disrupted the mission and had the potential for further destabilisation. The work of an independent Synod of Kafraria and discussions which had taken place in 1910 prefigured an independent church. Black people themselves grew to prefer the option of a black church.

The process towards union was not altogether smooth as we can note in a letter from Lennox to Ashcroft of the FMC (30 August 1922, Letterbook Mission Council, HPAL, UFH) for eventually: '. . . we came face to face with the actual facts of the situation, sound reason and good feeling prevailed, and the Commission seemed to pass into a region of good mutual understanding and determination to co-operate'.

Consummation of Union

The first General Assembly of the BPCSA

It had been agreed that 'the Synod and Presbyteries meet immediately before the convocation and General Assembly to resolve to dissolve with a view to uniting in the new church' (Commission on Union, 6 February 192, Box 12, F91-100, NAHECS, UFH). The women's associations were also invited to be present and conduct their own business concurrently, a practice which endured until the union with the Presbyterian Church of Southern Africa in 1999.

The convocation of Presbyterian missions met at Lovedale on the evening of 4 July 1923 with Rev. P. L. Hunter in the Chair. After Rev. J. Lennox gave a brief historical survey of the events leading to union, the uniting missions tabled reports. The Synod of Kafraria resolved to convey to the new church all of its properties; the Presbytery of Kaffraria tabled the disjunction certificates of all in the Presbytery except for Rev. J. Lundie of Malan, along with the disjunction certificates in favour of the Presbytery from the PCSA. The Presbytery of Mankazana tabled its disjunction. And it was reported that the Mission Council of Natal had not been able to meet and would report subsequently. The membership of the new body amounted to 25,000 souls. Rev. William Stuart of Burnshill was then unanimously elected Moderator of the General Assembly.

Stuart then formally constituted the gathering and gave his Moderatorial Address. He commented that the coming together of the UP and FC missions with the Mission Council of Natal was 'a forward step in the line of natural development' and a result of 'earnest and prayerful deliberation, full and careful consideration of the many interests involved and persons specially concerned'. The highest office was open to black people 'as it ought to be', so the new church retained the concepts of equality and parity. 'The Church of Christ is for any and everyone, . . . irrespective of nationality, colour or tongue' (Rev. W. Stuart, Moderatorial Address at 1st General Assembly, BPCSA 1923: 39), though van der Spuy (1971: 45) believes this remark would have been more appropriate in a united church. Many would disagree with this assessment (see below). Nonetheless the BPCSA 'was placed in a paradoxical situation for while it claimed universality and colourblindness, its very name, composition and future relationships proclaimed something different'. This was a rather negative view for it was open to all as many missionaries and a few non-missionary church workers discovered. Often the missionaries proved the truth of the statement for having served their working years in the BPCSA, many retired into membership and service within the PCSA.

Rev. J. Lennox was appointed Senior Clerk and Rev. M. Sililo of New Scotland, Natal, Junior Clerk. A number of representatives of other churches brought greetings to the General Assembly as did several tribal chiefs 'to congratulate the Presbyterian Missions on the step they had taken and to stimulate the newly formed Church to greater and nobler efforts for the spiritual uplift of the African races' (Sikutshwa 1946: 12). The FMC conveyed the Extract Minute recording its satisfaction with completing negotiations for union. In loyal addresses to the King and the Prime Minister there are references to the current situation in the country: 'unrest and bitterness so widely manifest in the social and political life of the world' and to moves being made 'to improve the relations between the different races in the land' that demonstrate the context in which the birth of the BPCSA has occurred and the church's social and political concern (BPCSA 1923: 46). These issues were not unrelated to the desire for ecclesiastical autonomy.

The name of the new Church

The final choice of name was 'The Bantu Presbyterian Church of South Africa', proposed by the Commission on Union and adopted by a large majority, then the General Assembly agreed to:

> ... instruct Clerks to inform the Government of the Union of South Africa of the step now taken in constituting this Church, so that the Church now formed may be officially registered under the new name. (BPCSA GA 1923: 25)

This would avoid complications which many of the South African initiated churches had encountered. Assembly further raised the status of mission stations 'under Native Missionaries' as soon as they demonstrated that they were self-sufficient (BPCSA GA 1923: 31).

Sikutshwa is circumspect in dealing with the name of the new church. Before the formation of the Church, the agreed name was 'The United Presbyterian Church of South Africa' in preference to the 'Native Presbyterian Church of South Africa' (Commission on Union, 15 August 1922, Box 12, F91-100, NAHECS, UFH) although there appears to have been ongoing discussions regarding this before union (Lennox to Soga, 25 November 1922, Letterbook, Synod of Kafraria, HPAL, UFH). It is of concern that the PCSA had an influence in the naming of a new black denomination and this further suggested an element of dependency on the one hand and the exercise of power on the other. They objected to the name United Presbyterian Church of South Africa, possibly because it might give the impression this new church was the focus of South African Presbyterianism. Its General Assembly had 'agreed to facilitate a Native Church in federal relationship with the Presbyterian Church of South Africa and that the name of the proposed new body failed to make this clear and further would lead to confusion in the public mind' (PCSA 1922: 34). 'Public mind' would have meant white mind' (Ac 1971/Ahl.3., WCL). Sikutshwa does not even mention this. He refers to churches being named after their founders, i.e. the retention of the designation 'Presbyterian' or 'Rabe'. However, he suggests that the name of the church has to be seen in the light of attempts at a solution of the 'Native Problem' and avoidance of 'political tactics' (Sikutshwa 1946: 13). Perhaps he comes nearest to the truth when he declared the importance of avoiding a name too similar to that of another church i.e. the PCSA. Here there could be confusion. The Commission on Union finally recommended the name of 'The Bantu Presbyterian Church of South Africa' (BPCSA). This became the final choice of name and it was adopted by a large majority over only six votes cast for 'The United Presbyterian Church of South Africa'. So it was designated a black church – a good thing to clarify that it was African, but a bad thing because of the racial connotation.

An order for the new Church

The new Church adopted the 'Practice and Procedure' of the UFCoS (1927) until it drew up its own *Manual of the Bantu Presbyterian Church* in 1958, and when it did so, the *Manual* closely resembled the Law of the Free Church of Scotland. It almost appeared as if anything distinctly African would be inferior to its European counterpart.

It was recommended and agreed that '. . . a Book of Order should in due course be prepared for the new Church itself, and that it should be in the Si-Xosa language' (Dewar, Committee on Creed and formula, Lennox papers, NAHECS). This would be based on the Books of Order of the UFCoS and the PCSA (Commission on Union, 18 August 1922, NAHECS). Meanwhile, a Basis of the church, a statement of Doctrine and Questions to be put at baptism, membership and ordination had been prepared.

Assessment of the Decision to Form a Black Church

From its inception, some considered its formation too spontaneous and without sufficient groundwork and preparation. However, this initiative in favour of forming a new church resulted from the desire to reward the loyalty of black ministers and members in the face of antagonism from Mzimba's followers besides the fear of further secessions. Yet, if this is true, then the initiative took twenty-five years to come to fruition.

Others considered it an expression of Black Consciousness that would achieve harmony (Rev. J. W. Househam, BPCSA 1923, minute 185); yet others considered it another secessionist church (Chief Native Commissioner of Natal to Lennox, 26 September 1923 and reply, file 'General Assembly', Lennox correspondence, Box F228, NAHECS). This would have been the first secessionist church formed as the result of lengthy negotiations and with the full assent of the sending church. Yet, the BPCSA was the only African church to have a voice in the 1923 Native Affairs Commission, while 'the Commission showed that in church matters, the South African government considered the voice of the missionaries more important than the voice of the indigenous church' (Millard 1995: 96–8). So it was not an AIC in the usual sense of the term. Then the BPCSA was ignored in the work of the 1925 Native Affairs Commission on AICs (Millard 1995: 96–8). Shepherd (1971: 89) concluded that it was 'the natural development of the hundred years of South African missionary work carried on by agents of the Churches in Scotland' though this opinion was not shared by all.

Burchell (1977: 57) claims that the establishment of the BPCSA was a compromise which allowed for the retention of substantial links with the Home Church and for developing closer links with the PCSA, and also for the Home Church to continue to exercise authority through powers committed to the Mission Council of Kaffraria. Union with the PCSA would have placed severe financial constraints on mission work and may have led to withdrawal of support from Scotland on the one hand and further disruption in the form of secession on the other. The possibility of further union was never rejected.

Brock (1974: 60), in evaluating the progress of the BPCSA, comments negatively that 'ecclesiastical separate development in the political circumstances of South Africa since 1920 have not given much scope to the Bantu Presbyterian Church and it has not proved itself a particularly inspiring example to follow'. However, at no time were whites debarred from membership. Those who wished to participate in this experiment had to know it was a black church they were associating with and not a body which provided an opportunity to exercise control over black people. Further, from its earliest times, the BPCSA has had a so-called coloured constituency. Perhaps if the history of the BPCSA has not provided an inspiring' example to follow, then this may be due to the continuing domination by the sending church through its Mission Councils and missionaries. Consequently, it had little opportunity to develop its own distinctive ethos had it chosen to do so.

The BPCSA has provided one 'workable answer to mission problems and tensions' (Burchell 1977: 57) which provided 'an independent African church in South Africa, controlling its own affairs and becoming ultimately free of white control and having, along with autonomous government, a federal connection with the Home Church' (Sikutshwa 1946: 6). Yet, the church was not free of white control either in terms of finance or personnel while the Mission Council continued in existence. But, it might also be considered a belated development in the light of the inability of the FMC to discover and come to terms with the total South African context in which the moves for the establishment of a Black church originated. It was a reactive development which had its roots, at least in part, in the growth of the AIC movement whose origins were traceable to the wider South African situation of the time. However, the Church of Scotland was prepared to accept the consequences of their mission policy in making the first experiment of an autonomous and segregated black church.

Faced with all this, the young church faced several problems including the need to secure its financial arrangements, the challenge of the political climate, its development within its own peculiar cultural milieu, the formation of a distinctive liturgy, musical tradition and theological expression, its internal responsibilities, the need to establish clear control of the appointment of overseas personnel and problems in its relationships with other reformed and particularly presbyterian bodies, especially the PCSA and PCA as well as its mission in general. This was a challenge which it had to respond to in the years following its birth. Burchell (1977: 60) is correct to a large degree in his assessment that 'the missionaries claiming superior understanding of the South African situation, had contrived to deflect the wider purpose of the Home Church and had foiled their efforts to introduce a policy which claimed to ignore racial difficulties'. However, it was the realisation in Scotland that there was a difficult situation which required to be tidied up that led to the decision about the Deputies' visit to South Africa in 1920 which brought the new church to birth, which in the period post-1923 remained 'under the guidance of the white church [UFCoS]. Independence could, therefore, only be obtained by establishing an independent church' (Millard 1995: 293).

Conclusion

The development in the formation of the missions into the BPCSA in 1923 after 100 years of missionary endeavour was long in coming to fruition but, between 1901 and 1909, when the FMC reaffirmed its commitment to union with the PCSA, and 1923, an inexorable process had begun. Numerous views exist about the decision to establish an independent black church, from the opinion that it was a racist act to a view which considered it a bold act of faith in the ability and potential of blacks to govern their own ecclesiastical affairs. It resulted from an emerging Black Consciousness in the sense of a developing awareness and desire amongst blacks in their ability to take control of their own affairs (cf. the rise of the AIC movement and particularly the Mzimba secession). But it was not secessionist because it did not disrupt the mission; rather it was the fulfillment of the early stated intention of the Scottish Mission in South Africa (cf. Shepherd 1971: 89). It might be claimed that the process took too long and was a late response arising out of practical necessity, considering that the mission was established in 1824 and the Mzimba Secession occurred in 1898. Nor was it a compromise (Burchell 1977: 57) for it was a clear alternative to union with a white-dominated PCSA. It was workable and independent to a degree but the continued existence of Mission Councils limited both its independence and the freedom of blacks to act without restraint and pursue their own policies and make their own mistakes and successes.

The BPCSA which grew out of the Scottish Mission actually became subordinate to the Mission Council after 1923 as the result of the latter's control of finance, property and missionary personnel. Its independence was restricted, therefore, by the control exercised by the UFCoS through the Mission Councils. Because Mission Councils were exclusive they existed taking no great account of the views of black people possibly not expressed in Presbytery as the result of 'intimidation' by missionaries who 'knew better' but often understood less. The position was worse with women who were not represented in any courts of the church. Little had been learned from the active role women performed, even in leadership positions, in the Scottish 'voluntary' societies or in the growing *uManyano* movement. The lay organisations in the church offered scope for development and leadership which found no easy or official recognition in the church.

Brock's (1974: 60) criticism about the BPCSA as an example of ecclesiastical 'Separate development' and not an 'inspiring' example at that is somewhat unfair. This was the first independent black church of its kind to be formed and it may be asked whether its actual development has been any less distinguished than many churches with a longer history and more varied experience?

Despite the lack of resources from the black community, the Mission grew before 1923 and the Church has survived and grown ever since its formation bearing witness to the many faithful blacks who carried the Gospel enthusiastically throughout their wider community. Despite reservations about the ability of blacks to handle their own church affairs, the birth of the BPCSA was a triumph of realism in the South African context.

CHAPTER TEN

Mission to Church – Church to Mission: The First Ten Years, 1923–33

Introduction

At the inauguration of the Bantu Presbyterian Church, the Moderator of the first General Assembly, Rt Rev. William Stuart, commented:

> Little wonder if the taking of this step had occasioned doubts, fears and anxieties in the minds of some of our people ... It has been well for ourselves and for these communities that the taking of this step has been a matter of long continued earnest deliberation, much consultation and many earnest prayers. (Moderatorial Address BPCSA GA 1923: 35)

Discussions, arguments, secessions and plans preceded this step. It had been a long, arduous and complex journey but one which eventually bore fruit. It was now up to the church to prove its worth by making its mark both in the ecclesiastical and wider context of South Africa.

Yet, this happened despite Elphick's (2012: 81) view that:

> By the 1920s, after Protestants had been conducting intensive missions in parts of South Africa for more than a century, the fulfilment of the implication of their gospel – that the equality of believers before God entailed equality of black and white in church and society – had been, it seemed, indefinitely postponed.

Whatever their personal reservations about Africans' abilities, no missionaries publicly advocated perpetual European domination of the African church, although they demonstrated little confidence in the short- and middle-term prospects of the success of such ventures as the formation of autonomous back churches. In theory, the principles of Christian universalism and the indigenous church dovetailed neatly, since the proclamation of a single gospel throughout the world would give rise to churches equal in stature though implanted in different cultures. In South Africa, however, where white Christians had founded well-endowed and cohesive churches, the two principles were in tension. Universalism in South Africa meant close fellowship and effective equality between white and black Christians, while the doctrine of indigenous churches implied that Africans, with their distinctive cultures, would go their own way, as whites would go theirs (Elphick: 94–5).

Therefore, the Bantu Presbyterian Church of South Africa (BPCSA) was birthed in the midst of racial tension, but also in the context of dependency and the argument for independence, two themes at the core of the Missionary Movement.

The First General Assembly of the BPCSA

The formation of the Bantu Presbyterian Church of South Africa was a momentous step forward and a sign of independence and autonomy. However, this view turned out to be mistaken as subsequent events would prove. For instance, one matter which remained unclear was the relationship of the General Assembly to the Mission Council of Kaffraria. This was a potential problem area and a joint commission was appointed to consider the matter (see below).

The Constitution of the BPCSA

The constitution adopted by the BPCSA was basically that of the United Free Church of Scotland (BPCSA 1925: 51–70). The Constitution was unashamedly Presbyterian (BPCSA 1925: 51). Its distinctive features included:

> 4. Congregations are not independent of each other, but are integral portions of one and the same Church having a common doctrine and being subject to a common government . . .
> 6. The constitution of the Church being entirely spiritual, appeal from the decision of any of the courts to the Civil Tribunals is regarded as an offence against the laws of the Church . . .
> 11. This Church has the inherent right, under the safeguards for deliberate action and legislation which it itself has provided to frame and adopt its Subordinate Standards, to revise and alter the same, whenever in its opinion the necessity for so doing arises, to interpret its Statement of Doctrine, to modify or change its Constitution, but always in agreement with the Word of God and with due regard to liberty of opinion which do not enter into the substance of the faith (BPCSA 1925: 51–2).

There was no concession to the African context regarding polity and procedure. This was in effect, a Scottish church in South Africa. Yet, the separation of the spiritual and temporal was a dissonant factor in an African church where as Magesa (2013: title) asked 'What is not sacred?'. In all of the discussions, negotiations, plans and hopes for the future, the concept of a church in Africa was not discussed. This may have been a form of response to the invasive effects of the Mzimba secession.

The role of missionaries

The place and function of missionaries had to be speedily resolved because, at the time of union, there were still many serving in South Africa and they were keen to continue in service. It was agreed that the following should have seats in the higher courts of the Church:

- ordained ministers in pastoral charges;
- theological tutors;
- representative elders from each congregation or mission;
- ordained missionaries appointed by the General Assembly 'with the view of giving all necessary advice and assistance, but they shall leave the conduct of business as far as practicable to the native members. (Plan of Union of the UFCoS, section on Administration of Missions, para, 6; minute 41,2(a), BPCSA, 1923)

In a letter to J. H. Oldham, Lennox (11 December 1922, Lennox papers, NAHECS, UFH; cf. Commission on Union, 15 August 1922, NAHECS) had claimed that at the time of union, missionaries would have seats in the courts of the church 'with full powers' which will decline in the course of time until 'they will no longer be required'. This area was problematic because no checks and balances were built in to limit the missionaries' exercise of power. It would be as difficult for them to accept a reduced role as it would be for black ministers to assert themselves. This was especially true when there had to be a debate about the status of Native assistants in courts of the Church before it was resolved to admit them to higher than associate status. It was agreed that 'ordained Native assistants be given seats in the courts of the BPCSA' (GA 1923: 23).

But this was not accepted without a challenge. Rev. T. B. Soga had expressed a desire for the blacks to have 'complete control in the Native Courts' because missionaries controlled the Mission Councils. He based his case on the fact that the Plan of Union for the Scottish churches in 1900 in which they 'imposed on us [missionaries] all the duty to leave the control of the Native courts entirely to the Natives' (Lennox to Ashcroft, 30 August 1922, Letterbook, Mission Council, HPAL).

But another aspect of the role of missionaries has to be understood relating to the retention of power by mission councils:

If the Bantu Church communicate direct with the Foreign Mission Committee on any matters which relate to the council's responsibilities, the Committee will necessarily require to pass such back to the Council, who are the Committee's local Executive, for their opinion before the Foreign Mission committee's answer to the Assembly can be given. (Mission Council of South Africa, Relation of Mission Councils to Bantu Presbyterian Church, FMC note 2154, Lennox papers, Box 12, F91-100, NAHECS)

This is significant because it strikes at the heart of the autonomy granted since a white group within the church has power to veto its decisions and wishes.

No parameters were defined to limit the missionaries' exercise of power. It would be as difficult for them to accept a reduced role as it would be for black ministers to assert themselves. However, the intention was for black Christians to take control of their own affairs and decision making. The problem was this was difficult for the foreign missionaries who were so used to deciding for local Christians, with or without consultation. The concept of partnership in mission was not yet at a stage of development it could be integrated into the life and witness of the missionaries and black ministers. This only began in earnest as Church of Scotland policy in 1947 (Duncan 2008: 109ff; Lyon 1998: 5) although what emerged was continued domination through control of personnel and finance. There was little or no control on the missionaries' use of finance or the deployment of personnel while the mission councils remained in place. Consultation was still a concept to be developed in the future of missionary outreach.

There was a difference between Missionaries and missionaries; the former being used to refer in documentation to foreign appointments, while the latter designated black ministers without a call to a congregation and appointed to congregations (cf. BPCSA 1925: 35).

Theological Education

Related to the above, theological education had become a contested field following the secessions of the late nineteenth and early twentieth centuries. Brian Stanley (1990: 134) has asserted that 'educated indigenous leadership was a prerequisite of progress towards autonomy'. As the need for an indigenous ministry expanded, so did the need for improved training facilities. Theological education had begun at Lovedale Missionary Institution in 1870 and remained so into the 1920s. The opening of the South African Native College, Fort Hare, in 1916, stimulated the drive for an educated black ministry and building Iona House, partly funded by the Women's Association, provided further impetus to the establishment of divinity at Fort Hare in the 1930s (Denis & Duncan 2011: 28). However, the curricula replicated those used in Scottish faculties and colleges. This had led to the unfortunate dispute between William Govan and James Stewart, Principals of Lovedale Missionary Institution in the mid-nineteenth century, regarding the value of continuing the teaching of Latin and Greek (Shepherd 1971: 27–31). Although Stewart won the dispute and the languages were displaced, there were no further substantial changes in the curriculum. This encouraged the continuation of dependency as no account was taken of contextual African factors. It also forced candidates for the ministry to adopt an Enlightenment paradigm which denied any possibility of the successful and faithful inculturation of the gospel by enforcing a European worldview in opposition to the forced demise of their African worldview. This was imposed on their congregations and converts and resulted in developing a false distinction between religion and culture. Little or no effort was made to investigate the role of the culture of the location of missionary outreach. It was simply dismissed to be replaced by mission Christianity imported from Europe.

The pastoral care of the Church

Seven presbyteries were formed for the care and supervision of the work of the Church – Kaffraria, Mankazana, Transkei, Griqualand East, Umtata, Natal and Zoutspansberg. Initially it had been planned to unite the Presbyteries of Kaffraria and Mankazana, but this was considered premature, though they were united later.

Regarding pastoral charges, it was felt that mission stations should be upgraded to full status as pastoral charges when they 'reached a stage of maturity to manage satisfactorily their financial responsibilities' (BPCSA1923: 31). Black ministers were to be paid by their congregations. The question arose about non-payment due to financial stringency. If this occurred, supplements would be paid from Assembly funds. This posed a potential problem because the stipends of missionaries were secured and poorer congregations were put in the position of becoming beggars. One matter which remained unclear was the relationship of the General Assembly to the Mission Council of Kaffraria. This was another potential problem area and a joint commission was appointed to consider the matter. Nothing substantial emerged from this decision and the *status quo* remained until 1978 when, on the appointment of Rev. Graham Duncan to the linked Lovedale District and Institution congregations (BPCSA1977: 27, 41), the General Assembly determined that his stipend should be remitted to the General Assembly office.

The business of the Church was dealt with by seventeen Committees: Life and Work, Finance, Board of Trustees, Welfare of Youth, Education, Training of Theological Students, Evangelists, Temperance, Statistics, Publications, Church Extension, Creed and Formulae, Presbyterian Hostel Fund, Preparation of Loyal Addresses, Relations with the Mission Council of Kaffraria, Representatives to the General Assembly of the PCSA and Committee for Work amongst Lepers at Emjanyana (BPCSA GA 1923: 22). However, there was no committee on missions. The mission of the denomination would be advanced by the Life and Work, Trustees, Welfare of Youth, Education, Training of Theological Students, Evangelists, Temperance, Publications, Church Extension, Presbyterian Hostel Fund, Relations with the Mission Council of Kaffraria, Representatives to the General Assembly of the PCSA and Committee for Work amongst Lepers at Emjanyana committees. A further important means of extending the mission would be through the church associations, the Women's Christian

Association, the Girls' Association and the Young Mens' Christian Guild. The church associations were the nearest the BPCSA came to indigenising the denomination. Here we note the first and virtually the only attempt to Africanise the liturgy. This demonstrated a high level of organisation and extensive interests both in church and community.

The pastoral care of the church was closely linked to finance. Black ministers were always vulnerable financially and dependent on the good graces of their missionary mentors who controlled the Assembly finances. This was an indirect means of control over the black ministry. This was an example of the maintenance of dependency through financial control.

The matter of shortage of ordained ministry significantly affected the pastoral care of the denomination through the administration of the sacraments in a scattered context. It was decided to restrict celebration of Baptism and Holy Communion to 'those who are clerically ordained' (BPCSA GA 1925–6: 21).

Pastoral affairs even extended into the field of politics when Rev. T. B. Soga issued a letter condemning the Pass Laws in 1925 and the BPC took up the matter to little effect. Another pastoral matter which exercised many assemblies was that of temperance (BPCSA GA 1927: 14, BPCSA 1928: 16–17).

Liturgy

A remarkable event took place in 1929 with the publication of *Amaculo ase Rabe*, the Xhosa hymn book which has stood the test of time and is still used by most of the Xhosa speaking churches today. This was a joint project of the 'Bantu Presbyterian Church, the Congregational Church, the Missions of the Free Church of Scotland and some other religious bodies' (BPCSA 1929: ix). It has to be remembered that the worship style inherited from Scotland and promoted in South Africa was formal in the extreme. As part of the Reformed tradition, the United Free Church was firmly based in Scripture as the Word of God. Formality reached its zenith in the celebration of the sacrament of Holy Communion. Worship was cerebral and intellectual with little space given to the affective domain. The expression of emotion was strictly circumscribed. This was another matter of control and exercise of power. The unrestrained freedom of the spirit in worship was evident only in the church associations, which for the most part the missionaries eschewed, particularly in their liturgy with the emphasis on *imvuselelo* (revival) and *umjikelo* (fund-raising revival). This would also gradually become part of the Sunday morning liturgy, except at the celebration of Holy Communion. This freedom extended to the associations of the BPCSA.

Church Associations

A further important means of extending the mission would be through the church associations:

> Church organisations and associations played a major part in the quest for social, moral and spiritual acclimatization. Choirs, bible classes, youth organizations and especially women's associations were all part of the Churches' response to urban [and rural] life. (Sundkler & Steed 2000: 734)

Although the women's organisations had been operating before 1923 (Nzo 2017: 77) they also united at the first General Assembly (BPCSA GA 1923: 23–4). It became the custom for a delegation of the Women's Christian Association to be received at each General Assembly where they would report on their work and donate for the work of the denomination. In 1924, they presented their Constitution and it was decided that the Business Committee should report at the next Assembly: 'On relations between the Conference of the Women's Association and the Assembly regarding issues wherein through co-operation between the two bodies can be furthered' (BPCSA GA 1925: 32). Their constitution stated that they would meet annually along with the General Assembly (BPCSA 1925: 71). This was the beginning of what would, in time, become a symbiotic relationship.

Along with the Women's Christian Association (WCA), the Girls' Association (GA) and the Young Men's Christian Guild (YMCG) also performed a missionary function in the church through their intensive evangelical outreach, particularly in worship with the adoption of the *imvuselelo* and *umjikelo* services. This was linked to the pressing need for pastoral care in the contexts of extreme poverty and racial discrimination to which they were subjected. One reason that the associations had freedom was that the missionaries had little or no experience of church associations and distanced themselves from them.

The Girls' Association was established in 1954, as a preparatory stage for membership in the *manayno* and for unmarried ladies.

Finance and Property

A basic approach to the sustenance of the denomination was agreed in 1925:

> ... it is the Christian duty and privilege of each member and candidate to give freely and liberally for the support and extension of the Work of Christ, through the Church according to their means; but that the offering shall not be regarded as a tax imposed by the Assembly, nor a payment for the privileges of Church membership. (BPCSA GA 1925: 38)

An initial principle was agreed that all the immovable property of the BPCSA should remain vested in the name of the General Trustees of the United Free Church of Scotland (BPCSA GA 1925: 37). However, by 1926, another view prevailed and it was proposed that:

> In view of the fact that at present the newly formed Bantu Presbyterian Church of South Africa has no direct control over the Property held in trust for them, the Assembly desires humbly to petition the Foreign Mission Committee of the United Free Church to associate the Trustees of the Bantu Presbyterian Church with the Representatives of the Home Church trustees for the South African property, so as to prepare ways and means on the question of transference of property. (BPCSA GA 1926: 12)

This was a forward-looking step as events transpired. Early on, property became a matter of dispute between the BPCSA and PCSA in Glenthorn in Mankazana Presbytery where recourse had to be made to 'the Bantu Presbyterian Congregation at Glenthorn, as shown by documents in the possession of the South African Representatives of the Board of Trustees of the United Free Church of Scotland' (BPCSA GA 1928: 22).

Finance took no account of the three-self policy regarding the BPCSA becoming self-supporting. Matters continued as before with the United Free Church (the Free Church [FCoS] united with the United Presbyterian Church [UPCoS] to form the United Free Church of Scotland [UFCoS] in 1900) continuing their financial support as previously despite their desire to reduce their financial commitment. There was no endowment to allow the church to develop its own approach to financial government. In addition, black people did not have the financial resources of white congregations so this necessitated a different approach to stewardship. A complicating factor was that, besides being forced to plead for grant assistance, the money given was sent to the mission council where missionaries controlled and disbursed it as they saw fit. This led to a situation where missionaries determined where the needs lay and not the communities (congregations, presbyteries, BPCSA) affected. To operate with regular grants from Scotland militated against financial independence and kept the BPCSA in servitude. This was demeaning and humiliating at any time but especially for a newly established denomination. This situation would continue until the 1970s.

Relationship with the UFCoS

While this appeared to be a matter settled on the formation of the BPCSA this was by no means the case. Pending the retirement of Rev. J. M. Auld from Columba Mission in 1927, the BPCSA requested that the Foreign Mission Committee (FMC) grant the congregation a right of call (Columba Min. 471, BPCSA GA 1927: 35). This was refused with the suggestion that the BPCSA form a:

'Native congregation' on the grounds that 'the area superintended from Columba, with its numerous schools, and its service for the European population, and other responsibilities, cannot be regarded as a suitable parish for a Native minister'. (Columba Min. 523, BPCSA GA: 1928: 25)

It was clarified that the European station, buildings and farm lands 'are not the property of a congregation' (Columba Min. 523, BPCSA GA: 1928: 25). Separate development was their view and nothing could be done without consultation with the Mission Council whose membership was predominantly white missionaries. The matter was referred to the FMC for reconsideration:

> as in the judgment of the Assembly, the Minute deprives the Bantu Presbyterian Church Assembly of rights in the control of congregations which Assembly has believed to belong to itself and the lower courts of the Church through and since the formation of the Bantu Presbyterian Church. (Columba Min. 523, BPCSA GA: 1928: 25)

Besides the financial issue, the United Free Church maintained its hold on properties in the young BPCSA. This could easily be construed as a racist stance. A further step was taken by Rev. William Gavin the next year when he proposed a South African body for resolving such issues by the Joint Committee of Assembly and that the Mission Council be consulted (BPCSA GA: 1929: 40).

The FMC (BPCSA GA 1929: 46–9) responded. First, they commended the competent manner the BPCSA had organised and carried out its affairs and patronisingly commented that the Mission Council 'will rejoice in every evidence of the growing ability of the Bantu Assembly to rule her own house, and that the Assembly will always cherish the affectionate and grateful feelings of a daughter to her mother' (BPCSA GA 1929: 46). However, the FMC 'cannot overlook the fact that the Native ministry is not yet adequate to undertake full responsibility for the whole work formerly administered and now in process by the Mission Council' (BPCSA GA 1929: 46). This raised the delicate issue of who decides when the black church is ready to take full responsibility for its own affairs and by what criteria? It raised the further question, Why was the BPCSA established if it was not competent to conduct its own affairs and reach its own decisions? This was no more than imposed dependency as there was no mechanism put in place to prepare black BPCSA ministers and members for transferring authority. It is a pity this had not been clarified before 1923.

To resolve the divergent views, the FMC suggested: 'the appointment of a Committee of Assembly (including Native ministers, elders and Scottish missionaries) to consider all questions in which the functions of Assembly and the Mission Council are intertwined' (BPCSA 1929: 47). The FMC blurred the issue by asserting that the BPCSA 'has autonomous powers in the organisation and government of the Church in all spiritual matters' (which were not defined) (BPCSA GA 1929: 47). The BPCSA was given authority over intangible (i.e. spiritual) matters while the missionaries controlled all property moveable and particularly immovable, such as land. The problem arose because of the involvement of Mission Councils as the FMC's 'representatives on the field' (BPCSA 1929: 4 para.5.(5)). Regarding property the FMC 'hold all the mission property as a trust, and they have the responsibility for seeing that it is used in the best interests of evangelisation in Africa' (BPCSA 1929: 4 para.5.(6)). This was the patronising policy of trusteeship at work in a crass manner. It enforced dependency and made no provision to end this approach to mission. There was no way in which the BPC could approach the FCoS directly:

> The Committee will be glad to receive communications from the Bantu Church direct, but suggest that all matters which affect the relations of the Bantu Church to the Council should be dealt with first by the proposed Special Committee, who will pass on their recommendations to the [Mission] Council and Assembly. If the Bantu Assembly communicate directly with the Foreign Mission Committee will necessarily require to pass such back to the Council, who are the Committee's local executive, for their opinion before the Foreign Mission Committee's answer to the Assembly can be given.

At every step there was a check in place to delay and limit independent decision making and action. This hardly demonstrates autonomy for the BPCSA. This was an issue that would endure until the dissolution of the Mission Council in 1981. The BPCSA was held in bondage by Mission Councils dominated by missionaries and, later, missionary opinion, and their *imprimatur, nihil obstat* was required before any policy decisions regarding property and finance could be made. The BPC had to copy the Mission Council regarding correspondence with the FMC, but the reverse was not required. This resulted in one-sided transparency by the BPCSA and one sided secrecy by the mission council. This was not a sound means of developing independence of thought and action or trusting relationships despite the mollifying language.

The following year, a report was received regarding this matter and the BPCSA Assembly requested:

> 6. ... that the Foreign Mission Committee consider the advisability of arranging for handing over, under legal title, the property of some station or stations as a first step towards more general transfer and in order to give the Trustees of the Bantu Presbyterian Church the opportunity of training in the management of property.
> 7. With a view to removing misunderstandings between the General Assembly and Mission Council and improving relations between these bodies, all correspondence to and from the Foreign

Mission Committee and Mission Council which affects the Bantu Presbyterian Church be submitted to the Special Committee to be appointed by the General Assembly. (BPCSA 1930: 45)

The existing situation promoted and maintained an imbalance in relationships. This was clear from a letter from Robert Forgan, Joint Convener of the FMC, to the BPCSA:

> ... I have sent a copy to Mr Godfrey thinking it right that the Mission Council should be informed of our action. We earnestly hope that the Bantu Assembly in September will be wisely guided, and that action may be taken on lines that will lead to united action in the future and prevent separate action on the part either of the Assembly or the Mission Council. (Forgan to Shepherd, 8 May 1930, BPCSA 1930: 45)

This seemed to mean that the BPCSA was to conform to the policy of the Mission Council. But the core of the matter was explained in a message sent by the FMC to the 1930 BPCSA General Assembly referring to the proceedings of the 1929 General Assembly:

> [i]n which several cases are recorded as giving rise to difficulty just because they were being dealt with separately by the General Assembly and the Mission Council ... Further the Foreign Mission Committee [confirms] the full recognition of the independence of the Bantu Church.

The heart of the problem was that the FMC did not envisage a situation where there is no need for a Mission Council 'where such Christian Natives were unrepresented' (BPCSA 1930: 52) where there is an independent church. This raises the question regarding the independence of the BPCSA and the purpose of the Mission Council other than to police the thinking of the BPCSA? Duncan (2016a: 22–32) has advanced an argument that the continued existence of the mission council as a 'self-perpetuating anachronism' hampered the mission of the BPCSA.

Rev. T. B. Soga, prepared a memorandum relating to the continued existence of the mission council in which he argued that the matter of relations between the BPCSA and Mission Council should have been finalised before the formation of the BPCSA. Hence,

> they are calculated to destroy the principle and autonomy of the Native Church in South Africa. As things are, evidently the Church Overseas has no intention of leaving these problems wholly to the discretion of the Bantu Assembly. (BPCSA 1930: 4)

He challenged dividing the mission areas to weaken them rather than consolidating them and of being anti-Presbyterian. What were *adiaphora* (matters of little consequence) before union are now of great consequence (BPCSA GA 1930: 49).

Members of Mission Council (MC) possessed double powers of voting. He summarises his view strongly; the Minute indicates:

> that should any disagreement arise concerning matters of Mission Council [MC] interest, the Bantu Assembly will have no say; but that such matters will have to be forthwith referred to the FMC, 'where the Bantu Assembly will not be represented again; and more weight will ultimately, be given to the opinion of the MC as such. This is what we understand by the Mission Council's executive powers in South Africa'; and it is an indirect way of nullifying the very autonomy of the Bantu Church. What the UF Church gives with one hand, it indirectly takes away with another ... these [lands] cannot be claimed by the Bantu Church as a right. (BPCSA 1930: 49)

Soga pointed out the resulting unhealthy relationship of distrust between the Mission Council and BPC which he determined to be a spiritual matter and a cause of 'estrangement between the Bantu Church and the Mission Council will remain forever' (BPCSA GA 1930: 49). Here we can see how enforced dependency prevented the development of good relationships. This would later be a prime problem with the concept of partnership in mission (Duncan 2008). Regarding the control of mission lands; 'one sees no end to conflict' (BPCSA 1930: 49). These were to be prophetic words. Loyalty was another issue raised by Soga who reminded the FMC that the missionaries 'have become members in full of more than one church' (BPCSA GA 1930: 50). Therefore, to whom did they owe their first loyalty? On which power did they depend for their ability to control – the UFCoS or the BPCSA?

Land was a sensitive issue, and one of which the missionaries and the FMC had little or no understanding. There was no comprehension that land was not the absolute property of the FCoS (but of God, Ps 24: 1) although they 'owned' it and used it as they saw fit. There was considerable ignorance of the spiritual nature and value of land (see Duncan 2016a). Soga (BPCSA 1930: 50) explained the significance:

> At the commencement of the Church's mission in South Africa the nation through their then chiefs marked out certain lands for the use of early missionaries and school people [*amakholwa*]. Later when the political circumstances changed, and rule was taken from Native hands, government authorities granted some tracts of lands for the use of missionary societies, and small allotments with commonage rights adjoining mission glebes were given to the individual Christian families within mission station boundaries separate from the rest of the district. This is the land now in question, and the missionary holds it to be the property of the Home Church, and that it must meet Mission Council interest.

Soga continued in this vein even mocking the FMC for delegating the 'higher' functions of spiritual oversight while withholding the temporal oversight of property. (BPCSA GA 1930: 51). He is scathing in his assessment of the FMC's power and dominance, through the Mission Council where it has 'liberty to tamper with our Assembly decisions exclusively, subsequently, and, privately' (BPCSA 1930: 52). He reiterates the point that 'the White [missionaries] belong to two churches legally, in Scotland and South Africa, where the Native does not belong so' (BPCSA 1930: 52–3). This was a very difficult memorandum to pen by one who held the Mission and the UFCoS in such high regard (BPCSA 1930: 53–4). His father, Rev. Tiyo Soga, was the first black person to be trained and ordained in Scotland and held a high, though ambivalent, view of the Scottish church.

The 1931 General Assembly agreed to copy its correspondence to the FMC also to the Mission Council (BPCSA GA 1931: 22). It further agreed that missionary Rev. Dr R. H. W. Shepherd's proposal be implemented:

> That the Assembly accept the principle of the demarcation of the present European mission areas into suitable parishes and refer the matter to the Committee on Relationships between the Assembly, the Foreign Mission Committee and the Mission Council for consideration and report to the next Assembly. (BPCSA 1931: 24)

Later, the same Assembly rejoiced in 'earnest and constant desire of the Foreign Mission Committee to promote both the spiritual progress and material prosperity of the Bantu Presbyterian Church' (BPCSA GA 1931: 37). The FMC response to T. B. Soga's memorandum indicated a clear change of policy for if communication from the BPCSA to the FMC was to be through the Mission Council they:

> shall be sent without any alteration by the Council. If the Mission Council desires to make any observations on such proposals from the Bantu Assembly they will be requested to do so quite apart from the proposals themselves. (BPCSA GA 1931487)

The FMC confirmed that the duty of superintendence is the function of the Presbytery. They reminded the BPC of the cost of trusteeship of property and asserted the long term time scale involved in transfer of property (this took until the 1970s and 1980s). This required that the BPCSA be registered as Trustees of property (BPCSA GA 1932: 35). At this Assembly the momentous step was taken to include 'Native members' of the Mission Council (BPCSA GA 1932: 35).

The only other denomination formed in the same manner was the Tsonga [Evangelical] Presbyterian Church in South Africa (Maluleke 1995). It also suffered identical problems about their relationship with the *Département Missionaire* of their Swiss mission church during the same period. Hence, the BPCSA provided a 'unifying centre' for developing black churches in South Africa.

Conclusion

The Bantu Presbyterian Church made a good start as an independent denomination. It had a strong Presbyterian ethos and this was reflected in its organisation. The lack of a separate mission committee meant that missions were treated on a business-as-usual basis. This was hampered by the tensions which existed between the Foreign Mission Committee of the United Free Church of Scotland, the Mission Council and the Bantu Presbyterian Church General Assembly. Continued and constant dependency characterised the relationship in the midst of contested loyalties and a lack of mutual trust, particularly in the areas of finance and property. The general missionary presumption was that the new church would conform to the standards and values of the 'mother' church in Scotland. Clearly, insufficient thought and action had taken place in the process helping to form the BPCSA regarding the potential problems that could arise. As far as the UFCoS and the Mission council were concerned it was business as usual. These were an enduring sore in the life of the BPCSA until the dissolution of the Church of Scotland South Africa Joint Council in 1981 and probably restricted her faithfulness as a missionary church. There is little evidence that the United Free Church of Scotland promoted the ideals expressed in the three-self policy of becoming self-supporting (finance), self-propagating (mission) and self-governing (polity). Despite all this, it was a 'unifying centre' for future ecclesiastical developments in South Africa, but the emergent Bantu Presbyterian Church was neither autonomous nor independent. It remained a dependent denomination in terms of staffing by Scottish missionary personnel, and regular annual grants. This was an increasing source of frustration and distrust and hampered the development of the missionary outreach of the Bantu Presbyterian Church of South Africa. Members of the BPCSA could see no future when they would be entrusted with their own affairs.

In broader perspective, the evaluation of Ott et al. (2010: 219) reflect Bishop Azariah's plea: 'Churches must relate to one another as equal partners in God's mission'.

CHAPTER ELEVEN

Reaching Out: The Bantu Presbyterian Church in South Africa and the Presbyterian Church of South Africa and Ecumenism, 1923–39

Introduction and Background

> The Lord, indeed, as he has done from the beginning of the world, can wonderfully, in ways unknown to us, preserve the unity of the true faith, and prevent its destruction from the dissensions of men . . . I should with pleasure cross ten seas, if necessary, to accomplish that object. (Letter XVII, Calvin to Cranmer, Archbishop of Canterbury, 1552)

This quotation summarises the reforming view of ecumenism since the sixteenth-century Reformation. It reminds us that the sixteenth century Reformations were an attempt, following many earlier attempts, to reform a corrupt church. There was no desire to establish new churches but to follow in the Lord's intention from creation:

However, in the course of time, the Reforming tradition developed a 'defective genetic tendency towards schism' (a term coined by the late Presbyterian Prof. Calvin Cook, Rhodes University, Grahamstown; cf. Muirhead 2015: 1–3, Burleigh 1960: 457).

Following the Scottish Reformation it was many years before mission became a viable prospect. As we have already seen the beginnings of mission to South Africa were delayed until 1824. Before this mission depended on forces outside the formal structures of the church; hence, the growth and development of interdenominational voluntary societies. From 1824, the Free Church of Scotland engaged in mission in South Africa.

At the Disruption (1843), the Free Church of Scotland came into being as the result of secession from the Church of Scotland. This had a significant impact on the Scottish mission in South Africa. The Glasgow Missionary Society had been active in South Africa since 1821 and from 1834 'the disputes of Scotland made themselves felt though restrained by the allegiance to a greater cause' (Drummond & Bulloch 1975: 166). In 1838 the Church of Scotland took responsibility for mission and subsequently 'the Glasgow Missionary Society (GMS) adhering to the Principles of the Church of Scotland' attracted five missionaries while the newly-formed Glasgow South African Missionary Society attracted two (Drummond &

Bulloch 1975: 166). Until 1842 the two missions operated as one presbytery. In 1845, following the Disruption and the closure of the GMS, three mission stations, Lovedale, Burnshill and Pirie, were transferred by the Church of Scotland to the Free Church of Scotland while two, Chumie and Qhibira, were in 1847 transferred to the United Presbyterian Church of Scotland, the 'Voluntaries', which was the progeny of the union of the Secession and Relief Churches (Hewat 1960: 180). The Free Church of Scotland and the United Presbyterian Church of Scotland united in 1900 to form the United Free Church of Scotland and in 1929 it reunited with the Church of Scotland. A remnant of the uniting denominations always remained outside the union.

Before the Formation of the BPCSA

Following its historic tradition of supporting ecumenical initiatives, the Scottish Mission was committed to ecumenism and supported the General Missionary Conference in South Africa (GMCSA) from its formation in 1904 whose stated aim was 'the establishment of Native Churches is the true aim and end of Christian Missions, and these ought to be truly African in character' (Thomas 2002: 8–9). The GMCSA was both an ecumenical and a missionary organisation which demonstrated the essential link between the two. Scottish missionaries were involved from the outset. Rev. Dr James Stewart of Lovedale was present and was appointed the chairperson (Shepherd 1971: 65, 82). His successor, Rev. Dr James Henderson was also closely involved as was his colleague Rev. John Lennox as Secretary and Treasurer (Shepherd 1971: 82). Rev. Brownlee J. Ross was also involved (Thomas 2002: 15) as were Dr Alexander Kerr, first Principal of the South African Native College (renamed Fort Hare University cf. Thomas 2002: 83), Dr Arthur Wilkie, Principal of Lovedale after Henderson (Thomas 2002: 61), Rev. James Dewar and Dr R. H. W. Shepherd, last missionary Principal of Lovedale Institution (Thomas 2002: 85).

In the successor to the GMCSA, the Christian Council of South Africa was established in 1936 (Thomas 2002: 90). It gave way to the South African Council of Churches in 1968. The BPCSA has been involved in and committed to ecumenism throughout.

It was also involved in the momentous World Missionary Conference (1910) through the presence and participation of Dr James Henderson of Lovedale (Stanley 2009).

First Attempts at Presbyterian Union in South Africa

The main protagonists in ecumenism during the early years of the BPCSA were the BPCSA itself and the PCSA where unresolved issues occupied the agenda of both denominations. We have seen that a first attempt at union took place in 1880. Nothing came of this attempt until, in 1891, a Federal

Council promoted union. At its fourth meeting, in 1895, a draft constitution was presented having been scrutinised by sessions, congregations and presbyteries. It was then sent to participating 'Churches and Presbyteries'. The Colonial Committee of the FCoS expressed its support particularly in terms of 'the christianisation of the native races, and the consolidation of the Christian communities in South Africa' (PCSA, Rae to Federal Council, Minutes 16 July 1895, 19 March 1895). At this stage the UPCoS missions decided to participate in the union although the UFCoS missions subsequently voted to remain separate as the Synod of Kafraria. It 'feared that the predominantly white PCSA would allow racial discrimination to determine its life and work, including its mission policy' (Hunter 1983: 1). The issue of status would be aggravated when the care of black PCSA Congregations was placed under the supervision of its Mission Committee.

The union of the Presbyterian Church of South Africa (often called the South African Presbyterian Church, e.g. Lennox 1911: 81, and what was 'termed the colonial Presbyterian Church' [Shepherd 1971: 88]) was consummated on 27 September 1897. It was clear from the beginning that issues of race and distrust were evident as seen from those who did not participate in the union. Yet, they were seen differently by white proponents of the venture. The PCSA General Assembly was not convinced of these arguments (Proceedings of the First General Assembly, PCSA [1897], WCL, Ac1971/Ah1.1: 26–7).

From its inception, the PCSA's mission work among the indigenous peoples became the responsibility of the Mission Committee, while mission work among whites was the preserve of the Colonial Committee – soon to become the Church Extension Committee. As a result those whose fears regarding union on the grounds of race were justified (Cory, MS Ac1971/Ag 2: 8).

The PCSA had a confused and confusing mission policy which depended on informal relations between white congregations and their associated black missions and, for many years struggled to resolve the problem of integration (Hunter 1983: 1). White Presbyterians regarded this as their missionary outreach and were satisfied as a result of the control they could continue to exercise over their funds within their designated mission as an extension of their congregational commitment.

Richard Elphick (2012: 7–8) makes the central claim:

> that the struggle over racial equalisation . . . was pivotal to South African history; that this concept was rooted in the missionaries' proclamation of God's love to all people, as manifested in the birth, crucifixion and resurrection of Jesus; that the ideal of equality was nurtured in large part by missionary institutions, even though missionaries themselves repeatedly sought to limit, deflect or retard its achievements . . . There is, therefore, a history of an idea in relationship with institutions and the people who ran them.

Although both branches of Presbyterianism viewed black people as objects of mission, the Scottish mission, through a combination of evangelism and education sought to raise black people to take care of their own affairs. It was a basic missionary principle that missions should establish local churches under local leadership.

This concept made union problematic as both Presbyterian bodies were operating from different discourses, the one colonial and the other mission-oriented. Elphick asserts that ecumenism was bound up with transferring property and power from missions to the 'native' churches they had founded, but in South Africa, as Thomas has demonstrated, ecumenism retarded indigenisation and prolonged missionary power. This was the case in the PCSA.

On a typical mission field, the distinction between mission and church was fairly clear. Under the three-self policy enunciated by English and American evangelical mission societies in the nineteenth century, missions would establish 'native churches' in regions far from their homeland and gradually transfer their authority and assets to them. Two such 'native churches' had been established by English-speaking missions in South Africa:

> one Presbyterian [BPCSA], one Congregational . . . in South Africa the model of 'indigenisation' was vastly complicated by the fact that most truly black churches, the so-called African Independent Churches, had not been founded by white missionaries at all, and hence had no need to assert their independence; viewed warily by missionaries and white churchmen, these churches played no role in ecumenical affairs until the 1960s. (Elphick 2012: 269)

Yet the independent churches were not totally indigenous as they were offshoots of missionary bodies and in many cases continued to replicate their practices. They were, however, initiated by indigenous peoples. These African Initiated Churches (AICs) added another dynamic to the tapestry of southern African Christianity, even within the Presbyterian *corpus* due to the Mzimba Secession of 1898 (Duncan 2013b).

The BPCSA and Ecumenism

The substantial reason for the emergence of two denominations originating from Scotland, the BPCSA and the PCSA, rather than one was racism but the semi-official reason was that union with the Presbyterian Church of South Africa was not in the best interests of the black people in the Scottish mission (*SAO*, November 1973: 2); the PCSA's desire to form a federal arrangement was rejected since such 'a relationship with the PCSA would in future discredit the witness of both churches' (*Imvo Zabantsundu*, 7 August 1923). In the first General Assembly of the BPCSA it was decided to 'have a special relationship with the Presbyterian Church of

South Africa' through mutual representation in each other's highest courts (BPCSA 1923: 20). This 'special relationship' was to be exposed to many strains and stresses in succeeding years. However, the PCSA's desire for union remained. It appears that fraternal delegates raised no contentious issues while attending one another's General Assemblies, which may have exacerbated the tensions that arose.

An early example is within the jurisdiction of the Presbytery of Mankazana (Baviaans River; see Soga 1862: 167). This was the presbyterial area where the two missions of the United Presbyterian Church (which aligned itself with the United Free Church of Scotland) and the Free Church of Scotland (which aligned itself with the Bantu Presbyterian Church) were active and where the stresses of presbyterian ecumenism were most deeply expressed. In 1925 the BPCSA General Assembly noted a decision of the PCSA General Assembly (PCSA 1924 Min 106):

> The Assembly heard with grateful appreciation the resolution of the Bantu Assembly regarding the ministers of the Presbytery of Mankazana, and requests such Ministers, who are Ministers of this Church, to intimate their acceptance of the position indicated, namely, that of Assessors, with full rights, in the Assembly of the Bantu Church and in the Mankazana Presbytery. (BPCSA 1925–6: 34)

The same agreement was made regarding missionaries serving white congregations. 'It was noted that the work referred to . . . does not come under the Bantu Presbyterian Church' (BPCSA 1925–6: 34). These were two projects under two denominations although there was to be a degree of mutual recognition of ministries.

An unfortunate situation occurred in 1927 when Rev. W. P. T. Ndibongo was regularly appointed as missionary to the BPCSA Glenthorn congregation and was denied the right to reside on the property. The Glenthorn congregation of the Presbytery of Port Elizabeth refused to consider an application to occupy land for this congregation. This led to the appointment of a joint commission to consider the matter (BPCSA 1928: 23). The commission found that the PCSA minister at Glenthorn had not been appointed to the native congregation. The commission found also that the property was vested in the PCSA as a gift from the FCoS and that in doing so they 'have an interest in the gift' (BPCSA 1928: 27). Appeals were made to both parties to accept the *de facto* situation and to exercise discretion in carrying out their respective duties. By 1930 there was no clear solution in view although several alternative possibilities were explored (BPCSA 1930–1: 35–6; BPCSA 1931–2: 45). Interestingly, no mention is made of this incident in either of the histories of the Glenthorn congregation (De Villiers 2011; Glen Thorn Presbyterian Church 1990).

This was followed by a confusing minute of the Assembly (Minute 584, BPCSA 1928: 46): 'Rev. T. B. Soga submitted correspondence regarding possible union with the Presbyterian Church of South Africa (Mzimba)'. What is confusing is that the PCSA and the Mzimba church (The Presbyterian Church of Africa [PCA] or the African Presbyterian church were two separate churches, one a settler/colonial church and the other a black church. The PCA was a church which split form the Scottish mission in 1898 and it is difficult to see how these were confused; it is also difficult to see how the BPCSA could contemplate union with the PCA because of the tensions still present. However, the name of Mzimba is problematic in this context. Again, a committee was formed to consider the matter and report in 1929. No report is recorded.

At this time the issue of BPCSA church members working in urban areas, particularly Cape Town, became manifest in their 'craving for their church' (BPCSA 1934: 29) for the BPCSA until this time had exercised its mission almost exclusively in rural areas. The view of the PCSA was set out in a decision made at its General Assembly on 18 September 1934 along with the desire that 'some day we hope to be one Church':

> When the General Assembly released the ministers and congregation of the Kaffraria and Mankazana presbyteries our understanding was that the Native mission work of our Assembly should be carried on and should have its natural development in the districts in which it was already established, the Bantu Church taking over the mission work in the areas where it had congregations.

By this arrangement:

> the Presbyterian Church of South Africa would be responsible for mission work in Cape Town and the western area of Cape Province, in Port Elizabeth District, in Durban, in the area embraced by the Orange River Native Presbytery, on the Witwatersrand and in Pretoria. Work in the Northern Transvaal was to be continued by both Churches, each in its own sphere, and development there was to proceed according to opportunity and success, each Church being careful not to intrude upon the area occupied by the other or to interfere with the natural growth of each other's work. (BPCSA 1934: 47–8; cf. PCSA 1934: 47)

There appears to be no evidence that the BPCSA ever accepted this 'understanding' or arrangement although they were aware of it (Minute 1080, BPCSA 1934: 28) although Xapile (1999: 82) claims they did, but without citing a reference (cf. Xapile 1994: 29). It is difficult to contemplate how this could be considered an equitable arrangement while the membership of the BPCSA was mobile in terms of work migration and the PCSA had congregations both in urban and rural areas. For them it was a win-win situation while the BPCSA lost valuable income while their members spent their working lives in PCSA congregations, which they supported financially, and returned to their own BPCSA congregations when they ceased to be wage earners. Hence, in the rural areas, BPCSA congregations consisted predominantly of the elderly, women and children, none of whom were wage earners. As a result, these congregations found it difficult to maintain a minister without support from their relatives who were working in urban areas and also supporting the congregations they were attending. Thema (2021: 25) is of the view that: 'Black ministers viewed this arrangement as demeaning and disparaging'. This was to become a constant thorn in the flesh of attempts at union until the negotiations which brought the UPCSA into being in 1994–9.

The Presbytery of the Ciskei petitioned the BPCSA Assembly regarding their place of membership. In an attempt to reconcile the situation, Rev. W. P. T. Ndibongo (BPCSA 1934: 29) gave notice of motion:

> I beg to move that the Bantu Presbyterian Assembly should respectfully ask the Presbyterian Church Assembly to meet each other half way, by peacefully handing over all their Native congregations to the Bantu Presbyterian Church, and that the minister or Ministers of the Presbyterian Church in charge of the Native Congregations be a member or members in the Bantu Presbyterian Assembly as it was in the then Mankazana Presbytery. (BPCSA 1934: 29)

This was a conciliatory move to restore the anticipated harmony between the two presbyterian denominations. It was followed by a proposal that in the absence of clear boundaries between the congregations of the two denominations, a joint council be established in order to 'discuss distribution of forces for the highest interests of the 'Kingdom of God' (BPCSA 1934: 37). This was agreed. However, Rev. S. W. Njikelana and fourteen others entered their dissent with others claiming this decision was flawed due to, *inter alia*,

> There are no defined boundaries between the Bantu Presbyterian Church and the Presbyterian Church of South Africa, insomuch as the Presbyterian Church of South Africa has invaded Bantu Church congregations in the Mankazana Presbytery or Presbytery of Adelaide.

As the people of Cape Town had left the Presbyterian Church of South Africa in a regular manner, having been furnished with disjunction certificates by the Kirk Session of Cape Town, it is irregular to decline serving ordinances to them for any period however short the time may be (BPCSA 1934: 37).

It was recommended and agreed that a Joint Council be formed:

> On which both churches shall be represented and which shall be charged with the duty of reviewing the whole field, and considering how the available forces of the two Churches can best be distributed so as to make the most effective contribution to the work of the Kingdom of God. (BPCSA 1934: 54)

Despite this, a report was received in the 1935 General Assembly of the BPCSA from the Joint Council formed in 1928. It stated:

That the speedy organic union, considerately proposed, affect for the future only the Bantu and the Presbyterian Churches of South Africa, Native Mission work and property and that alone.

That in the very critical and complex situation which has arisen, places like Cape Town, Johannesburg be henceforth created into Preaching Stations with respective Sessions coming directly under this Bantu General Assembly, and that ultimately this Assembly resolve that these be sent down to the Appointments Committee for settlement. (BPCSA 1935: 35–6)

The view was taken that the only solution to the constant internecine conflict was organic union (Xapile 1999: 85). An unfortunate situation arose from a proposal, by Dr Arthur Wilkie of the BPCSA rejecting union, resulting from this report relating to proceeding to union and resignations from all committees ensued (BPCSA 1935: 36–9). The General Assembly of the PCSA continued with its view on the value of union with the BPCSA (BPCSA 1935: 40–1) but an *impasse* had arisen. 'The occasion had underlined the fact that there was resistance within the Church to any union with the PCSA' (Xapile 1999: 86).

In a sterling effort to resolve this crisis, Rev. Holfort Mama produced a principle for consideration which was agreed. This would attempt to safeguard the close co-operation which 'each has at heart':

> where the Presbyterian Church of South Africa is firmly established, and into which the Bantu Presbyterian Church has recently entered, Mr Mama advocated that the agents of the latter Church be withdrawn, and that members of that Church, coming into these areas, be received as members of the Presbyterian Church [of South Africa], and be ministered to by the Minister of that Church ... Put briefly, his policy is, that where the one Church is in numbers and organisation clearly more fitted for undertaking the work, the Other Church should withdraw and the arrangement outlined be given a chance to work. (BPCSA 1938: 18)

Such members would simply be under the care of the other church during their stay in the urban area (and be placed on a separate roll), and would be expected to contribute towards the minister's stipend. This arrangement would apply specifically to the Cape, the Reef and Port Elizabeth (including Tarkastad and Glenthorn). Then the Joint Council committee framed a policy agreement in these words:

> A co-operation that would admit of members of the one Church, while maintaining their identity with that Church, being received as members of the other and a co-operation that would ensure due recognition of the rights of the Church so loaning and gifting its members the sister Church to an equitable distribution of that support every church has the right to expect of its members. (BPCSA 1938: 19)

This seemingly innocuous arrangement, however, had a negative side. First, it has to be recognised why these members were moving from rural to urban areas. Because of the rise of industrialisation and urbanisation (the 'pull' factor) the rural areas were becoming increasingly impoverished and people had to move to the towns to secure work areas (the 'push' factor). This migratory mobility had serious detrimental effects on rural congregations (mainly of the BPCSA). Ministers' stipends in urban areas was an issue but a more serious issue was who was going to pay for ministers' stipends in rural areas? Hence, the issue was an economic one. Members would normally return to their rural homes on retirement or when unable to work, e.g. through injury or retirement, and still could not support the life, work and witness of their rural congregations. The PCSA benefitted from this arrangement over many years. The overriding concern expressed was 'the maintenance of harmony between the two Churches' (BPCSA 1938: 19).

The BPCSA (1938: 18–19) responded with a list of comments relating to the policy advocated by the Joint Council:

1. It be understood that where one of these sister churches first occupied a field as in these specially affected localities the Ministers of that Church be allowed to take charge of that work for the Church which entered the field later, i.e. that the Bantu Presbyterian Church congregations in Cape Town, Tarkastad and Glenthorn be under the supervision of the Presbyterian Church of South Africa Ministers who may be already labouring in the said localities, and on the distinct understanding that they will have a separate and a distinct organisation from that of the PC of SA Congregation, and shall be known as Bantu Church Congregations.
2. That these Bantu Church Congregations worked by the PC of SA Ministers will have the same status as all Bantu Church Congregations and be responsible to the Bantu Church Assembly and abide by its constitution.
3. That contributions received from such Bantu Church Congregations be remitted to the Bantu Church Assembly for their disposal and having due regard to the necessity of meeting expenses of the Presbyterian Church of SA Minister.
4. That in large centres of labour such as Johannesburg which permit of many churches this procedure shall not apply.
5. The Congregations already formed by the Bantu Presbyterian Church be allowed to continue under the direct ministration of the Bantu Presbyterian Church Ministers and in that case it would be advisable for the Presbyterian Church [of SA] Assembly to hand over the empty buildings in those areas for the use of the Bantu Congregations, and the Presbyterian Church continue to do its work on the Rand as before.

The suggestion about the work in Johannesburg is made in view of the fact that we have already an old and a large Mission Field in Northern Transvaal which may easily be coupled with our work already begun in Johannesburg.
6. We would further remark as the Rev. J. Y. Hliso is working in the Bantu Presbyterian Church Congregation at Port Elizabeth, the work of the Presbyterian Church of SA there could be placed under his supervision with the same privileges as those applicable to the Presbyterian Church of SA Ministers in charge of work under the Bantu Presbyterian Church as in the case of Cape Town, etc. In our view an agreement on these lines will result in the settlement of the present conflict in the field and provide the basis of harmony in the future. (BPCSA 1938: 20–1)

The PCSA accepted this proposal but a major BPCSA concern here was the fear that their congregations would lose their full status and be reduced to the status of missions (point 2 above) and lose much-needed income for the support of their ministers (point 3 above). Point 4 attempted to begin with a level playing field for missionary outreach in a context where many denominations were operating. Point 5 followed from this and sought to preserve the integrity of work already established in urban areas. Point 6 referred to a specific case where PCSA work could be entrusted to the care of a BPCSA minister in an urban area. These issues emanated from a position of lack of trust and insecurity regarding the future development of the BPCSA. The fact that these issues were raised in the first place indicates that the long-term view remained that of separate churches rather than one united denomination.

The Joint Council met at the University of Fort Hare on 3 May 1939 and considerable disagreement regarding the best way the two denominations could both relate to one another while they tried to witness to the gospel emerged (Xapile 1999: 90). Xapile (1999: 91) summarised the impasse correctly: 'It is evident that the Bantu Presbyterian Church from now on did not take the union seriously'. Two senior BPCSA ministers revealed this in different ways. Rev. W. P. T. Ndibongo maintained his 1934 position that the PCSA should transfer its African work to the BPCSA (Robertson 1994). This view was supported by the majority of BPCSA members (Xapile 1999: 96). Rev. D. V. Sikhutshwa wrote an article in the *South African Outlook* (*SAO* December 1939) in which he stated that union was an 'absolute impossibility'.

Matters deteriorated when it was reported to the 1939 General Assembly of the BPCSA that the PCSA Presbytery of Port Elizabeth had placed a minister in New Brighton, which had been a vacant congregation when the Joint Council provisions had been agreed. This was a charge where the PCSA had been active earlier than the BPCSA/PCSA agreement (1939: 23): '. . . what this really implied was that very few congregations, if any, in the cities would be BPC as it was obvious that the PCSA had had an earlier presence' (Xapile 1999: 92). The result was a reversion to the 1938 decision which meant that by 1940 all the African congregations formed the PCSA'S Presbytery of Mankanaza, as per the recommendations of Rev. Holfort Mama. From this point little progress was made on the ecumenical front and negotiations ground to a virtual halt.

It was at this time (1937) that the Faith and Order Conference met in Edinburgh (Best 1992). It noted three models relating to church unity – co-operative unity, mutual recognition and organic union. In the South African context the first worked sporadically; the second was a reality and the third at this stage was seemingly unattainable. Yet, Xapile (1999: 99) was confident:

> A union was possible. It was necessary in order that both blacks [sic] and white Christians stand united not only as regards ecclesial matters but also as a united front against apartheid. Some members of the BPC were not convinced that a united church would help them towards their goal. They wondered if it would not add to their suffering. Sadly, those who held this view won. The people of God, the church, had to wait for politics to dictate how they should do things.

Matters became further complicated by the application of a number of BPCSA congregations to rejoin the PCSA. While integration of black and white congregations had been impossible at the time of the formation of the PCSA, Hunter (1983: 284) noted that:

> By 1940, all the African mission congregations from the PCSA's Presbytery of Mankanaza that had entered the BPC in 1923, had requested to be received back into the PCSA. Though different issues motivated the return to the PCSA, in each case the African members had recognised that the PCSA's policy of integration, albeit it limited and defective, had proved more beneficial to African mission work than the BPC's policy of separate parallel development.

It is not clear from the evidence that this actually was the case. The desire for reinstatement within the PCSA may have been influenced by the financial and other benefits available under the PCSA arrangement, especially with regard to the payment of the minister's stipend.

Conclusion

While there was the persistent desire for union with the Scottish mission from the beginning of its negotiations in 1891, and more so after its formation in 1897, this was not reciprocated by the mission or the BPCSA before and from the time when it was established in 1923. What became clear before and after 1923 was that there was a clear problem of distrust on the part of the BPCSA ministers and members linked to being oppressed by racist white Christians and a clear unwillingness to share power, property and other assets by white PCSA leaders. These two concerns meant that progress was virtually impossible. This was the beginning of a century-long (1891–1999) project that later involved the PCSA, the BPCSA, the Congregationalists and the Swiss Mission (Tsonga, later Evangelical Presbyterian Church). It would be marked at times by enthusiasm, frustration, procrastination and thrawnness (Scottish: stubbornness, obstinacy) which would prevent union until 1999 when the PCSA and the BPCSA united to form the Uniting Presbyterian Church in Southern Africa.

CHAPTER TWELVE

The Bantu Presbyterian Church in South Africa and Ecumenism, 1940–99

Introduction

Following the tensions which arose between the BPCSA and the PCSA, Xapile (1999: 98) was confident:

> The challenge was to see the union in the context of the struggle of the oppressed who needed their freedom desperately before they could form unions and maintain such unions as equals with their oppressors. It was necessary to seek this union in South Africa so as for the church to witness as members of God's family. This would have brought a strong sense of credibility in a country where the church was also instrumental in dividing communities. A union would have created space and a forum for Christians to learn to speak and act together.

This was reached after a number of years of striving for a form of organic unity within Presbyterianism in South Africa. Xapile emphasised the political dimension of requirements to be met in order to give serious consideration to the question of union – political liberation was a prerequisite to uniting on the basis of human equality. This view was adopted by the BPCSA even before the institution of grand apartheid with its legislated and enforced policies of segregation. The other issue was that the BPCSA was still a young denomination and finding its way in mission and unity matters.

Onward Christian Soldiers

The 1941 General Assembly remitted the matter of union to the next assembly and distributed the draft basis of union to commissioners to Assembly (BPCSA 1942: 47); the 1942 General Assembly resolved that: 'this matter be allowed to remain on the table until such time as the Bantu Presbyterian Church is sufficiently established to take its full share in such matters as Union with other Churches' (BPCSA 1942: 23). Clearly the BPCSA would not be coerced into any union before it felt it had reached a stage of sufficient maturity to play its full part in any union. In 1944, the General Assembly received a notice of motion 'That the Assembly review minute 1669 (BPCSA 1942: 23) with the object of opening negotiations with the

Presbyterian Church of South Africa' (BPCSA 1944: 13). This matter was not dealt with and remained dormant.

Rev. B. B. Finca (2021: 1) reflected on the ministry of his grandfather, Rev. T. P. Finca, in relation to church unity. He was:

> outspoken on matters of church and state. From very early in my life I came to understand that the difference between the BPC (as it was then known) and the PCSA was not based on any polity or doctrine. But it was the product of the South African government's policy apartheid and racism.

This was possibly the outcome of a particular view of church and state relations that precluded meaningful ecumenism. Finca (2021: 1) futher stated that:

> There was a generation of the 'BPC church fathers' who believed that it will be impossible to have a genuinely United non-racial church in an apartheid country. They articulated in the 1960s a conviction that later became a rallying slogan of the Black sporting bodies in the 1980s when they said 'there can be no normal sport in an abnormal society.' They argued that such a United church will be fake. It will sing on Sunday: 'In Christ there is no East nor West ... but one fellowship of love' but live daily a life of racial segregation. They will say 'we are not divided, all one body we, one in hope and doctrine, one in charity', but it will continue to mirror in its practical life the divisions of the apartheid policies.

These 'BPC Church Fathers' reflected what Vellem (2013: 146) in his *Black Theology of Liberation* described as 'the irruption of faith that refused patronage, rejected racial inequality and signification by others'.

> Although they politely took part in the union negotiations, they were sceptical of the union that will only lead to a structural and cosmetic unification that is devoid of fundamental transformation. They taught us that the 'Bantu Church' was diametrically opposed to the apartheid policies and to racism. It could not tolerate a system in which white congregations are formed for white members and black congregations for black members; the pattern of appointment of ministers that follow the racial divisions of apartheid; the payment of stipends and benefits will result in white ministers being paid better than black ministers; the separate training of candidates for the ministry with white students going to first grade universities and black students going to so-called 'bush universities'; and be part of a church that appoints white ministers to be military chaplains to render spiritual support to the SADF in the war against our liberation fighters. (Finca 2021: 1)

In 1956, a decision was reached to engage with the PCSA, taking account of '(a) The competition between the two Churches, and (b) The constitutions of the two Churches' (BPCSA 1956: 34). During the following year, the PCSA presented 'minimal terms for union' and it was agreed to prepare a response (BPCSA 1958: 35). At the same Assembly both the Free Church of Scotland (a small mission church of the continuing Free Church of Scotland in Scotland) in South Africa and the Presbyterian Church of Africa (PCA) expressed interest in union with the BPCSA (BPCSA 1958: 35–6). Discussions continued and in 1959 the Church of the Province (Anglican) requested a meeting with representatives of the BPCSA and PCSA to discuss 'a clearer understanding between the churches and that the Union for which we all pray might be forwarded' (BPCSA 1959: 45). The BPCSA acceded to this request. The PCSA received a report under its African Missions committee in 1959 that the Tsonga Presbyterian Church might be prepared to join with the BPCSA in talks regarding possible union (PCSA 1959: 76). What is noteworthy here is that this was regarded as part of the PCSA mission to other Africans.

By 1960, matters had advanced apace and the BPCSA agreed 'to proceed with the negotiations towards full union on the basic principle of the equal status of all ministers, elders and members'. An earlier decision to attempt 'a five year period of union at Presbytery level and separate Assemblies' was dismissed (BPCSA 1960: 22). This Assembly also agreed to continue to negotiate with the Presbyterian Church of Africa (PCA – the church which seceded from the Scottish Mission in 1898). A significant development occurred in 1962 with the agreement that in a united church there would be equality of status in the ordained ministry (PCSA 1962: 217). There was little substantial progress except that in 1964, the BPCSA General Assembly recommended that contact should be made with sister congregations of the PCSA and the Tsonga Presbyterian Church (TPC) (BPCSA 1964: 19).

However, progress was intermittent. The PCSA sent what amounted to an ultimatum to the 1965 General Assembly of the BPCSA, informing them that if they did not ratify the resolution on union they would proceed with negotiations with the TPC, 'but assures the BPC in this event its return to the negotiations will be welcomed at any time it feels able to do so' (BPCSA 1965: 25; PCSA 1965: 42). The BPCSA responded with a resolution assuring the PCSA 'that the proposed church union must be one of depth which involves a real conviction of oneness in Christ and not merely an association for the sake of administrative efficiency' (BPCSA 1965: 29). The issue related to property issues in the Draft Basis of Union (paragraph 3 of Schedule J, p.42) which the PCSA viewed as 'a matter of detail' (PCSA 1965: 222–3). The BPCSA believed differently. For them it was unacceptable that white congregations be able to hold their own title deeds while they, as a black church agree to their properties being held by the General Trustees of the denomination. This was exacerbated by different perceptions of the nature of land ownership in the black community where land was held in trust for the entire community. The PCSA viewed this 'either as a misconception of the situation or on the premises which are quite unknown to us' (PCSA 1965: 223). But the Draft Basis of Union was sent down to presbyteries and congregations with the commendation to work towards closer co-operation.

At the same Assembly, it was reported that Presbyterian (BPCSA, PCSA, TPC) conversations with the Anglicans had progressed to the stage of the formulation of a Statement of Belief and a proposed Covenant. It was further agreed to engage in internal discussion for three years. The two main points of discussion were the role of episcopacy and intercommunion (BPCSA 1965: 33). In 1966, the BPCSA resolved 'to take such steps as its constitution requires to secure the approval of the Bantu Presbyterian Church to the Draft Basis of Union' (BPCSA 1966: 34). This was a significant step forward. The following year it was noted that of the seven presbyteries, four accepted the basis of union while one rejected it with two not replying. The status of the laity was raised with the PCSA (BPCSA 1967: 41). The draft Basis of Union was again sent down to presbyteries in 1968 (BPCSA 1968: 40). Comments received were remitted to the unions committee to be reported on in 1970 (BPCSA 1969: 31) when:

> By 35 votes to 12 the Assembly accepted the Basis of Union as in the printed booklet and sends down to Presbyteries the Final Basis of Union for approval or otherwise and report to the next Assembly.
> The Rt Rev. J. Y. Hliso entered his dissent. (BPCSA 1970: 45)

The status of this dissent is unclear as the Moderator of General Assembly had no deliberative vote, and hence no right of dissent. While four presbyteries voted in favour of union in 1971, there remained a general lack of unanimity. Over a third of the Assembly voted for a deferral of a final decision and 'the Assembly, realising the unhappy atmosphere' again remitted the matter to presbyteries for another year. Visits were again to be paid to congregations to assess their views on union (BPCSA 1971: 33–4). The PCSA had voted in favour of union by a substantial majority in 1970 (PCSA 1970: 109).

Concurrently, events were proceeding apace in the Church Unity Commission (formed in 1968) (Wing 1990: 1) of which the BPC was a member along with the PCSA, the Tsonga (later Evangelical) Presbyterian Church, the Methodist Church of South Africa, the Church of the Province (Anglican) and the United Congregational Church. In 1972, the BPCSA General Assembly affirmed the CUC Declaration of Intention:

> Believing that a union of churches in Christ involved a full and deep fellowship among [sic] of all races and a brotherhood crossing all barriers of race, and believing that there is not at the moment sufficient evidence of brotherhood even in the congregations of our different Presbyterian Churches in the various places where they exist side by side,

And believing that justice and peace among all the peoples of this land are supremely important and that our churches have not given sufficient attention to these matters,

And believing that fellowship among Christians of all races is a necessary preliminary to a meaningful structural union.

Assembly resolves:

> To seek a deeper fellowship and brotherhood among Churches at all levels ... (BPCSA 1972: 29)

This was sent down to Presbyteries for study and comment before sending down the Plan of Union with encouragement to participate in local initiatives (BPCSA 1972: 30).

This step indicates that the BPCSA was not against union in principle because it had also engaged the Anglicans, but it also indicates that in the particular case of union with the PCSA there were unresolved issues that appeared to be intractable. Later that same year the PCSA approached the BPC with a request for comments on their proposal to resite their General Assembly office in Johannesburg. The BPC was of the opinion that the office should remain in the centre of Johannesburg for ease of access (BPCSA 1972: 454).

The relationship between the BPC and the PCSA deteriorated further at this time because some people blamed the BPC for preventing the union in 1972. But there were also several events initiated by some members of the PCSA that were interpreted by the some in the BPC as undermining its autonomy and jurisdiction.

In 1973, Rev. Douglas Bax moved a notice of motion in the PCSA General Assembly meant to allay the fears of the BPCSA regarding his perception of fears concerning union with a white denomination:

> We understand the hesitations those who fear that even in a united church the White members will show prejudice and discrimination against, or paternalism towards, the Black members. We understand the doubts of those who fear that the White members will assume an automatic right to all the real power in a united Church and refuse to share it fairly with Black members.
>
> We confess that there is ground for these fears because our Church and we who are White in it have not been free of them because of faults in the past. (PCSA 1973: 65–6)

This motion emanated from one of the most liberal voices in the PCSA. It was paternalistic and devoid of any repentance or intention to change. As sensitive as it seemed in its confession, it simply reiterated the *status quo*. Bax's statement made it clear that he, and possibly others, were aware of the BPCSA's concerns. When the notice of motion was debated, it was agreed to 'pass from the matter' (PCSA 1973: 80–1) without any consideration of action that might have been taken to resolve the well known, but unspecified, issues. In any case, the proposed confession was not accepted by the majority in the PCSA, since the matter was passed from. It is easy to see how the BPCSA found it difficult to move forward towards union in such a climate of distrust and a lack of commitment to transform.

A little later in 1973, the BPCSA agreed to discharge its Presbyterian Negotiations Committee since its work was complete and '[t]hat the Basis of Union negotiations discussions between the Presbyterian churches be kept an open possibility before the three churches' (BPCSA 1973: 19). Regarding the CUC union negotiations, it was decided to withhold a response until all presbyteries had responded (BPCSA 1973: 40). Progress was slow and no advance was made in 1974.

In 1975, General Assembly agreed to remit the 'Scheme of Union' to presbyteries for ratification (BPCSA 1975: 35). On another front, however, progress was made when the Business Committee approved the merger of the Congregational Adams College with the Presbyterian St Columba's College at the Federal Theological Seminary of Southern Africa (FedSem) (BPCSA 1975: 44). This was the most successful ecumenical theological education venture of the twentieth century in South Africa which involved Anglicans, Congregationalists, Methodists and four Presbyterian churches. Founded in 1963, the BPCSA committed the totality of its financial resources and personnel along with the other black churches (the EPCSA and the PCA). The other churches diversified their theological education programmes predominantly on racial grounds. Including the PCSA. From the late 1980s a Cluster of Theological Institutions was formed in Pietermaritzburg with the Lutheran dominated Faculty of Theology at the University of Natal, The Evangelical Bible Seminary of South Africa and the Roman Catholic St Joseph's Scholasticate Seminary. The BPCSA's commitment to union was sorely tested when the non-Presbyterian churches and the PCSA withdrew their support for FedSem and closed it in 1993. Yet, the church remained open to the opportunities of ecumenical theological education in its return to the University of Fort Hare in 1994 and continues to do so by now training its ministers at the universities of Stellebosch and Pretoria where it has exposed itself to working cooperatively with churches of the Dutch Reformed tradition and others. The priority of theological education in an ecumenical context has been further evidenced in the BPCSA/RPCSA involvement in the National Committee on Theological Education (NCTE), the Association of Southern African Theological Institutions (ASATI), and the South African Council on Theological Education (SACTE).

Ongoing ecumenical discussions led to The First Draft of the constitution of the United Church in Southern Africa (Presbyterian/Congregational) being sent down to Presbyteries. The 1976 General Assembly resolved that if the Scheme of Union was accepted the BPCSA would enter negotiations with the TPC and UCCSA which had already accepted it (BPCSA 1976: 33). The Assembly was in favour of organic union and rejected any federal scheme. However, it was recognised that 'the Church as a whole is not entirely in favour of union' (PCSA 1980: 70). This referred to lack of support at grassroots level. Yet, some also commented that 'not one of the arguments raised against union has focused on a major theological difference'. Interestingly, some also noted that 'there are more theological differences within the PCSA than there are between the PCSA and the other three denominations in the union negotiations'. Hence, the reasons had to be articulated in a more localised manner in terms of structural and financial concerns (PCSA 1980: 72).

No further significant movement took place until 1982 when it became evident there was no clear commitment to unity. The Reformed Presbyterian Church in Southern Africa (RPCSA, the BPCSA having changed its name in 1979) Assembly established a committee with a specific mandate:

(a) to formulate a strategy for continuing with the search [for unity]
(b) to open negotiations with the black Churches of the Reformed family as a first stage in the fulfilment of the strategy
(c) monitor matters relating to Church Union
(d) and to report to the Assembly. (RPCSA 1982: 23)

While the RPCSA General Assembly still appeared to be committed to organic unity, it was clear that this enthusiasm was not shared at presbytery and congregational level. Rev. B. B. Finca commented:

> When I became a minister and was later appointed by the General Assembly to be the Convenor of the Ecumenical Relations Committee for several years in the 1980's, I noted that there was very [little] appetite in the RPC for ecclesiastical union with the PCSA. The Committee on Priorities & Resources had relegated both the work of the Church Unity Commission and the bilateral negotiations with the PCSA to the periphery of the agenda of the church. The vote against union that was taken at the 1972 General Assembly at Gillespie Mission had firmly closed the chapter of seeking a structural union with the PCSA. Even the ardent supporters of union had come to accept that there cannot be a 'normal united and nonracial Presbyterian Church for as long as the cloud of apartheid and racism continued to hover over our country'.

While the RPCSA General Assembly still appeared to be committed to organic unity this enthusiasm was not shared at presbytery and congregational level. This was partly due to the intensifying political situation and continuing distrust of white Presbyterians. Hence, the move to negotiate, in the first instance, with black Reformed sister churches. The state of the nation was of greater concern to church members than matters of unity. In 1982, there was growing opposition to apartheid and the church was deeply involved in this. This was an area where, mostly, the churches, except for the Dutch Reformed family, were working ecumenically, although internally there were tensions relating to race issues throughout the churches of European origin.

In this context the United Democratic Front (UDF) was founded in 1983 as:

> a mass based organisation launched to coincide with the government's introduction of the tricameral legislation in August for the Coloured and Indian communities. [It] opened up a new space for national organisations, the UDF and the National Forum (NF). Of the two movements, the UDF proved to be the most successful . . .
>
> The UDF repeatedly called for the ANC and other political organisations to be unbanned, and refused to negotiate with the South African government in the absence of 'recognised leaders of the people,' who were imprisoned or in exile. (https://www.sahistory.org.za/article/19 76-1983-mass-democratic-movements)

This was a catalyst for the involvement of the white population and it was divisive in this context.

In the PCSA, by 1982, opposition had grown considerably although it was agreed to proceed with negotiations (PCSA 1982: 235). The issue was that there appeared to be a lack of knowledge and understanding of the thinking behind the move towards union (PCSA 1982: 235, 236). The General Assembly Moderator was charged with providing a sounding board for those with concerns regarding union. He reported a number of issues in 1983. He recommended 'to the church that it should suspend the present programme until the 1986 General Assembly when a decision can be made' (PCSA 1983: 184). This was agreed.

The outcome of the RPCSA Assembly decision (RPCSA 1982: 23), was the formation of the Ecumenical Relations Committee (ERC) which was to oversee all developments in the sphere of ecumenical relations. This aimed to produce a more coherent approach to the ecumenical movement. The first term of reference was 'To promote, foster and maintain good fraternal relations between the Reformed Presbyterian Church and other denominations of the Universal Church of Jesus Christ' (RPCSA 1988: 56). It placed no limitation on who it would negotiate with. The ERC report in 1985 (RPCSA 1985: 30) showed part of the extent of ecumenical relations which included the World Council of Churches (WCC), the Alliance of Black Reformed Christians in South Africa (ABRECSA), the Church of Scotland, and the denominations with which the BPCSA was in union negotiations. In addition, the RPCSA was a member of the World Alliance of Reformed Churches (WARC) and the World Council of Churches (WCC). It had close relations with the Presbyterian Church of the USA, the Mennonites in the USA and the Presbyterian Churches in Australia and Aotearoa/New Zealand. Within the African continent, it was a member of the All Africa Council of Churches (AACC) and had many informal relations with churches in Africa through these contacts, particularly with the Church of Central Africa Presbyterian (CCAP).

The relationship between the RPC and the PCSA remained volatile during the 1980s because there were several events initiated by some members of the PCSA that were interpreted by some in the RPC as undermining its autonomy and jurisdiction. There was an incident at Edendale congregation in the RPC Presbytery of Natal where hundreds of disgruntled members were received by PCSA without disjunction certificates. There were several other similar cases:

> We had to deal with cases where 'fugitives of discipline' in the RPC were allegedly accepted by the PCSA without following the normal protocols for transference from one denomination to the other. These events created hostilities in some circles and gave credence to the belief in some among us that the PCSA was trying to destroy the RPC. This undermined the cordiality between the two churches and subverted the agenda of union negotiations even more. (Finca 2021: 2)

Within South Africa, the BPCSA was closely involved in the ecumenical movement. It was an active member of the Christian Council of South Africa and its successor, the South African Council of Churches (SACC) and its regional branches. At the local level it was at its most effective, especially during the apartheid years. The BPCSA was represented at the historic Cottesloe Consultation organised under the auspices of the World Council of Churches in 1960. Perhaps it was during the apartheid era, in the face of the challenge to the very existence of the church, that it was easier to form a common commitment to develop because of the mutually experienced threat than in less troubled times.

At the local level there was the reappearance of issues with the PCSA regarding interference in its congregations which led to a complaint being lodged with the PCSA about 'repeated pastoral interference' at Ulundi, in addition to attempts 'to resolve outstanding problems' with the PCSA (RPCSA 1985: 30). By this time negotiations had been entered into with the Evangelical Presbyterian Church (EPCSA) (RPCSA 1984: 30).

The PCSA described the progress of union negotiations from 1959 until 1984:

> From 1959 onwards there were union negotiations Involving the PCSA, the BPC and the Tsonga Presbyterian Church (which arose out of the work of the Swiss Mission in South Africa and is now called the Evangelical Presbyterian Church). The BPC was not able to muster enough support for the union and withdrew from the negotiations in 1972. The following year negotiations were restarted this time involving the United Congregational Church of Southern Africa as well. These followed a complicated course with strong feelings being aroused in the PCSA. In 1981 the RPC withdrew from the negotiations and the

EPC opted for observer status only. The PCSA and UCCSA continued until 1984, when a majority of our Presbyteries turned down the Plan of Union. (PCSA 1989: 41)

As seen, during this period relations with the PCSA reached an all-time low except for an attempt by the PCSA Moderator of General Assembly, the Rt Rev. Glen Craig, to reopen discussions (PCSA 1987: 76). There is never any explanation given to the nature of the 'strong feelings aroused' in the PCSA.

By 1987, the Assembly noted that a draft constitution for union with the EPC and 'declare[d] that the Reformed Presbyterian Church is now ready on its basis to unite with the Evangelical Presbyterian Church' (RPCSA 1987: 25). In 1988, the ERC reported regarding union with the EPC that it was 'not able to report progress this year' and reaffirmed its decision to unite. The EPC had withdrawn largely due to impending problems arising from its close relationship with the Gazankulu homeland government, but they did not feel free to communicate this to the RPCSA officially. There was no advance by the time of the 1989 or the 1992 General Assemblies (RPCSA 1992: 45). A meeting was scheduled with the PCSA with the prayer 'that the Holy Spirit will guide them into all truth in dealing with the issues that have hindered proper relations between our two sister Churches' (RPCSA 1989: 35). Preliminary meetings led to a Basis of Agreement that both denominations should make a fresh beginning by focusing on past failures, long term relationships and a commitment to greater cooperation (PCSA1990: 18). It is interesting to note that 'the Presbyterian Black Leadership Consultation was asked to spearhead the implementation of the Agreement' (PCSA 1991: 22) with the black RPCSA to fulfil its 'commitment to the rebuilding of trust and fellowship and co-operation, [as] a living reality' rather than organic union at this stage (PCSA 1992: 127). However, it was conscious of the immensity of the task in the prevailing climate politically marked by:

> Callous and cynical violence, revelations of corruption and theft of the nation's assets on a vast scale, the politics of accusation, threat and manipulation. Is this not the time when the Church is called, even more urgently than before, to demonstrate the real meaning of reconciliation? (PCSA 1992: 127)

One issue that was a recurrent source of friction was the PCSA asking one of its associations to 'spearhead' union negotiations with another church rather than on a church-to-church basis. This led to a view in the RPCSA that it was being treated with contempt as a junior rather than as an equal partner.

Following the transition to a democratic South African society in 1994, the black RPCSA exhibited a greater confidence and generosity in union talks.

Rev. B. B. Finca, Convener of the RPCSA Ecumenical Relations Committee, took the view that:

> [w]hen the great 'miracle' happened to South Africa in 1994 and the historic moment of the irreversible demise of apartheid was realised with the holding of the first democratic election and the swearing in of Nelson Mandela as the President of the republic, a new era dawned for our country, but also for union negotiations between the RPC and the PCSA. The nation that had been torn apart by decades of apartheid and centuries of racism was bleeding and in need of healing. 1994 presented to us a unique challenge and distinctive opportunity to make a decisive break with the past and embrace a new vision of peace, unity, and reconciliation. The national question that weighed heavy on all of us was to heal the division of the past to transform the quality of life of all South Africans. In this situation God presented to all of us another Kairos moment and the call was to discern again the signs of that moment.

Here was a more positive attitude towards matters which would bring the different race groups together. This was particularly true in the black community. This attitude was evident in the RPCSA adopting a more positive approach towards union and so, by 1995, interest in union with the PCSA was again on the agenda. The PCSA was anxious to respond positively but realised that in the new prevailing climate they were not in a strong position to approach a black church with a view to union. None of the other denominations previously involved became part of this process.

By the 1996 General Assembly, union negotiations between the PCSA and the RPCSA had taken a more serious turn. The principle of union was agreed and a Central Committee was appointed to carry the process forward. The Basis of Union was adopted by the RPCSA in 1997 and it was sent down to Presbyteries under the Barrier Act, which is a necessary procedure when matters of considerable substance are being considered (RPCSA 1997: 51). The 1998 General Assembly, taking account of returns from presbyteries and after an intense discussion voted in favour of union. (RPCSA 1998: 57). The PCSA had already voted in favour of union (RPCSA 1998: 147). The union took place in Port Elizabeth on 26 September 1999.

Conclusion

The period from 1897 until 1999 was fraught with difficulties for the two Presbyterian denominations which united in 1999. Political, i.e. racial issues intruded into an already tense situation. In some senses it is difficult to understand how union could have come about without passing through the purifying fire of 1994. This gave the RPCSA courage to approach the PCSA on an equal footing, while earlier it had been in the position of the underdog responding to pressure from the PCSA. So union resulted from political change. What is unfortunate is that the union did not include the Evangelical Presbyterian Church, the Presbyterian Church of Africa and the United Congregational Church of South Africa, the denominations with whom the uniting churches had been in conversation sporadically over the years; plus the Methodist and Anglican churches of the Church Unity Commission.

CHAPTER THIRTEEN

The End of Mission Councils: The Church of Scotland South Africa Joint Council, 1971–81

Introduction

The Church of Scotland South Africa Joint Council (CoSSAJC) was finally laid to rest on 1 May 1981, fifty-eight years after the formation of the Bantu Presbyterian Church of South Africa (BPCSA) on 4 July 1923 (BPCSA GA 1923: 6). During this intervening period, the Mission Council exercised control over the affairs of the Church of Scotland (CoS) mission with varying degrees of effectiveness. This hampered the opportunity for developing indigenous leadership, polity, liturgy and theology. The continued existence of a Mission Council prevented free communication between the BPCSA and the CoS. Despite its grand title, it did not contribute to God's mission, particularly through the agency of black Christians, despite some senior black ministers being co-opted on to the CoSSAJC which continued to exercise power and control through the means of personnel, finance and property. Integration of the work of the Mission Council and the church was planned to take place in 1971. Yet, inexplicably, new constitutions were approved for the CoSSAJC (BPCSA 1972: 40–2) and the Missionaries' Committee (BPCSA 1972: 43–4) in 1972. Incidentally, a new Scottish member of personnel was about to arrive who was to represent and foster the maintenance of the *status quo*. However, it is first necessary to understand the position of the CoS regarding integration and partnership in mission from the 1910 World Missionary Conference held in Edinburgh.

Partnership in Mission

Following the 1910 Edinburgh World Missionary Conference, the International Missionary Conference (IMC) was established, and from 1928 at its Jerusalem meeting, the concept of partnership in mission was placed firmly on the agenda. The Church of Scotland was an active participant in all of the IMC meetings. It had led the way in the 1920s by beginning the process of integration in Nagpur, India (Lyon 1998: 44), but this was the exception – the rule came much later. By the 1930s, there was an awareness that change in mission policy was imminent though the conservative Church of Scotland could not openly admit this: 'neither the Mission Councils nor the Foreign Mission Committee as such have any acknowledged part in the control or administration of Church affairs' (CoS GA 1935: 615). This implies the opposite of what was actually true for considerable power was exercised over mission churches' affairs (Duncan 1997: 104ff) for there was still a belief that indigenous nationals were not yet capable of managing their own affairs unaided. Further, CoS policy stated: 'Any policy of forced precipitate severance of missionary work from the churches in the field comes into conflict with obstinate facts and with a true conception of the church and its work' (CoS GA 1935: 616). No further elucidation was given to what were the 'obstinate facts'; at best, they were most likely missionary interpretations. At the end of the Second World War, the time was ripe for integration that would facilitate a new form of partnership. Hence, a special committee was established in 1945 by the Foreign Mission Committee to investigate possibilities for change in India. This was achieved by the formation of the Church of South India in 1947 and perhaps because of it, there could be no doubt regarding ownership and responsibility within a united church. It was 'the precursor of attempts at practical partnership' (Duncan 2008: 113). Mission Councils in India were terminated because they were no longer 'an integral part of the life and work of the indigenous church' (Lyon 1998: 43). Lyon (1998: 46, 47) absolutely clarified the position. The development of policy:

> meant in practice continuing to exercise the control from which it had seemed to be saying it wanted to withdraw. No rhetoric of partnership could conceal the reality that the Church of Scotland through its missionaries and its grants of money, still exercised an inappropriate control.

In Scottish mission, 1947 was an important year because it culminated in integration resulting from the formation of autonomous churches globally. In this process, the Rev. James Dougall, Secretary of the Foreign Mission Committee of the CoS, played a significant part by promoting integration. Dougall often quoted the Foreign Mission Committee Minute of 1947 that stated:

> The Church of Scotland has from the beginning regarded its foreign missionary enterprise as an integral part of the life of the Church, springing of necessity from the nature of the Church itself. It has in the same way placed at the centre of its concern the bringing into being of living branches of the Church in other lands which should accept for themselves the same missionary obligation, the discharge of which is one of the essential marks of a living Church. (Church of Scotland Foreign Mission Committee, Minute 8799, April 15, 1947: CoS GA 1957: 453)

Lyon (1998: 276), however, pointed out the risks of integration: 'being seen by sending churches as a branch of colonialism, and by the proponents of nationalism, it was interpreted as liberation from foreign hegemony'. Despite this, the 1947 General Assembly of the CoS noted that 'The Presbyterian churches of the Dominions are all of them the offspring of the Church of Scotland and delight to acknowledge their parentage' (CoS GA 1947: 421). Mutuality and interdependence still had to battle with paternalism and trusteeship for supremacy.

However, the rapidly changing global context was crying out for a change in mission policy. Dougall liked to quote the new definition offered by Lesslie Newbigin, who described the missionary as 'the agent of the help which one part of the Church sends to another for the discharge of the common missionary task' (quoted in Dougall 1963: 93; Newbigin 1958: 47). Dougall stated clearly:

> Enquiry starts from the assumption that the world in which the Church lives has so changed that the particular form of the mission of the Church to the world has to be re-examined and restated ... It is impossible to escape the conclusion that the missionary task for this generation involves new perspectives, means and methods if we are to be faithful to the Truth which marches on. (CoS GA 1952: 352)

This task was marked by:

(1) changes in global economic, social and political conditions
(2) growth and development of younger churches and their desire for self-government
(3) establishment of the World Council of Churches (WCC) and its relationships with these churches
(4) declining financial support from older churches.

In addition, policy had to respond to rapid change in Africa because: 'Strife for political power has embittered race relations' (CoS GA 1951: 371).

In the African context, the rise of nationalism was a potent force in the drive towards ecclesiastical independence.

Duncan (2008: 115) expressed the following opinion:

> ... the integration of Church and Mission meant that the Younger Church had become a responsible partner to be consulted in all decisions, and its resources in personnel and experience now more clearly defined and limited the direction and scope of missionary activity. The Foreign Mission Committee had to ask of every undertaking how far it could enlist the interest and increase the vigour of the church on the field and how much that church could now and in the future make itself responsible for a significant share in the undertaking.

The Willingen Conference of the International Missionary Council in 1952 caught the spirit of the time when it pronounced that 'we should cease to speak of missions and churches and avoid this dichotomy not only in our thinking but also in our actions. We should now speak about the mission of the Church' (IMC, Willingen 1952: 40).

A meeting of missionaries held in Nagpur in January 1959 summed up the situation:

> We think that 'the mission' (and we consider that this, in the senses we use it, continues despite integration) with its impressive organisation and structure of institutions, its foreignness and its influence closely connected to financial power stands counter to mission. As things are, the Church does not know itself (always it has its eye on what 'the mission' expects it to do or say) and cannot act or speak in freedom. We are still far from a free and equal partnership. The situation is bedevilled by what is sensed as imperialism, spiritual, moral and financial, on the one hand, and by humiliation and a simmering rebelliousness on the other, this despite every effort we make in personal ways on both sides. (in Lyon 1998: 333)

In 1962, Neil C. Bernard, Africa Secretary of the Foreign Mission Committee of the CoS, offered a definitive standard for integration (Cory PR10432, South Africa Mission Council 'Integration in South Africa', 22 June 1962). Regarding South Africa, his approach to integration was contextual, drawing on past experience in other lands:

> ... integration of the Mission into the Church should be in accordance with government policy. On the other hand there seems to be doubt as to how far government will give responsibility to these tribal areas [homelands] ... the establishment of a joint council as the first step towards integration 'taking account of' the total situation in South Africa at the present time ... It should be stressed that where joint councils have been established in the past they have never been regarded as of other than temporary duration.

Bernard's approach marked the beginning of power sharing by involving the BPCSA as a temporary but necessary partner in the context of apartheid whose Group Areas Act was a hindrance to integration, particularly regarding hospitals, educational institutions and farms and other lands.

And the concept and theory of partnership in the Gospel was regularly developed. Under the annual Overseas Council report theme 'Together in a Divided World' (1976), it was defined as 'the mark of mission' (CoS GA 1976: 324), i.e. 'that which defines mission and it would indicate that it is partnership which constitutes the church in its missionary and ecumenical relationships. It provides hope in a sadly divided world'. The role of the sending church is 'to respond costingly to the demands partnership makes' (CoS GA 1976: 324), i.e. kenotically. The diminishing direct control over mission is not the end of missionary responsibility in a context of the:

growing and already enormous demands the opportunity for mission world-wide lays upon the whole Church of God . . . At the same time we hear them say to us that we must be prepared to receive from them what we need, so that together we may be better equipped to share the Gospel, and to participate in God's mission of healing and saving to the end of the world. (CoS GA 1976: 324)

Then there was a constant stress in the Overseas Council on openness to receive 'what our fellow Christians can give to us for our strengthening' (CoS GA 1977: 330). The sending church never defined what it needed and this has always been a problem in partnership. Receiving churches needs are clear – they require personnel and money. But what do sending churches need, and who determines those needs and how, if at all, are they communicated? Had it been possible to answer this question, many of the subsequent misunderstandings might never have arisen. Again, the need for sensitivity is stressed but it is never clear how this worked out in practice and how receiving churches viewed this approach. The reciprocity of mission was in its infancy in the Church of Scotland. Besides a few overseas bursars and Operation Faithshare, a three-month programme for the CoS to receive members of partner churches, little else happened. The Bantu Presbyterian Church was involved in both of these schemes.

Good communication was vital with the necessity of being 'sensitive to the issues and problems facing its partners, and must be ready to respond with understanding, a process that often involves not just long correspondence, but consultations and visits' (CoS GA 1976: 325). Personnel continued to play a pivotal role: 'The Churches want missionaries and ask unequivocally for them' (GA 197: 325). However, the Overseas Council acknowledged that:

'Even the word "partnership" has been suspected to be a hypocritical camouflage for unwarranted interference' (CoS GA 1977: 330) despite the emphasis on its laudable aim which it saw as 'to strengthen the Churches overseas . . . and to encourage members of the church here [Scotland] to appreciate that the mission to which all are committed is one mission whether at home or abroad'. (CoS GA 1978: 316)

The CoS mission policy constantly faced the Scylla of paternalism and trusteeship and the Charybdis of integration and partnership.

The Last Decade

The Foreign Mission Committee of the Church of Scotland was replaced with the Overseas Council within the revised structures of the Church of Scotland in 1964 at a time when Mission Councils were disappearing globally (Duncan 2008: 123). The prime focus on partnership resulted from the development of national leadership in African and Asian nations and transferring membership and ministry by many missionaries to younger churches 'who by this time were directing their own work' (Duncan 2008: 123). Further, the global political scene had undergone significant changes in every continent. Two-way relationships were emerging, and younger churches had begun a conversation with each other, as in the formation of the All Africa Conference of Churches in 1963. This ecumenical development had the potential to become a mutually enriching experience (CoS GA 1963: 427). During the 1960s, it became Overseas Council policy to make block grants to mission churches which allowed churches to draw up their own budgets based on their own discerned needs. However, there was no involvement in the decision-making process concerning the amounts given. This was inimical to developing partnership relations. (Duncan 2008: 123–4)

The BPCSA (Min 504, CoSSAJC 4–5 July 1971) recommended the local appointment of a 'Treasurer of the Joint Council and Treasurer of the BPC'. This appointment was probably proposed to facilitate the transfer of Joint Council finances and integration. A local person was interviewed and 'found unsuitable'; however, an offer of a candidate from Scotland was received and agreed (Min 558, CoSSAJC ExCom 21 November 1972).

On 6 November 1973, it was reported to the Business Committee of the BPCSA 'that the Church Accountant, Mr Matthew I. Stevenson, had arrived' (BPCSA GA 1973: 40) and filled an important vacancy in the church. Matt Stevenson played a significant role in the last years of the CoSSAJC. He presented his first report of the Joint Council in 1974 (BPCSA GA 1974: 19–21) and demonstrated his command of the complex affairs of the Joint Council. From this point, there was a certain tightening of arrangements as to the disposition of Ellesmere Farm at Gordon Memorial Mission at uMsinga in Natal:

> ... it was decided that this matter should be dealt with by the Secretary/ Treasurer ... That all future correspondence should be between the Council and the appropriate department of the KwaZulu government. (Min 629, CoSSAJC 21 May 1974)

This arrangement would lead to a difficult situation with the Missionary-in-charge, Rev. James Gossip. The Treasurer was urged to progress the transfer of Joint Council funds to the BPCSA and report diligence to the executive (Min 654.5, CoSSAJC 23–24 July 1974). By this means, the BPCSA was thereby removed from having an effective opinion or interest in the matter. Then, an unfortunate personnel situation involving two missionaries arose at Nessie Knight Hospital in the Transkei. This situation was taken up by the Joint Council which is unprocedural because it was neither part of its remit (Min 668.5, CoSSAJC 23–4 July 1974; cf. BPCSA GA 1972: 40–4; Min 693, 702, 743 CoSSAJC 26 November 1974) nor even that of the Missionaries' Committee. This interference became the norm as in the case of Rev. James Gossip at Gordon Memorial Mission in 1976 (Mins. 784, 800

CoSSAJC 7 April 1976). The Secretary was given powers to act with others. If the personnel were members of a presbytery of the BPC then it would have fallen to them to deal with the matter; otherwise it would fall to the Kirk Session of the congregation of which they were members. As far as can be ascertained, this issue never came officially to the notice of the BPC. Failing all else, it was for the Overseas Council to resolve. The Secretary of the Joint Council seemed to arrogate to himself, or was given powers not rightly his. This was an innovation in procedure and led to an unfortunate escalation involving more personnel than was necessary.

At this juncture, Rt Rev. Gladwin T. Vika gave his Moderatorial Address at the 1974 General Assembly entitled *Whither Bantu Presbyterian Church?* based on a question posed earlier by a representative of the Church of Scotland in a time of crisis. Vika examined the question from the viewpoint of the role of the church in terms of government action in the removal of church lands, and church personnel, particularly in a period of integration as responsibility was being transferred from a white to a black body. In such a situation, he affirmed 'the Christian at its most demanding and at its most uncompromising' in its promotion of God's kingdom in the world (cf. Matt 10: 34–9) (BPCSA GA 1974: 50). Vika cited a comment from a founding document of the BPCSA:

> So the 'mission' from Overseas fosters a new Native Church, and as the latter increases in strength, the work of the 'mission' reaches completion, and a time comes when the Native church is able to take upon itself its full responsibilities ... However, a two-fold problem faces the BPC in the advent of integration: Increased responsibility and a lack of man-power to meet the increased responsibility. (BPCSA GA 1974: 53)

Rt Rev. Gladwin T. Vika, General Secretary of the BPCSA and Moderator of the General Assembly of the BPCSA, who was also Convener of the BPCSA Integration Committee, concluded his Moderatorial Address with a challenge to lay and ordained alike to sacrifice in the name of and for the sake of Christ through service within the BPC. Neither of the two problems enunciated by Vika were of substantive importance. The whole point was to increase responsibility within the black *corpus*, and there would have been no shortage of able manpower had the missionaries performed their work effectively. White missionaries were holding on to senior posts instead of empowering successors as conceptualised in authentic partnership.

On 26 November 1974, the Secretary of the Joint Council presented a report 'for information' as if this was not of substantial importance to the BPCSA (BPCSA GA 1974: 19) and its future planning. He reported that transfer of funds was progressing, while on 27 May 1975 a portfolio of trust funds was handed to the Rev. Vika. A further schedule of grant balances was presented later in the same year. Monies from the sale of congregational lands were transferred as they became available (Min. 717.g, CoSSAJC 27 July 1975). During 1975–8, the takeover of mission hospitals at

Nessie Knight (Sulenkama), Donald Fraser (Gooldville) and Tugela Ferry (Msinga) was planned. However, the 'homeland' governments adopted a different approach to take over. They wanted the land to be donated to them, as with Lovedale Institution and Ellesmere (Gordon Memorial) Farm (BPCSA GA 1974: 19). This transfer raised the sensitive issue of who historically owned the land, and how and why the church acquired it, other than to benefit the local people. Regarding integration, it was noted that despite progress made it 'will take time to implement' (BPCSA GA 1974: 20).

By 1975, Joint Council funds had been transferred to the BPC except for travel expenses, secretarial expenses, assembly expenses and estates (Church of Scotland Trust). It is not clear why these funds were retained but this was 'Noted with satisfaction' (BPCSA GA 1975: 19), such was the trust in which the Joint Council Treasurer was held. These funds could easily have been operated by the BPCSA except perhaps for the estates that could have been administered by the church attorneys. Then, the Joint Council could have been dissolved, and the church lawyers, Hutton & Cook, in consultation with the Church of Scotland Overseas Council could have transferred properties in consultation with BPCSA officials. However, fund retention allowed the Joint Council Treasurer considerable latitude in their use without supervision, especially when he was travelling on business outside the remit of the Joint Council (e.g. performing work as financial adviser to the Federal Theological Seminary in seeking compensation for the expropriated from its site in Alice in 1974) (Denis & Duncan 2011: 5). Rev. Ian Moir, recently appointed Africa Secretary of the Overseas Council, stated 'I only wanted to open the way for you to cut down your travelling' (correspondence, Moir to Stevenson, 15 July 1976, Cory, File 02/5), which was considered excessive according to Stevenson. He continued with this work after he left the BPCSA and worked as Financial Manager of the South African Council of Churches for a period from 1979.

It was reported in 1976 that 'the Council continues to serve both Churches in the sphere of land and property, together with the important matters of people and personnel' (BPCSA GA 1976: 20). Meanwhile, personnel were further reduced by the refusal of permits to the Revs James Gossip (Missionary in Charge at Gordon Memorial Mission) and Ewan Campbell (Missionary in Charge at Lovedale Institution). A replacement was sought for Mr Campbell (BPCSA GA 1975: 44). Rev. James Kincaid resigned as Missionary-in-Charge at Cunningham Mission in July 1976 (BPCSA GA 1976: 16); Mr Victor Crawford, missionary printer, also resigned (BPCSA GA 1976: 17) as did Miss Fiona Hamill and Dr A. T. Cameron at Tugela Ferry Hospital (BPCSA GA 1976: 19). The following missionaries remained:

Miss EJ Phillip at Tugela Ferry, due for UK leave in August, 1977;
Mr HA Kingcome at Lovedale, due for UK leave in August, 1978;
Mr MI Stevenson at Umtata, due for UK leave on 4 November 1976.

Agreed that Mr Stevenson be invited to come back. Dr AM Sammon at Tugela Ferry, will complete his contract on 21st January, 1977. (BPCSA GA 1976: 19–20) ... Assembly agreed to ask missionaries going on leave to return if conditions permitted and that replacements be found possible and that replacements be found for those whose contracts had expired. (BPCSA GA 1976: 20)

In the event, seven missionaries were lost in a short time because Ms Phillip (BPCSA GA 1977: 20) and Dr Sammon did not return to missionary service and the only replacement already requested was for the post of Missionary-in-Charge at Lovedale.

Rev. James Gossip was 'relieved of his duties at Gordon Memorial on 30 April 1976' at the request of the Business Committee of the BPCSA (BPCSA GA 1976: 19). Gossip's departure had its origin in a dispute that involved the local magistrate and a land issue. Gossip, being a missionary, was responsible to the Overseas Council. It is not clear how the matter came to the Business Committee without reference from the Presbytery of Natal. It came to Stevenson's notice because Gordon Memorial Mission was a property of the Church of Scotland. From then, the situation deteriorated rapidly. Stevenson took grave offence on behalf of the Joint Council and the BPCSA and concluded this had precipitated an 'irrevocable breakdown of relations between the Church of Scotland and the BPC' (correspondence, Stevenson to Moir, 28 June 1976, Cory, File 02/5). There was no supporting evidence for Stevenson's assertion and relations continued normally. Stevenson was upset because he was not party to the confidential correspondence between Moir and Gossip. Moir responded with:

> My last letter to Jim was an attempt at a pastoral letter. There is nothing in this letter which you do not know about. To send copies of this personal letter to other people would have destroyed the effect. The other reason for not sending you a copy was to try to show Jim that the BPC and the Overseas Council are not involved in a conspiracy against him. (correspondence, Moir to Stevenson, 15 July 1976, Cory, File 02/5)

Moir further pointed out that 'the Overseas Council concurs with the recommendation of the BPC'. There is no evidence to suggest a rupture in Overseas Council and BPCSA relations besides Stevenson's claim. This lack of evidence suggests that Stevenson fomented a breach because he needed to be in control and speak for both the Joint Council and the BPCSA without authority or accountability.

The Overseas Council stated the following about their future: 'It has been the hope for some time that the Council would be dissolved and that its responsibilities pass to this Assembly' (BPCSA GA 1977: 21). The council proposed arrangements for transferring the management of Impolweni Farm and Lovedale Press. This was referred to the Integration Committee. It is difficult to understand why the process of integration was not completed at this time as had been the case in other countries. The BPCSA moved towards establishing a finance department (BPCSA GA 1977: 40) with M. I. Stevenson as potential Treasurer. This would become a source of dissent that eventually led to Stevenson's resignation (BPCSA GA 1978: 37–8; cf. Min 936 CoSSAJC 22 August 1979). Clearly, there were financial problems in the denomination, but a greater difficulty arose out of a poor personal relationship between Matt Stevenson and the new General Secretary, Rev. S. B. Ngcobo who had replaced Rev. G. T. Vika on his resignation to join the Transkeian homeland government on 1 January 1978. Of note was the close relationship Stevenson and Vika enjoyed as colleagues over the period since Stevenson arrived in South Africa. It is difficult, otherwise, to explain Stevenson's resignation as he was about to occupy one of the most senior positions in the BPCSA, and he had the support of the denomination.

The General Assembly, in 1978, agreed to change the name of the BPCSA to the Reformed Presbyterian Church in Southern Africa (RPCSA) with effect from 1 January 1979 (BPCSA GA 1977: 33). Before the appointment of a Missionary-in-charge at Lovedale, it was agreed that the person appointed would take care of the linked Lovedale District and Institution congregations (BPCSA GA 1977: 41). Subsequently, it was noted that 'The Revd G. A. Duncan was ordained to the Holy Ministry on 12 March 1978 at Burnshill Mission in the Presbytery of the Ciskei. He is Moderator of the linked Lovedale congregation' (BPCSA GA 1978: 17). It was further noted in the Joint Council report of 1978 that Duncan accepted his role as Missionary-in-Charge at Lovedale Institution and was elected Chair of the Joint Council (BPCSA GA 1978: 19, 20).

In April 1979, Revs Ian Moir and Iain Paterson, representing the Overseas Council, visited South Africa to hold a consultation with the Joint Council to consider how to allocate the funds derived from the sale and transfer of Church of Scotland properties in South Africa. The basic premise of the discussions was that funds would not be transferred to the Church of Scotland but allocated to projects of the RPCSA. A number of funds were established for this purpose. No reference to this consultation was made in the subsequent General Assembly of the BPCSA until 1980 when only some funds established were mentioned specifically:

> The Overseas Council has agreed to the transfer of R196,000-00 (this being compensation from the sale of Nessie Knight Hospital) to the Reformed Presbyterian Church. The Overseas Council has accepted the RPC's request that R100,000-00 be allocated to the Maintenance of the Ministry Fund, and R96,000-00 be allocated to the Training of Ministry Fund. (RPCSA GA 1980: 20)

By this time, Matt Stevenson had left the service of the RPCSA without leaving an updated report on the work of the Joint Council: 'The Rev. G. T. Vika in the absence of the Secretary of Joint Council submitted the report' in 1979 (BPCSA GA 1979: 17). Stevenson's resignation was not unexpected. On 24 November 1978, the Business Committee received a letter from the General Secretary of the South African Council of Churches, Bishop Desmond Tutu, that requested Matthew Stevenson be seconded to the South African Council of Churches as Deputy General Secretary. This appointment was refused because the BPCSA's need was greater. Stevenson submitted his letter of resignation with immediate effect. Business Committee requested Mr Stevenson to remain until November to give a special committee time to meet with him (BPCSA GA 1978: 44–5). The Joint Council received the letter of resignation from the Overseas Council on 22 August 1979 with its request that Stevenson be released on 22 September 1979. The Chair was requested to contact the Overseas Council to make transitional arrangements. Rev. G. A. Duncan was appointed Secretary/Treasurer 'subject to the approval of the OC' (Mins. 936, 937 CoSSAJC 22 August 1979).

On 19 July 1979, at a meeting of the Business Committee, Mr Stevenson informed attendees that he resigned as a missionary of the Church of Scotland and requested to be relieved of his post as General Treasurer. This resignation was accepted with regret. The General Secretary along with the Joint Treasurers was appointed to fill the vacancy (BPCSA GA 1979: 41). At the subsequent General Assembly in 1979, the first following Stevenson's resignation, a minute was passed:

> Recognising the important role that the Joint Council, and its predecessors, the Mission Councils have played in the past, it was unanimously agreed to recommend to the Overseas Council and to this General Assembly that Church of Scotland Joint Council be dissolved effectively from the 1st January, 1980, or as soon thereafter. Agreed. (BPCSA GA 1979: 18; cf. Min 935.c CoSSAJC 22 August 1979)

No further obstacles to integration remained. Remaining business was to be assigned to a Property and Assets Holding Committee (Church of Scotland) that would attend to matters relating to impediments arising out of the Group Areas Act and incomplete negotiations for compensation and realised assets not transferred. The committee was to consist of an equal number of Overseas Council and RPCSA nominees and was to be reappointed annually if necessary (BPCSA GA 1979: 18–19). At the Business Committee in November 1979, an attempt was made to rescind the minute regarding the dissolution of Joint Council because all land assets had not yet been transferred. This was rejected on the basis that 'dissolution, whenever, it takes place does not stop the envisaged transfer of Assets' (BPCSA GA 1979: 44).

In 1980, Rev. Ian A. Moir, Partnership/Africa Secretary of the Overseas Council, attended the RPCSA General Assembly, held at Gillespie Mission and 'handed over to the Church, through the Moderator, the certificates of Assets totalling R196,000-00. These were received with thanks. Mr Moir said that the interest would follow in due course'. The date for dissolution was set as 1 June 1981 (BPCSA GA 1980: 20):

> Anticipating that this will be the last report of the Joint Council to the General Assembly, the council wishes to place on record its thanks to those ministers and elders who have served and contributed to its work over the years. (BPCSA GA 1980: 20)

However, Joint Council matters were not yet complete. In November 1980, financial irregularities were reported to the Business Committee arising out of the audit of the 1979 Joint Council accounts; the 1979 Overseas Council grants had not been paid to the RPC; the second, third and fourth quarter grants were used to pay accounts without the RPC's authorisation; the first quarter grant 'has not been used to pay accounts yet it has not been paid to the Church either' (BPCSA GA 1980: 42). These irregularities were inexplicable besides the poor relationships in the General Assembly office. The outcome included:

> After a lengthy discussion, the Joint Council Treasurer agreed to investigate this disturbing matter further and was prepared to pay what was due to the Church once it was ascertained what the position was.

Further to that, the Business Committee agreed to note the situation with grave concern and await the outcome of the consultation of the Church auditors and the Joint Council auditors. It was, further, agreed that the Church of Scotland should be informed about this disturbing situation (BPCSA GA 1980: 42).

Mr Stevenson refused to account for the irregularities and the CoSSAJC auditor, Mr Gordon L. Laurence of Brandt, Bowling & Tagg (firm of accountants in Grahamstown, who had been consulted by the BPCSA and the CoSSAJC for many years) resigned immediately after he received queries regarding his audit. The 1979 grants were paid before the Business Committee met on 30 July 1981 (BPCSA GA 1981: 34). Subsequent to this, the Overseas Council approved the dissolution of the Joint Council (Min1001 CoSSAJC 1 May 1981). This momentous event took place without ceremony on 1 June 1981 and, after 58 years of existence, the RPCSA took full responsibility for its own affairs.

One of the first matters that required attention following the dissolution of the Joint Council was a report which arose out of the ongoing matter of the disposition of Lovedale Institution. The report was submitted by Milton M. Khala, a senior sales representative of Lovedale Press, who had had a meeting with Chief D. M. Jongilanga, Minister of Education in the Ciskeian Legislative Assembly, on 22 May 1981. The Chief expressed his frustration with the 'Lovedale authorities' for delaying a resolution of the disposal of Lovedale and accused them of waging a 'cold war' against the Ciskeian government. The 'Lovedale authorities' asked for R1,500,000 for the property, yet they had recently offered it to the University of Fort Hare for R100,000 (Cory, PR 0432, L6, 27 May 1981). This issue was sensitive because it placed the BPCSA in a potentially vulnerable situation. It was one legacy Stevenson left behind to be resolved. Within days of Khala writing this report, the CoSSAJC was dissolved and the matter was expedited by Robert D. N. Stanford, of the churches' attorneys, Hutton & Cook, King William's Town, in consultation with the General Secretary of the BPCSA, Rev. S. B. Ngcobo. Stanford had dealt with the sale and transfer of Church of Scotland properties for some years and was best qualified to finalise the sale and transfer. This demonstrated there was no need for an intermediary body to effect integration.

Conclusion

Partnership in mission was the broader context in which integration occurred. Yet, it only marginally affected the process of integration whose aim was to develop independence and mutuality and strengthen the integrity of churches derived from the missionary movement. This led to a constant struggle with meaning of partnership in practice and also to a paradoxical situation of integration by guaranteeing the continuing involvement of the CoS and at the same time promoting the right of independent churches to exercise prime responsibility for mission in their own areas. Looking at the global context, it appears that in countries with higher levels of racism there were higher degrees of control exercised externally. In South Africa, much delay occurred due to the existence of apartheid. However, CoS policy played into the hands of those who believed that black Christians were incapable of dealing with their own affairs or of determining their own political future. The CoS and Joint Council attitudes were tantamount to collaboration with the *status quo* rather than the presentation and promotion of an alternative way of demonstrating Christian witness in the South African context. There was a sufficient cadre of beneficent white Christians and an emerging body of black professionals with legal and financial expertise who could have facilitated integration and allowed the BPCSA to stand on its own feet and demonstrate that they could indeed do so. What is of concern in terms of partnership is that there was a lack of partnership between the Joint Council and the BPCSA. By listening to and being guided by one missionary in the closing years of the Joint Council, the CoS refused to initiate and participate in this act of faith in the future of African Christianity and became reactionaries in the original sense of the word.

CHAPTER FOURTEEN

A Young Church in Mission or Maintenance Mode? The Bantu Presbyterian Church of South Africa, 1923–99

Introduction

> The ecumenical movement does not derive simply from a passion for unity; it sprang from a passion for unity that is completely fused in the mission. (Le Guillou cited in Boegner 1970: 269)

> The fact that it was largely the missionary endeavours of churches and missionary societies during the eighteenth and nineteenth centuries which gave birth to the ecumenical movement of the twentieth century, is generally accepted today. (Saayman 1984: 8)

This is true of any Reformed church community, the subjects of mission and unity are integrally interrelated as seen from the Scottish mission to South Africa. Scottish Presbyterians were always prepared to work with others in pursuit of their mission all in the same of seeking the unity of Christ's church. The overlapping agenda of the Church in Scotland was easily transportable to South Africa. However, Africans were also confused by the different versions of Christianity they were presented with. In their traditional contexts they were not exposed to different versions of African traditional religion. In some ways these imported traditions actually militated against the ecumenical impulse.

Up until this point we have been looking mainly at external developments in the outreach of the RPCSA in relation to other South African denominations. However, there was also a considerable amount of effort being expended both in its internal missionary and evangelical outputs and in developing its own distinctive tradition.

The story of the first hundred years of the Scottish mission in South Africa has been discussed. This led to the formation of the Bantu Presbyterian Church of South Africa in 1923 (Duncan 2016b). In her study of the history of the Scottish mission in South Africa, Sheila Brock (1974: 60) contended that 'ecclesiastical separate development in the political circumstances of South Africa since 1820 have not given much scope to the Bantu Presbyterian Church and it has not proved itself a particularly inspiring example to follow'. This chapter challenges Brock's assertion by examining the extent to which the BPCSA remained true to its Constitution 'in the form of a self-governing Native Church' (BPCSA 1958: 113) and 'an autonomous branch of the Holy, Catholic Church' (BPCSA 1958: 114) 'labouring for the advancement of the Kingdom of God throughout the world' (BPCSA 1958: 115) from its formation in 1923 until union with the Presbyterian Church of Southern Africa (PCSA) in 1999. The mission of the church is summarised in section IV of the Constitution (BPCSA 1958: 117):

> The vocation of the church is joyfully to bear witness to its Lord, to worship God in His Name, to build up its members in Faith and righteousness and the spirit of unity, to proclaim His Gospel to the ends of the earth, to give loving service to mankind for his sake, and to watch and pray for the coming of His Kingdom.

The ecumenical responsibility of the BPCSA was a traditional component of Reformed churches and presaged its regular involvement in church unity initiatives. It also spoke to the reconciliatory mission of the church within and beyond its borders 'to the ends of the earth, to give loving service to mankind' (see Duncan 2017, 2018b). However, reconciliation was difficult to achieve in the prevailing South African context.

The Beginnings of the Mission of the BPCSA

Duncan (1997: 150–1) has described the emphasis on the inclusive nature of the new denomination in the way Rev. William Stuart, first Moderator of the General Assembly of the BPCSA, formally constituted the gathering and gave his Moderatorial Address in which he discussed the inaugurated approach of reconciliation by commenting that the coming together of the UP and FC missions with the Mission Council of Natal was 'a forward step in the line of natural development' and a result of 'earnest and prayerful deliberation, full and careful consideration of the many interests involved and persons specially concerned'. The highest office was open to blacks 'as it ought to be', so the new church retained the concepts of equality and parity. 'The Church of Christ is for any and everyone, . . . irrespective of nationality, colour or tongue' (BPCSA 1923: 39). Nonetheless the BPCSA 'was placed in a paradoxical situation for while it claimed universality and colourblindness, its very name, composition and future relationships proclaimed something different'. This was a rather negative view for it was open to all as many missionaries and a few non-missionary church workers discovered. Often the missionaries proved the truth of the statement for having served their working years in the BPCSA, many retired into the service of the PCSA.

However, the missionary dimension was evident in Stuart's reference to the 'inaugurated approach of reconciliation'.

In loyal addresses to the King and the Prime Minister there are references to the conflictual situation in the country: 'unrest and bitterness so widely manifest in the social and political life of the world' and to moves being made 'to improve the relations between the different races in the land' that demonstrate the context in which the birth of the BPCSA has occurred and the church's social and political concern (BPCSA 1923: 26). Fundamental to the birth of the new denomination was the ongoing role missionaries were to play in this new context.

The Role of Missionaries

There were still a number of missionaries serving who wished to continue in the service of the BPCSA. They were granted seats in the courts of the church 'with the view of giving all necessary advice and assistance, but they shall leave the conduct of business as far as practicable to the native members' (BPCSA 1923: 24). In a letter to J. H. Oldham, Lennox (1922): claimed that the 'full powers' accorded to missionaries would decline in the course of time until 'they will no longer be required'. This area was problematic because no limits were built in to restrict the missionaries' exercise of power. This was a situation which was fraught with tension which continued at varying levels of intensity during these years (see Duncan 2016a), particularly as the number of serving missionaries increased.

Rev. T. B. Soga expressed a desire for the blacks to have 'complete control in the Native Courts' because missionaries controlled the Mission Councils. He based his case on the fact that the Plan of Union for the Scottish churches in 1900 'imposed on us [missionaries] all the duty to leave the control of the Native courts entirely to the Natives' (Lennox to Ashcroft, 1922). Elphick (2012: 2) drew out the contradictory situation the missionaries found themselves in: 'The seed of South African egalitarianism was the theological proclamation of the early missionaries: that Jesus died on the cross for people of every nation and race, not for whites alone; and that, in consequence, all who accepted him were brothers and sisters'. The missionaries had an 'ambiguous relationship' with equality regarding black believers and presented a 'counter-ideology of equality'. Contrary to white missionaries, 'Black Christians, . . . tended vigorously to assert that equality in the eyes of God should evolve into social and political equality' (Elphick 2012: 2). This had begun post-1853 and the granting of 'responsible government', where: 'An emerging black leadership [educated at mission schools] was convinced that Christianity, Western education, and the colourblind franchise would open the way for blacks to attain equality with whites in common citizenship' (Elphick 2012: 3). The issue here, as expressed by Soga relates to the autonomy of the BPCSA. The situation was encapsulated in Rousseau's comment: 'Man is born free, but everywhere he is in chains'.

But another aspect of the role of missionaries has to be understood relating to the retention of power by mission councils. The missionaries in the mission council were the sole conduit through which all communication had to pass from the RPCSA to the Church of Scotland (BPCSA 1929: 49). This is significant because it strikes at the heart of the autonomy granted since a white group within the church had power to veto its decisions and wishes. At the heart of the debate was the liberation of black Christians from missionary domination exercised through mission councils, which had been a significant factor in the secessionary church movement in the late nineteenth century. Sadly, this problem was only resolved with the dissolution of the Church of Scotland South Africa Joint Council in 1981.

However, mission did not arrest. Following the missionary era, the RPCSA maintained its strong interest in the main areas of missionary endeavour – education, health, agriculture and industrial education. Through its ongoing commitment to Lovedale Press and publishing, the RPCSA made a substantial contribution to education and the development of vernacular languages, particularly *isiXhosa*, with its promotion of black writers.

The Role of Evangelists

From the earliest days of the Scottish mission in South Africa, indigenous Christians performed the role of 'evangelist' as catechists, teachers, pastors and ministers. In time the specific role of evangelist emerged in areas not reached by the mission and where extension work was thought to be feasible. The office of Evangelist emerged as a response to the need to provide ministerial assistance in large and widespread rural congregations. Significant work was done by a body of unsung heroes and heroines (although women were denied recognition for their sterling contributions in this role). The General Assembly took a broad view of the participants in evangelism: 'The Assembly enjoins on all ministers the remembrance that they are Evangelists and encourages them and their sessions in this the first task of the Church' (BPCSA 1936: 16). But it established a committee to focus on the needs and methods of evangelism that may be experimented with in congregations. It also appointed a Mission Committee to 'review and help all mission work' besides conveying 'to the members of the Church information enabling them to take a warm and practical interest in the work' and to supervise the work of evangelists (BPCSA 1936: 17). The evangelistic needs outlined above became the subject of a Missionary Night held at the 1938 General Assembly (BPCSA 1938: 31) which also received a report on a 'valuable survey of evangelistic work' (BPCSA 1938: 32–4). Elders and deacons were encouraged to join in the training of evangelists at Lovedale Bible School opened on an ecumenical basis with the basic remit of preparing evangelists for service. The Assembly also decided: 'That Sessions do their utmost to encourage the Women's Christian Association and the Young Men's Christian Association to engage actively in evangelism'. This was to be achieved by holding conferences 'for the deepening of the spiritual life' be held in congregations for office-bearers and members (BPCSA 1938: 32). The following year, the General Assembly decided:

> Kirk Sessions are earnestly urged to take active steps to bring the claims of the gospel to,
> (a) The mass of Heathens in our missions
> (b) Our young 'school' Africans.

This would be facilitated by at least one evangelist in each congregation (BPCSA 1939: 20). This salutary aim was never realised.

However, plans were also afoot to re-establish lay education programmes, including those for the training of evangelists. From the late 1970s, there was a plan to replace the now-closed Lovedale Bible School expropriated by the government to facilitate development at Fort Hare University in 1974 along with FedSem (BPCSA 1974: 46). In the following years plans to open the Lovedale Lay Education Centre were approved (RPCSA 1979: 26). This was to replace the Lovedale Bible School. After a promising start in planning, the project was abandoned in 1982 due to 'the unsettled political situation surrounding [the sale of] Lovedale (RPCSA 1982: 19).

Church Associations

The Women's Christian Association (WCA) and the Girls' Association (GA) will be considered in the final chapter on the role of women in leadership in ministry in the RPCSA.

Young Men's Christian Guild (YMCG)

The concept of an organisation for young men originated in the areas where men had left their homes for economic reasons in order to earn a living in response to the draw of the mines in the Free State and the Transvaal following the discovery of diamonds and gold in the second half of the nineteenth century. Distanced from their families and church connections they came together in their hostels for communal worship, prayer and preaching. This was one of the main means of keeping alive their faith and church commitment in areas where the churches were only at the beginning of the missionary and extension process by the established missions like the Free Church of Scotland Mission and the not yet established Presbyterian Church of South Africa. These men's groups were self-sustaining as there were no ministers available at the early stage of their development to lead them. Some of these men would have been ordained elders and would possibly be familiar with liturgy and pastoral care.

The idea of establishing a Young Men's Christian Association (YMCA) was first mooted in 1935 'to coordinate the evangelical word under the Church'. Draft proposals were requested at the 1936 Assembly (BPCSA

1935: 35). In 1947 (BPCSA 1948: 9) the name of the men's association was changed to the Young Men's Christian Guild. Its constitution was ratified by the 1958 General Assembly with aims similar to those of the WCA:

(a) To advance the Kingdom of God in our church, in other sister Churches and throughout the world.
(b) To deepen the spiritual lives of our young men and to promote the study of the Scriptures among them and the intellectual, social and physical well-being of our youth.
(c) To foster loyalty to our Church and to the church of Christ as a whole. (BPCSA 1958: 39)

This expresses a universal obligation to promote God's mission within an ecumenical perspective as it follows the pattern of Jesus' holistic development, spiritually, physically, intellectually and socially (cf. Luke 2: 52).

All three associations found it easy to cooperate with their partner associations in their activities, for example in sharing to gather in the Women's World Day of Prayer. They often also cooperated at times of bereavement and in various community activities.

Printing and Publishing

Shepherd (1940: 62) informs us that Rev. John Ross arrived in South Africa with 'a small Ruthven printing press with a supply of type, paper and ink. Ross described this as a 'powerful auxiliary'. This inaugurated the work of the Lovedale Press which became a powerful instrument of mission. As the missionaries learned local languages they were anxious to commit them to written form in order to evangelise the indigenous peoples. By 1861, Rev. William Govan, Principal of Lovedale Institution, also having 'recognised the power of the written word' (Shepherd 1940: 400) opened the printing and bookbinding departments and so began the work of Lovedale Press.

The major aim of the Press was to provide 'the ministry of the printed word to the African people' (Shepherd 1971: 102). There were two subsidiary aims: that books which were to be paid for and used by South Africans should be printed and bound by African workers as far as was possible; the other was that African authors should be encouraged to submit manuscripts for publication. Lovedale Press bore the cost of publication and paid royalties on sales. One of the main successes was the publication of a large number of textbooks and readers for schools, especially the *Stewart Xhosa Readers*.

The press expanded under Govan's successor, Dr James Stewart, and it was during this period that 'South Africa's oldest continuous mission journal' (Switzer: 119) 1993: began to be published – The *Kaffir Express* (1870), renamed the *Christian Express* (1876) and later the *South African Outlook* (1922). Shepherd (1945: 12) claimed that the purpose of this venture was to spread ideas in 'the moral wastes and desert places of heathen ignorance' and contribute to the general missionary work of South Africa. The *South African Outlook* became the official mouthpiece of the General Missionary Conference of South Africa and the Christian Council of South Africa. The *Outlook* drew on the wisdom of Lovedale and Fort Hare academics who were active in studying the racial problems of South Africa, some of whom were experts in specific fields such as education, health and economics. They met regularly to discuss current racial issues and:

> to formulate, on behalf of the missionary and other religious forces, the policy which it was felt should be adopted towards the Government measures affecting non-Europeans, as well as to consider means for non-European advancement. (Shepherd 1971: 104)

For some time, the 'devotional, evangelical and primary educational themes acceptable to the missionaries continued to dominate book and pamphlet publication in the vernacular at Lovedale (Switzer 1993: 121). Consequently, the Xhosa contribution to the development of literature was considerable during the first half of the twentieth century. These developments continued under the succeeding Principals of Lovedale.

Strict editorial policy was implemented and maintained in order to ensure that no anti-Chrsitian material was published. However, Shepherd contributed greatly to the dissemination of vernacular literature:

> In all its efforts for the spread of literature Lovedale recognised that there was a danger lest the missionary agencies, having in their schools taught vast numbers to read, should leave non-Christians and even anti-religious elements to supply the reading matter ... While in school and when they left it it was imperative that they find within their reach literature suited to their every need, in order that they might have an understanding grasp of Christian life and morals. (Shepherd 1971: 104)

This signified considerable ecumenical co-operation at a time when the Christian Council of South Africa was about to be formed.

The Lovedale Press also engaged in book colportage which enabled its publications to be accessed by people who lived in remote areas. The colporteur, Mr G. A. Gush, also conducted services in English, Afrikaans and Xhosa.

Bible Translation

This was another of the projects missionaries engaged in with enthusiasm in their desire to convert the indigenous population (Shepherd1940: 65). John Bennie was deeply involved in Bible translation and the translation of the Xhosa Bible was complete by 1887. The evangelistic power of this work was pre-eminent and was based on the following principles:

- The primary aim of the missionaries was to spread the gospel and also influence the Xhosa to accept an international way of life that would be acceptable to the civilized world. (Jafta 1971:14)
- The literary development of the Xhosa cannot be separated from the missionary endeavour. (Jafta 1971: 6)

Because the work of Bible translation was centred at Lovedale this had been a project of the Mission Council of Kafraria. This was transferred to the BPCSA in 1926 as the revision of the Xosa Bible was proceeding. The same was the case with the Xosa Hymn Book (BPCSA 1926: 34–5).

Theological Education

Since the opening of the South African Native College at Fort Hare in 1916, it was anticipated that the new denomination would have a formal relationship with the college besides its training centre at Lovedale. It was decided to enter discussions with the Presbyterian Church of South Africa regarding co-operation in theological education (BPCSA 1924: 20–1). A new syllabus was also to be considered (BPCSA 1924: 22) in a context where the European model of theological education had already been adopted and implemented. This became problematic regarding entrance qualifications which were retained at a high level reflecting European standards (BPCSA 1930: 34). One of the first practical tasks in theological education was to determine the best manner probationer ministers could be incorporated into the life and work of the BPCSA (BPCSA 1924: 19). A committee worked on this. The nature of the high calling was expressed by the General Assembly in 1935 (BPCSA 1935: 20) as a matter for serious prayer and consideration as it commended:

> the vocation of the ministry, with its opportunity for heroic and sacrificial service. The Assembly affirms its conviction that such service of Christ demands the highest possible training together with special qualities of consecration and spiritual experience, and therefore appeals to young men aflame with love for Christ for the dedication of their lives to His Ministry.

This indicates a strong awareness of the necessity of spiritual maturity besides educational ability for the demanding work of God's mission which it describes as 'heroic and sacrificial service'. Besides the BA (Theology) course, students were also enrolling for a Diploma in Theology at the University of Fort Hare by 1940 (BPCSA 1940: 5, 8). The students were allocated to their respective church hostels for accommodation with a warden who supervised their progress on behalf of the Church. Presbyterian students resided at Iona House.

A *Special Commission on the Church Ministry* reported to the General Assembly in 1971 (BPCSA 1971: 48–9) arising out of a concern for the lack of candidates offering for the ordained ministry. Several relevant issues were raised but the matter of the lack of lay education, 'a priceless contribution to God's work' (BPCSA 1971: 48), was highlighted as a vital component of mission work. This was a hindrance to mission besides the discerned problems of lack of contact and poor impact of ministers due to having to minister to large extensive congregations. Lay leadership was vital in congregations where, apart from servicing a mainstation, ministers may have up to fifty outstations to care for, often at a considerable distance from the mainstation. Elders who lived in these outstations would care for their members there but, until recently, little training was offered to them.

Substantial progress was made to further mission and unity when the establishment of the Federal Theological Seminary was proposed (BPCSA 1960: 270; Denis & Duncan 2011: 41–7). This was to become an experiment in mission and ecumenism which provided a serious challenge to the apartheid government. The proposed site was at Lovedale on land held in trust by the Church of Scotland for the BPCSA. A site was chosen nearby adjacent to the University of Fort Hare. This site, opened in 1963, was expropriated in 1974 due to a refusal to sell the land in order that expansion could take place at the adjacent University of Fort Hare, although the reason may have been the Seminary's role in providing sanctuary to students during periods of unrest. FedSem moved temporarily to Umtata and then Edendale in Natal, before settling more permanently at Imbali in Pietermaritzburg. An example of both ecumenism and mission is to be found in the work of the ecumenical Young Men's Christian Guild which met weekly on Sunday evenings and went into the community every Wednesday evening to offer support to families undergoing traumatic events. This was especially helpful during the latter part of the 1980s when there was conflict in the Inbali/Edendale areas between the African Natinal Congress and the Inkatha Freedom party which led to many deaths. Students were often called to conduct funerals when the pressure of funerals on ministers became heavy. They learned their ministry in a troubled and violent context which was a good preparation for ministry in many communities around South Africa during the apartheid period.

The seminary closed in 1993 (RPCSA 1993: 75). Consequently, the training for ministry programme of the RPCSA, EPCSA and UCCSA was transferred back to the University of Fort Hare (RPCSA 1994: 30). At this time the original expropriated FedSem Campus was symbolically returned to the churches. There were several reasons for the closure and the ending of apartheid was one of them (Duncan 2004: 1–31). Another was the lack of support from the Anglican, Methodist churches along with the Presbyterian Church of Southern Africa now that the universities were open to students of all races.

Life and Work

The supply of ministers in large and widely scattered remote parishes was met by a decision to allow licensed probationers to celebrate the sacraments in such places (BPCSA 1924: 19). Mission was at the heart of the Committee on Life and Work's interest as seen from a deliverance of the 1938 General Assembly (BPCSA 1938: 13): 'Office-Bearers and Ministers should use their best mental faculties in discovering special methods of wooing young men and women for Christ. The Church needs live young folk to step in and take the vows for the furtherment of our Church'. The Assembly replaced the word 'Native' with 'African' in its usage (BPCSA 1938: 16).

The 1971 General Assembly received a significant historical report (BPCSA 1971: 54–70), *Bantu Presbyterian Church of South Africa: Origin and progress*. In a section headed *Workers and their achievements: Minister and Elders* the important work of church extension (mission) was attributed to ministers (missionaries and black ministers) who had taken an active and enthusiastic role in missionary work. Many elders were also praised for their contributions. The report concluded:

> When we remember those gone before us, and the splendid work done to the glory of God and the spiritual benefit of our people, we should double our efforts and in our time pray for the Spirit to lead us to greater achievements. (BPCSA 1971: 70)

While some were quick to conclude that little spiritual growth had taken place in the BPCSA, the church itself, perhaps best placed to make the judgment, concluded positively regarding ' the spiritual benefit of our people' and regarding the need for constant vigilance in this ongoing concern. Mission was based in the solid work done in the past to promote the gospel leading eventually to the foundation of an autonomous church. Brock's assertion regarding the poor performance of the RPCSA could be interpreted to mean that all was well under the close supervision of the missionaries while an autonomous church governed by black people was not up to the task. Yet, mission was integral to the work of the church as it had been in the past and would remain so for the future.

This view was consolidated in 1974 (BPCSA 1974: 56–7) as the result of the report of an ad hoc committee which led to the affirmation of several functions of the denomination:

(a) To convert people to Christ . . .
(b) To encourage and strengthen those who are already members of the church . . .
(c) To serve the community in all its aspects: – spiritual, social, physical and mental . . .
(d) To be a conscience to those in authority . . .

(e) To promote and have fellowship with other church bodies in South Africa and throughout the world . . .

This was a comprehensive missionary mandate for the BPCSA to embark upon as it entered its second half-century since its foundation. It was evangelical and committed to challenging injustice. In this the work of the church associations would play an important role within the denomination and beyond it in the community.

A significant change occurred in 1978 with a decision to change the name of the BPCSA to the 'REFORMED PRESBYTERIAN CHURCH IN SOUTHERN AFRICA' with effect from 1 January 1979 (BPCSA 1978: 22). This was partly to take account of the negative connotations of the term *Bantu* besides the desire of some who were prepared to accept the homeland system which would make the inhabitants of so-called bantustan citizens of balkanized states in southern Africa rather than South Africa citizens. The relationship with the so-called 'independent' homelands was a source of ongoing conflict in the RPCSA. It allowed for latent tribalism within the RPCSA to come to the surface as the move came from the dominant Xhosa-speaking section of the church. It was spearheaded by Rev. Gladwin Vika and Mr Matthew Stevenson, leading homeland supporters. Vika was to become Minister of Health in the Transkei government and later, Minister of Foreign Affairs. The strong view in the church opposed the Nationalist government policy. The change of name raised up issues which challenged the traditional Xhose domination of the RPCSA.

Temperance

The General Assembly of 1926 called for total abstinence and for the introduction of unfermented wine at Holy Communion (BPCSA 1926: 32–3). This remained the policy of the BPCSA even when it was obeyed more in the breach than in conformity. This was a long standing problem among the working classes of South Africa where alcohol had been used as a means of payment, especially on the wine farms of the western Cape and as a means of controlling workers in their occupations which were seasonal. This also was a means of ensuring ongoing poverty. In 1927, the General Assembly reminded 'Congregations, kirk sessions, Deacons' courts and Ministers that it has been the inherited and established custom of the Bantu Presbyterian Church to insist on total abstinence from intoxicating liquors . . .' (BPCSA 1928: 16). This decision was strongly supported by the WCA (BPCSA 1928: 50) who related conformity to abstinence to personal purity (BPCSA 1931: 61). This became a regular theme in their annual meetings. At this time temperance was interpreted to mean 'total abstinence'. This was a missionary activity because alcohol was the cause of many other related social issues including marriage problems, poverty and unemployment. The Assembly was concerned for the welfare of its members as seen from the decision to petition the Prime Minister regarding the extension of the tot system (a system used by employers to give a daily amount of alcohol as part of wages) which was common, particularly in Western Cape vineyards:

> The Assembly views with amazement and sorrow the proposal to extend the tot system to the Transvaal and to give facilities for the spread of the drinking of European liquors amongst the Natives ... (BPCSA 1930: 16)

But this prohibition was extended in 1930 to include 'the practice of grinding beer, drinking and hiring people to work for *utywala* (an indigenous form of beer) within mission boundaries' (BPCSA 1931: 20). This had a deleterious effect on migrant workers and their families. It also had serious implications for the status of the Christian family as one agent in promoting the mission of the church. In the Mamabolo area in the northern Transvaal, the congregation were forbidden by the minister from taking 'intoxicating and stupefying beverages'. 'They could not escape the verdict of exclusion from the Church. So strict was the minister against the use of liquor and drugs that the Church lost some members' (Thema 2021: 50). The General Assembly decision was regularly reaffirmed (e.g. BPCSA 1959: 15) throughout its existence.

Conclusion

From the above it is clear that the Bantu/Reformed Presbyterian Church was engaged in mission throughout her lifespan in a wide variety of ways involving different sections of the denomination. Despite limited resources, declining support from the Church of Scotland, and in the face of intensified oppression as apartheid was introduced and consolidated she fulfilled her God-ordained mission of promoting and extending the kingdom of God within her capabilities. While foreign missionaries remained in declining numbers, the black membership took an increasingly responsible role in the governance and witness of the denomination as an agent of mission in South Africa. The mission of the BPCSA/RPCSA was not limited to purely ecclesiastical issues. It extended into the sphere of socio-political issues.

CHAPTER FIFTEEN

The Bantu/Reformed Presbyterian Church and Socio-political Issues

The legal enactments on African affairs during the 1950s amount to a frighteningly long list, including most importantly in regard to Church life: the Group Areas Act of 1950, extending residential and occupational segregation; the Bantu Education Act of 1953, whereby mission schools were taken from the hands of missions in order to produce more effectively an education 'for Africans only (mission schools at various educational levels had for a century been fundamentally important for Africans); and the Native Laws Amendment Act of 1957, which brought apartheid to one of its ugliest consequences – the infringement of religious freedom.' (Sundkler & Steed 2000: 821)

The mission of the RPCSA was expressed in its proud record of resistance to injustice, not only as a denomination but also because of individual and congregational commitment. The deliverances of General Assembly are often a poor guide to the actual process of resistance, yet they bear collective witness of the denomination to the struggle against manifest evils in society. The words of Rev. G. T. Vika, in his Moderatorial address, *Whither Bantu Presbyterian Church?* in 1974, may express more than the actual truth for that time: 'Apart from a few Christian protesters in isolated cases the church has done nothing to improve the position of our unjust society' (BPCSA 1974: 53). This was written in the context of 'current events that pose a challenge to the Church in this country, and call for it to declare its stand in the face of what seems to be a church-state confrontation'. This resulted in the termination of the policy of sending 'loyal addresses' to the State President, regularly followed since 1923, due to them being remitted to the Department of Bantu Administration where they were simply filed.

The social justice issues focused on the matter of racial segregation, both official and unofficial, before 1948 when the Nationalist Party came to power and promoted its apartheid policy as official policy afterwards. This affected the church at large in various ways. Vika declared:

> ... Government continues, through legislation, to create more problems for us as the process of visas and permits through which workers from abroad have to pass is becoming more stringent by the day. (BPCSA 1974: 50)

This was a reference to the problems experienced in securing entry and reentry permits for missionaries and other foreign church visitors. There is anecdotal evidence that, on more than one occasion, the assistance of 'friends' in Pretoria was solicited through contacts in the PCSA. It also referred to the problems experienced by BPCSA ministers who were sent abroad to represent the denomination at meetings of ecumenical bodies. Vika noted how much division this had caused both within the church and beyond (BPCSA 1974: 50–4) as it affected both the membership of the RPCSA and the possibility of attracting missionaries. He commented on how it had 'been the tendency of the Church for too long in our country to soft pedal any areas which are likely to irritate the government of State'. Referring to the detrimental influence theologically of a strong pietism and individualism, he accused the BPCSA: 'The problem is that the church is too Christian to be involved in matters, yet the Galilean Boy became a controversial figure from the age of twelve' (BPCSA 1974: 51). His address was a clarion call to the BPCSA to reorient itself for mission in areas hitherto considered secular, despite the potential threat of reprisals from the government. An inhibiting factor here may have been the predominantly rural population of the RPCSA which may not have been as directly impacted by apartheid as those living in urban areas.

Notwithstanding the above, successive General Assemblies, at the very least, noted and objected to matters of national and international interest and concern, including the Group Areas Act, influx control, conscientious objection, bannings and the role of ministers as marriage officers, unrest in Natal and capital punishment.

Passive resistance

In response to a national movement against the restrictive apartheid legislation, the General Assembly took a strong stand in favour of passive resistance because it was sanctioned by scripture as a response to gross injustice, not sourced 'in the lower nature of men, but in their partial grasp of the transforming truth that they too, are people of God and sons of the highest' (BPCSA 1952: 36). The Assembly noted the gravity of the situation:

> As the campaign intensifies the difficulties and incitements will increase, and only as our people can continue to behave non-violently and without bitterness to any man, will their endeavours be found worthy of the blessing of God the Father, Who in the person of His Son, Jesus Christ, died upon the cross that we might be reconciled to Him and to each other. (BPCSA 1952: 36)

Here we have the essence of God's mission in which the church is the main agent. The ultimate aim of God's mission is reconciliation. This offers a *rationale* for socio-political engagement based on the BPCSA's adherence to the supreme authority of the scriptures. The use of violence was eschewed, partly because it would have been an extremely controversial issue and many would have argued that it was contrary to scripture.

Bantu education

The Bantu Education Act of 1953 was a blight on the distinguished mission work in education by a number of churches, not least the Bantu Presbyterian Church. It evoked an immediate response from the General Assembly in 1954:

> The General Assembly place on record its regret that the government has embarked on a scheme of education which seems to place emphasis on preparing pupils for a subordinate role in the country's life rather than giving them the common culture of the Christian West . . .

This could have been accomplished without displacing missionary management of existing schools, particularly as only one third of Bantu children were in school (BPCSA 1954: 22). However, the government was well aware that the success of mission education lay in its development of both conformists and free thinkers, the latter much in evidence in the African National Congress, the Pan Africanist Congress (PAC) and other anti-segregationist bodies.

A decision was made not to sell church properties which housed schools, but to lease them to the government. Some retained control of their hostels to continue to influence the Christian life and character development of the students. The Bantu Education Act undermined one of the most significant and successful means of promoting ecumenism and mission within the total community for mission schools were not restricted to BPCSA members' families. Concerns were expressed regularly at General Assembly (e.g. BPCSA 1976: 290). Schools and colleges directly affected were Emgwali School for girls, Pholela institution, Blythswood Institution and the renowned Lovedale Missionary Institution. In 1976 when students protested against the enforcement of Afrikaans as the medium of instruction in schools the General Assembly issued a statement:

> . . . after several years of Bantu Education we find it unacceptable, and request the government to give our children the same education as given to other races in South Africa. (BPCSA 1976: 32, 36)

This was a rather mild rebuke for a situation in which children's life prospects were being severely diminished. One response of parents was to move their children to mission schools because they were situated in rural areas and less likely to experience unrest.

Pass laws

Pass laws, which controlled the rights of movement of the black population in South Africa originated in the eighteenth century and over the years their purpose changed. When the pass laws were implemented at the beginning of the twentieth century, they operated as part of the push-pull economic system to force the flow of labour into 'white' agriculture and industry and to redistribute labour into geographical areas where needed. This process would last until the 1950s, when the government changed the system which became a means of exclusion as it focused on removing Africans from 'white' areas and 'pushing' them into the homelands, especially if they had ceased to be productive contributors to the economy. Under this scheme, black South Africans had to carry passes on their persons wherever they went.

The 1927 General Assembly passed a resolution: 'That Mr [Rev. T. B.] Soga's protest be sent to the press and that a protest against members of the Assembly requiring to carry passes be sent by the Assembly to the authorities responsible for the regulations' (BPCSA 1927: 12). This was a deviation from the principle of freedom of movement which would seriously hamper the missionary work of the BPCSA. Related to this the General Assembly deplored the passing of the Group Areas Act again as it would also interfere with the missionary outreach of the church:

1. Contrary to the righteous will of God which calls his children to act with equal justice towards their brothers, in those proclamations so far made under the Act certain sections of the community are being unjustly penalised.
2. The work of several of our congregations existing for many years is to be disrupted by the removal of the members, the cancellation of long established business interests and the expropriation of extensive church buildings without adequate compensation. (BPCSA 1958: 24)

This matter was extended as government-initiated forced removals took place displacing many members from their traditional homes. The relationship of justice to the mission of the church is emphasised as the historical work was undermined and restricted. The land issue demonstrated the government's lack of understanding and sensitivity in a matter which was not only social and economic, but also deeply religious.

The ANC and PAC launched anti-Pass Law campaigns to be held on 21 March 1960. An incident of state-sponsored murder occurred at Sharpeville where police shot on protestors and killed 69 people, of whom 50 were women and children. This caused a grave crisis nationally and internationally and led to the Cottesloe Consultation later in 1960.

The Cottesloe Consultation, 1960

The consultation was initiated by the World Council of Churches (WCC) as a result of growing tension within South Africa between the Dutch Reformed Church and the Churches of European Origin (CEO). The WCC was concerned to attempt to heal the divisions among its member churches and assist in reaching a just stance on racial issues. Dr Robert Billheimer, sent by the WCC on a mission of fellowship, stressed the need for interchurch dialogue; he proposed that a meeting be held 'to discuss the churches' responsibility in the time of crisis' (Ryan 1990: 55). The WCC required member churches 'to draw up memoranda on the five points to be read at the very important December meeting' (BPCSA 1960: 20). The points were:

- The factual situation in South Africa;
- Christian understanding of the gospel for relationships among races;
- An understanding of contemporary history from a Christian viewpoint, especially with regard to rapid social change;
- The current emergency and our understanding of it;
- The witness of the Church in respect of justice and co-operation. (WCC 1960)

The BPCSA appointed a group of senior ministers 'to edit and coordinate the memorandum' and elected representatives to attend the conference to be held from 7–14 December 1960; Rt Rev. J. A. Anderson (Moderator), Revs D. V. Sikutshwa (Senior Clerk), B. M. Molaba, W. P. T. Ndibongo, T. P. Finca, J. S. Summers, G. G. Ndzotyana, A. F. Chisolm, D. W. Anderson and C. D. Zulu (BPCSA 1960: 20).

Among the outcomes of the discussions, it was affirmed that:

- All races have equal rights to share in the rights and privileges of their nation;
- No Christians can be excluded from churches on the basis of race;
- There are no scriptural reasons for prohibiting mixed marriages;
- The migrant labour policy is not acceptable;
- Job reservation for white people should be replaced by a more equitable system of employment;
- South Africans have a right to own land within the republic;
- All South Africans have a right to participate in government.

The consultation had a very negative outcome despite the degree of unanimity reached. The participating Dutch Reformed churches rejected the consultation outcomes, thereby nullifying the proposals which emerged from the consultation.

Forced Removals

The Nationalist government's forced resettlement policy instigated another form of forced migration. Between 1960 and 1982, 3,500,000 people were forcibly relocated from their ancestral homes (Davenport 1991: 404). It was punitive, led to enormous deprivation and caused untold losses of various kinds – land, property, wealth (livestock), families, health, traditions and culture. This, of course, affected churches as their members were involved, and caused denominations to follow their members in an attempt to mitigate some of the negative effects. This impacted on the BPCSA far more than the PCSA (in urban areas and on productive land) due to its concentration in the rural areas where resources were poor and limited.

The area to be designated as the Ciskei (south of the Kei River in the Eastern Cape) where the Scottish mission began its work, an area devastated for over a century due to the wars of dispossession and the cattle-killing tragedy, is worthy of some consideration. The Ciskei was described as deprived of 'virtually all the attributes of a viable economy' (The Quail Commission Report, cited in Switzer 1993: 334). Yet it became a 'dumping ground for Xhosa refugees' (Switzer 1993: 336). Migration was the common feature of life in the Ciskei. White farmers and town dwellers left for the metropolitan areas. Farm workers, especially those who were retired, women and children were forced into the reserve. Inhabitants of African locations in the East London metropolitan area were 'consolidated' in Mdantsane (the township near East London, second in size only to Soweto). African refugees from the Herschel and Glen Grey areas were resettled. The Surplus People Project stated that there were at least forty-four resettlement sites in the Ciskei reserve, not including the forced movement of people before the 1970s or those who moved within the reserve (Switzer 1993: 336–7). In the 1980s, forced migration focused on those living outside the Ciskei, especially those who worked in Cape Town. In 1962, the community of Maphuto (Palmiefontein) in the northern Transvaal was forcibly removed to Solomondale (Thema 2021: 38). This affected the BPC community and they built a new church at their resettlement area. All of this negatively affected the church life of the BPCSA. Particular examples are Dimbaza on the outskirts of King William's Town, where Pirie mission extended its work to include an outstation there, and Mgwali:

> A Presbyterian settlement in the 'white corridor' between East London and Queenstown, which occupied land originally given to the Xhosa minister and hymnologist Rev. Tiyo Soga by Sandile, the Xhosa paramount, and kept by the residents as a reward for their loyalty during the cattle-killing of 1857. (Davenport 1991: 405)

Paradoxically, in this punitive migratory progress, only the mission offered some form of positive and palliative migratory progress in the sense of escape from the regular vagaries of war and deprivation.

World Council of Churches (WCC): Programme to Combat Racism

The World Council of Churches Programme to Combat Racism was launched in 1969 in response to a mandate from the Council's Fourth Assembly in Uppsala in 1968, Sweden. In the 1970s and 1980s, the Programme played a highly visible and controversial role in international debate about white-minority rule in Southern Africa. It supported reflection and action among churches in Southern Africa, provided direct humanitarian support to liberation movements, and was a leader in international campaigns for economic disengagement from apartheid. This programme, involving grants made, became a source of intense discussion and action by churches in South Africa.

This was discussed in depth at the 1970 General Assembly of the BPCSA on the basis that grants had been made to:

> certain organisations to aid them combat racism and help the victims of racial injustice in Southern Africa, as well as other parts of the world. The money is given only to be used for educational and medical assistance, although certain, though not all, of the organisations are committed to the use of violence to achieve their ends. No check on the actual use of the money is planned. (BPCSA 1970: 41)

The issue at stake was the use of violence and the concern that funds donated by South African Christians would be used for this purpose. The BPCSA expressed a strong abhorrence to the use of violence since this was the method adopted by the Nationalist government to promote the policy of apartheid, 'which violence has the effect of mocking God through the physical and spiritual violence and indignity done to His children'. (BPCSA 1970: 42)

After thanking the WCC for its support in the past for assistance given to support South Africa and other nations, it resolved to remain a member of the WCC in order that it might continue to contribute to global ecclesiastical debates. Further to this:

> Assembly recommends that the grant for 1971 to the World Council of Churches be held in reserve, pending the opportunity of discussion with representatives of the World Council of Churches and to correspond immediately. (BPCSA 1970: 42)

The BPCSA had refused to compromise its stand on violence even if it meant losing financial support. It would not sacrifice this principle when South Africans had themselves suffered so much violent abuse at the hands of an oppressive government.

Unrest in Universities

University protests provoked a sharp response from the General Assembly in 1972 (BPCSA 1972: 33), instigated by the students at the Federal Theological Seminary (BPCSA 1974: 53). The students regularly provided sanctuary to protesting Fort Hare students and this challenge to the Fort Hare authorities became one of the excuses for the expropriation of FedSem in 1974.The Assembly urged the opening of South African universities to all based on applicants meeting entrance requirements and the avoidance of racially based measures which would provoke the students.

Prelude to States of Emergency: 1985–7

As the situation in the country deteriorated under the increasing encroachment of apartheid policies on the life of South African citizens, the General Assembly of the RPCSA sent an appeal to the State President. In 1984. It challenged the government regarding its legislated separatist policies as a threat to the mission of the church:

> The mission of the church is severely restricted by apartheid laws which affect the movement and deployment of Ministers . . .
>
> In order to satisfy the demands of Apartheid; people are divided White, Coloured, Indian and Black and the Blacks are further divided into ethnic groups; communities especially black communities are forced to move from their land to areas earmarked for them. Such forced removals destroy the communities affected, reduce them to poverty by imposing building programmes they can ill afford, deny them the basic right to settle where they choose to settle; generate bitterness, hatred and insecurity; impose untold suffering and disrupt the work of the church. (RPCSA 1984: 45–6)

It is interesting to note that the Dutch Reformed Church, a church historically renowned for its commitment to mission beyond the borders of South Africa (Saayman 2007: 45–68), should place such restrictions on mission within its borders. The missionary intent of the appeal was clear:

> The Church in terms of the great commission Matt 28:16 is commissioned to preach the gospel to all nations; therefore the apartheid prescription you [Dutch Reformed Church] preach to your own people, is a violation of Christ's commission.
>
> The Church is called upon to proclaim and practise reconciliation. The God who was in Christ reconciling the world to Himself has entrusted unto the Church the same ministry of reconciliation. Apartheid forces Christians to believe its heretical pronouncements that people are irreconcilable. (RPCSA 1984: 45)

The missionary commitment of the RPCSA was to a reconciled community. In this it was to remain committed to one South African society and therefore opposed the homelands policy although this was to become a contentious issue among certain groups even within the BPCSA, e.g. the pro-homelands Chief Kaiser D. Matanzima Transkei National Independence Party supporters (BPCSA 1976: 4). The BPCSA refused to distinguish between peoples, even black peoples.

When states of emergency were instituted, the General Assembly noted: 'with regret that since the introduction of the state of emergency regulations a great number of blacks have been victims of the so-called state of emergency' (RPCSA 1987: 33). Such wording indicated that the General Assembly did not trust the authenticity and integrity of the state of emergency or the government's use of such a mechanism to control the population.

Cumulatively, these responses were part of the General Assembly's repeated 'stand against apartheid as a heresy and the source of violence hatred and oppression in our country' (BPCSA 1984: min. 5886.3). Perhaps the closest the denomination came to actual physical participation in the violence was in the formation of the Standing for the Truth Committee with its remit 'to discuss the witness of the RPC against apartheid and formulate proposals to promote this' (RPCSA 1989: min. 6198) with the further concern that since 'at most of our Assemblies resolutions on the socio-political problems are passed without sufficient knowledge and information hence the reluctance to implement the decisions at grassroots level'. It was agreed that the Social Responsibility Committee should report on the state of the nation annually at General Assembly (BPCSA 1990: min. 6262.1).

The Kairos Document (1986)

It was in this context that the *Kairos Document* (*KD*) (1986) was adopted by the General Assembly of the RPC held at Tiyo Soga Mission in Cape Town in 1986 (cf. RPCSA 1995: 4). The *KD* arose within the scope of work of the Institute for Contextual Theology and was essentially a grassroots project. The *Document* constituted 'a Christian, biblical and theological comment on the political crisis in South Africa today' in a context which they described:

> In June 1985 as the crisis was intensifying in the country, as more and more people were killed, maimed and imprisoned, as one Black township after another revolted against the apartheid regime, as the people refused to be oppressed or to co-operate with oppressors, facing death by the day, and as the apartheid army moved into the townships to rule by the barrel of the gun, a number of theologians who were concerned about the situation expressed the need to reflect on this situation to

determine what response by the Church and by all Christians in South Africa would be most appropriate. (Kairos Theologians 1986: Preface)

There were very few academic theologians in this group. The term refers to those who were reflecting critically on their current situation. The *KD* challenged what it described as State Theology as 'the theological justification of the *status quo* with its racism, capitalism and totalitarianism', (*KD* 1986: 3) and Church Theology: 'this theology is critical of apartheid. Its criticism, however, is superficial and counter-productive because of engaging in an in-depth analysis of the signs of our times, it relies upon a few stock ideas derived from Christian tradition and then uncritically applies them to our situation', (*KD* 1986: 9) and promoted Prophetic Theology which 'concentrates on these aspects of the Word of God that have an immediate bearing upon the critical situation in which we find ourselves. The theology of the prophets does not pretend to be comprehensive and complete, it speaks to the particular circumstances of a particular time and place – the KAIROS' (*KD* 1986: 17). This was a watershed moment for both the churches and the nation. The response of the RPCSA (1986: 27) was brief and clear: 'That Assembly receive the KAIROS DOCUMENT and support it'. This was a natural response from a denomination that was a victim of apartheid. Apart from this response, a number of RPCSA ministers had signed the Document. In general the *KD* received strong support within and beyond South Africa, although it was also 'viciously attacked' by conservative church communities'. However, it provided a stimulus to people's faith and a dimension of mission (*KD* 1986: Preface II). Perhaps the most significant contribution of the *KD* is that it provided a new methodology for people to do theology as they: 'reflect on their own situation. They have begun to criticize the traditional, historical alignment of the Church with Western ideology, institutions and governments' (*KD* 1986: Preface II):

> the Kairos Document had agitated the masses of the black community to mount a titanic struggle against racism and the apartheid policies and the RPC was right in the thick of it because as the 'Bantu Church' it located itself at the centre of the struggle and the suffering of the victims of apartheid and racism. (Finca 2021: 2)

Throughout South Africa, rising protests became common as black Christians mobilised in church, religious and secular organisations. A number of RPC leaders were already playing a pivotal role in the anti-apartheid struggle. One result of this was a raid conducted by the Transkei Security Police in the middle of the night at the Church Offices in Umtata, the residences of RPC ministers, Rev. S. B. Ngcobo (General Secretary) and Rev. G. T. Mcoteli (Youth Organiser), and the manse of Somerville Mission where Rev. B. B. Finca lived. Materials were confiscated and these ministers were detained. The Rev. Chris Nissen, who was a thorn in the flesh in the Northern Transvaal Presbytery, was detained several times. Rev.

D. M. Soga was infamous in the Port Elizabeth region as the revolutionary leader of IDAMASA (the interdenominational ministers' fraternal), at the same time as the Rev. Sam Ngcobo was at the forefront of the Transkei struggle as President of the Transkei Council of Church. Rev. Finca led the onslaught against the Ciskei regime as the President of the Border Council of Churches for ten consecutive terms. Rev. A. N. Maja was detained for a lengthy period in the Transvaal as a regional leader of the Northern Transvaal Council of Churches and leader of the Ecumenical Council in Limpopo (Matlala 2016: 63–8). The men in these positions were vulnerable to vicious attacks and they were all targeted by the Security Police and subjected to untold suffering:

> For the RPC the struggle was not located in the arena of conference resolutions, position papers, delegations and statements. But it was in the praxis of struggle. (Finca 2021: 2)

The Truth and Reconciliation Commission, 1995

> Without confronting the injustices of the past – and going through remorse, reparation, and restoration – reconciliation and transformation is not possible. Reconciliation and unity is not easy. Instead of anger, disillusionment and despair, we need sons and daughters that will prophesy, young men and women that will see visions, and the old men and women that will continue to dream dreams. Genuine unity instead of assimilation is possible, I believe, because God is continuing to give to His people Kairos moments. (Finca 2021: 4)

The Promotion of National Unity and Reconciliation Act, passed in 1995, following the advent of democracy in South Africa, led to the appointment of the Truth and Reconciliation Commission (TRC). An RPCSA minister, Rev. B. B. Finca, was appointed one of the members of the commission. Despite four members of the Commission being Christian ministers, Maluleke (1997: 110, quoting Prof. Dirkie Smit) cautioned that the TRC: 'is after all a juridical and public instrument, not a spiritual and Christian instrument'. The aim was to grant amnesty 'at a price' of full disclosure and to offer a place for victims of human rights abuses to give voice to their trauma with the hope of reparation. Meiring (1999: 378) made it clear that: 'The Truth Commission was not a perfect commission . . . It was an Act of comrpomise'.

The RPCSA made a submission to the TRC. It was prepared and presented by three senior ministers: The Right Rev. Dr G. M. Khabela – Moderator, the Rev. D. M. Soga, the Rev. J. V. Mdlalose – General Secretary. They noted that the formation of their church:

> was a call for the liberation of African people from domination by white people in a white-led church. In the African Church, Africans

would take charge of their destiny and shape their faith in the way suitable to them[selves].

While today, this position may sound as support for the 'Apartheid's Separate Development policy,' at that time it was the most radical thing one could do about the liberation of the African people. The advocates of this position argued that there was no community in South Africa in which black people and white people lived as equals. There was also no culture of worshipping together between Europeans and African converts. (RPCSA 1995: 1–2)

With regard to its participation in the struggle, the RPCSA referred to its ecumenical credentials as its rationale:

The RPC, as a member of the South African Council of Churches (SACC), has acted according to the understanding of the South African political situation by this Body. Like other member churches of the SACC, the RPC has been faithful in its preaching of peace and reconciliation. (RPCSA 1995: 2)

The RPCSA lamented its lack of constructive engagement in the struggle against apartheid as the result of having been inculturated into a culture of:

formalities which were far removed from the hard realities of daily life of its members. The trouble with this kind of religion is that it fails to listen to the cries of the oppressed. It was this kind of abstract Christianity that allowed the apartheid regime to carry on for so many years. For that we also wish to apologise unreservedly. (RPCSA 1995: 3)

With regard to the use of violence, the RPCSA rejected the argument that church leaders and theologians had supported the armed struggle and defended its adoption of a century's old traditional stance:

The church understood violent resistance against apartheid in the light of the 'just war theory.' Broadly, it is because of its understanding of 'a just war' that the church sends or refuses to send chaplains to the armed forces. Specifically, the RPC understood the violence of the military wings of Political Movements in the context of this theory. It was also because of its understanding of 'the just war theory' that the WCC launched its Programme to Combat Racism in the early 1970s. (RPCSA 1995: 3)

It also rejected the mob violence approach and 'condemned "necklacing" and other forms of killings the mob had resorted to' (RPCSA 1995:3).

It confessed and regretted its ambivalent stance as a black denomination whose members were victims of the apartheid system:

Although from time to time, the RPC made public statements condemning human rights violations committed by the apartheid government, it failed to formulate a specific programme of action which reflects a church which is in solidarity with the struggles of the oppressed. Our teaching, preaching and witness did not differ from that of the so-called multi-racial churches. For this we must confess and repent. We did not stand firmly and unashamedly on the side of those who were the victims of apartheid atrocities. We lived with them every day but we did not embrace their struggles as a black church would have done. (RPCSA 1995: 4)

It also referred to the co-option of many of its members into the homelands system either wittingly or unwittingly:

We repent for those who are the members of the RPC who have not had the courage to repent for themselves. We also have to repent for the manner in which we failed to support those who took a position of faith and stood up to oppose the system of apartheid. (RPCSA 1995: 4)

Here was a confession of failure to offer appropriate support to those who suffered for a just cause. The only mitigation offered was that many people's actions, or lack of them, were the result of the effects of propaganda. Yet, 'The response of the RPC to the gross human rights violations caused by the apartheid system grew with the level of awareness' (RPCSA 1995: 4). This was the context in which the decision was taken to terminate the process of sending loyal messages to the State President.

In 1978 the Moderator of the General Assembly, Rt Rev. D. M. Soga declared that a Kairos moment had arrived in South Africa. This marked a change of attitude and action for the RPCSA.

With regard to healing throughout the nation, the RPCSA favoured the development of a theology of reconciliation (RPCSA 1995: 6–7) with a paradigm shift focused on the philosophy of *Ubuntu* – of peaceful harmony in society where the community is the basis on which the individual finds true identity. The submission was clear that what was presented could not be the last word on the matter: 'Last – What is it that we should have said that history will charge us for having omitted?' (RPCSA 1995: 8).

Conclusion

The Truth and Reconcilition Commission presented the RPCSA with an opportunity to review its history in the light of its history of oppression both prior to and after the formation of the BPCSA. The submission of the RPCSA to the TRC, which was historically accurate, honest, frank, humble and moderate, was the culmination of its response to racism and the resulting apartheid system which had been imposed on the nation throughout the twentieth century, first at the hands of the British and from 1948 under the Afrikaner Nationalist Party. Black people had participated in the hegemony of neither of these regimes. Yet, it took responsibility for its actions and lack thereof.

Throughout its existence the BPCSA and RPCSA acted responsibly and with integrity in relation to the struggles of its people in socio-political matters as part of their total commitment to Christ and his mission of reconciliation.

CHAPTER SIXTEEN

Bantu/Reformed Presbyterian Church Women in Leadership in Ministry

Introduction

There are certain issues that disturb the peace and equilibrium of denominations. Most are not of the 'substance of the faith' (*Westminster Confession of Faith* 1645). They are *adiaphora*, inconsequential matters. However, they have the potential to disturb the peace and unity of the church. This, in a way, is strange since, when it comes to the position of women in the church, they have been integral to the faith community since the election of God's people and have, in many and various ways exercised leadership (ministry) though this has often been suppressed in a male-dominated patriarchal environment. While some may consider the ordination of women contrary to scripture, the matter is somewhat outdated for the biblical and theological arguments have been long won in women's favour as in the case of the Bantu/Reformed Presbyterian Church in South(ern) Africa. It must be noted that ordination to the ministry in the Presbyterian tradition includes the ordination of women to the function of ruling elder, in addition to that of teaching elder (minister of word and sacrament). The main focus of this chapter is on the teaching eldership and ordination to the ruling eldership will be discussed where appropriate. It begins with an attempt to understand some of the prejudices against a woman-liberated view of scripture because such continues to be promoted as a rear-guard action against the promotion of women in church leadership. The issue of women in leadership within the non-ordained Women's Christian Association, though no less significant, will be considered in this chapter.

The Hermeneutical Perspective

'Leadership in the Christian church has taken different forms in various periods of history' (Purvis 1995: vii) as the church has responded to threats, challenges and contextual circumstances. Before there was clear evidence of ordination, the roles of men and women in the life of the church appear to have been fluid. Even when theological and biblical objections were overcome, there remained insuperable barriers to actual ordination (Purvis 1995: viii) as the result of 'white male privileged hegemony' (Purvis 1995: xi). It is not possible to discuss the leadership of women in ministry without taking account of the biblical and historical hermeneutics of women's lack of power and authority in terms of what might be described as conservative evangelical or fundamentalistic interpretations which promote the verbal inerrancy of scripture.

The enemy here is Christian fundamentalism which is well described by Purvis (1995: 52) as:

> ... based on a narrow range of theological and ethical convictions that are not to be subjected to intellectual interrogation from other perspectives. It is the perception that when faith and reason are at odds, which they often are, faith wins, even at the cost of anti-intellectualism. It is the perception that lines of human authority are clear, and ideas and convictions come already interpreted and ready to be put into practice without further reflection. It is the perception, at least, that Christian fundamentalism is triumphalistic, inward-looking, intellectually shallow, inappropriately emotive ...

The issue is well articulated as a matter of the authority of scripture by Bellis (1994: 16–20). Presbyterian feminist theologian, Letty Russell (1985: 12), expressed the dilemma when it comes to interpreting the role of women both biblically and historically:

> ... the Bible needs to be liberated from its captivity to one-sided white, middle-class, male interpretation. It needs liberation from privatized and spiritualized interpretations that avoid God's concern for justice, human wholeness and ecological responsibility; it needs liberation from abstract doctrinal interpretations that remove the biblical narrative from its concrete social and political context in order to change it into a timeless truth.

This is problematic for patriarchal fundamentalists who:

> ... say that the preserve cannot be altered; it must be maintained intact. 'Scripture is fixed; you must not change the text. You cannot make it say what it does not say'. This apodictic protest initiates a second theological reflection. A fixed unchangeable text is neither possible nor desirable. For better or worse, be it conscious or unconscious the text is always being changed. Although translators and interpreters readily acknowledge this truth at some levels, they resist its validity at others. Nevertheless, theological warrant for changing the text lies at the heart of scripture and faith – the name of the Holy One. (Trible 1985: 148)

Here the issue is the rigid non-negotiable fundamentalist position which only arose in nineteenth-century USA (Wuthnow 2014: 136–40) which was at odds with the teaching and interpretative approach of the sixteenth-century Reformers who based their interpretation on the hermeneutic of 'let scripture interpret scripture' (Driscoll 2013; UPCSA 2007: 6, 13).

Yet, Russell affirms inclusivity as integral to her hermeneutic:

> There is much to learn about paradigms of authority from communities of oppressed people such as the Black community, whose members listened to the Bible not for doctrinal propositions but for 'experiences which could inspire, convince and lighten'. What is needed is ... the development of new questions and paradigms of authority, which are functional in the communities of struggle wrestling with the biblical text ... *liberation is an ongoing process expressed in the already/ not yet dynamic of God's action in the New Creation.* (Russell 1985: 17) [emphasis in original]

Historical Overview

Long before biblical times, patriarchal society assigned women less status and scripture maintained the already-established status quo. But in the Hebrew Bible, women were used by God in order to further his purpose for his people of Israel by using women in positions of leadership. Deborah was a judge, prophet ('a channel of communication between the human and the divine worlds' [Bronner 1994: 174]) and woman of 'independent power' in ancient Israel 'teaching and leading the people of Israel in a time of crisis' (Bronner 1994: 174) as well as exercising legal, administrative and charismatic military functions (Russell 1985: 84). In the New Testament we note the work of many women; Prisca (Acts 18: 24–6), Lydia (Acts 16: 14–15), Phoebe (a deacon, Rom 16: 1–2), Mary (Luke 1: 46–55), Mary Magdalene (John 20: 18), Martha (John 11: 27), Joanna and Susanna (Luke 8: 3), Junia, Tryphaena and Tryphosa (Rom 16: 121), Julia (Rom 16: 13,15), Nympha (Col 4: 15), Euodia and Syntyche (Phil 4: 2–3) and female prophets were leaders in the New Testament church (1Cor 11: 5); and Philip had four prophetess daughters (Acts 21: 9). This despite Paul's injunction against women speaking in church meetings (which was directed at promiscuous women disturbing the worship of the redeemed community); Acts 1: 12–14, 18: 24–6, 21: 7–9, Romans 16: 1–16). Yet, Paul acknowledged the role of female prophetesses in Corinth. A far more significant innovation of Paul occurs in Galatians 3: 27–8, which relates to the equal status of women and men, all of whom have 'put on' Christ (Corrington 1992: 138) and live 'in Christ'. Here Paul broke loose from patriarchal mores as he forged a new Christian paradigm. In the early church no distinctions were drawn in the ordering of ministry. The only qualifications required related to the possession of gifts (special charisms – teaching, apostolicity, prophecy, evangelism, pastoral care [Eph 4: 11]). Women were elected as deacons (1Tim: 8–13), a position from which they could exercise 'the right to be heard on matters of the Christian faith (1Tim 3: 13). Women took up leadership positions in the Early church, e.g. Priscilla, Quintilla and Maximilla in the Montanist movement (Encyclopædia Britannica sa;

Corrington 1992: 137, 144, 186; Jensen 1996: 14); many, such as Perpetua and Felicitas, were martyrs for their faith (Christian History sa; Corrington 1992: 24).

Then women played a largely unacknowledged role in the Reformation and beyond including Jane Grey, Katherina Von Bora, Elizabeth I of England, Marie Dentière, Katharina Schutz Zell and Ursula von Münsterberg (Holcomb 2015: 1). Later female leaders included the Methodist, Selina, Countess of Huntingdon. This was a natural outcome of Luther's concept of 'the priesthood of all believers'.

Women (though not ordained) played a significant role in the many 'voluntary' societies which took up the challenge of mission before their denominations saw the need to engage in foreign missions. 'Voluntary' indicated 'a concept that does not inhibit their birth and a style of church organisation that is not embarrassed by their activity' (Walls 1996: 225). These societies came into being before denominations took up the cause of world mission and 'outflanked and subverted by this novel form of 'Protestant association' (Walls 1996: 225) whose membership was open and provided an opportunity for lay leadership including 'women's energies and gifts' (Walls 1996: 253). Significant in Scottish mission history is the role played by the Glasgow Missionary Society which operated from the closing years of the eighteenth century (Walls 2002: 206) and was instrumental in the establishment of the mission to South Africa which eventually, in 1923, led to the formation of the Bantu Presbyterian Church in South Africa.

Developments in the original sending church, the Church of Scotland were only a few years in advance of events in South Africa. On Wednesday 22 May 1968, the General Assembly of the Church of Scotland passed a deliverance that women should be eligible for ordination to the Ministry of Word and Sacrament on equal terms with men. The enacting legislation brought to an end decades of campaigning and debate. It opened doors to new opportunities and challenges for women, for congregations – and for a ministry which had for centuries been exclusively male. It changed the face of the national church. After the vote, Mary Levison, who had been prominent in the final years of 'wrestling with the church' for recognition of women's vocation to ordained ministry, commented: 'the Church no longer regards women as second class citizens. I hope this decision will have a liberating effect right through the Church'. In 1970, Rev. Dr Ian Fraser, during a seminar on the ordination of women, asked some still pertinent questions:

> Add a few ordained women to an unreformed ordained ministry and how much further forward are you? . . . all that you have is a face-saving operation. You fail to deal with that godly dissidence and frustration which belong, to my mind, to the Holy Spirit's pressure to reform radically church institutions. It is when the question of the ordination of

women is seen in its total context of reinheriting the whole people of God, and then seen as a dimension of the quest for the reinheriting of the whole of humanity. (CTPI: 1)

Reid is commenting on the resignation of women within their new role rather than the acceptance of the Spirit's challenge to use it as a transforming dynamo within the traditional church institution.

Within the African context, we note the contributions made *inter alia* by Kimpa Vita (Donna Beatrice), Alice Lenshina, Mai Chaza, Gaudencia Aoko, Mwilu Marie Kimbangu (Daneel 1987: 59). In South Africa similar contributions were made by Ma Nku (Daneel 1987: 59), Charlotte Maxeke (Millard 1999: 39–41) and Vehettge Magdalena Tikhuie (Millard 1999: 69–72). All of these aforementioned women were people of independent spirit.

Having established the historical and traditional place and role of women in ministry, we turn to the South African Presbyterian churches.

Dr Jane Waterston: Prototype Presbyterian Woman in Leadership

Jane Waterston (1843–1932) is significant for this study as she was a prototype leader in women's ministry, though never ordained. She arrived at Lovedale, a missionary of the Free Church of Scotland, in 1866 and in 1868 'opened a Girls boarding school with her own vigorous and original personality' (Shepherd 1971: 28). This was the beginning of her strong advocacy for the higher education of women (Bean & van Heyningen 1983: 279–87). In 1880 after having qualified as a medical doctor, she opened a medical department at Lovedale Missionary Institution (Shepherd 1971: 43) and ran both departments concurrently until 1883 (Shepherd 1971: 28, 34, 107, 151,157). In 1879, Waterston went to Livingstonia in Nyasaland (Malawi), but she soon returned to Lovedale having failed to find the degree of acceptance as a woman that would facilitate God's missionary purpose. From 1883, she practised medicine in Cape Town where she lived until her death in 1932. On moving to Cape Town, she left the Scottish mission and joined St Andrew's congregation which became the mother church of the Presbyterian Church of South Africa. Hence, she bridged the gap between the two Scottish branches of South African Presbyterianism. Van Zyl (1985: 6) has aptly described her as 'a remarkable woman – intelligent, courageous, determined, full of energy and committed to serving the Lord'. Bean & van Heyningen (1983: 12) refer to 'her competence [and] ... strength of character' as well as her 'rare determination, courage and intelligence' (Bean & van Heyningen 1983: 11). Waterston made an important contribution to feminist, medical and social development. Together these are significant qualities in the exercise of women's leadership in ministry.

Many other women, black and white, though less dynamic in personality than Waterston, followed in her footsteps and made significant contributions to God's mission in South Africa.

Bantu Presbyterian Church of South Africa (BPCSA)

One of the ecumenical issues raised by Murray (PCSA minister 1973: 11) is that 'the BPC would strongly oppose the ordination of women'. This was patently untrue as subsequent events revealed, although the ordination of women to the eldership is said, from the perspective of twenty-five years later, to have occurred 'only after a heated debate' (UPCSA 2001: 119). From the perspective of the later Gender Issues committee of the UPCSA, RPCSA proposals for equity in Presbytery were 'in advance of anything proposed in the PCSA . . . Unfortunately, however, the rule has not been carried over into the UPCSA, which has thus fallen back from it' (UPCSA 2001: 119).

Charity Majiza was the first woman to be ordained in the BPCSA. She came from Burnshill congregation in the Presbytery of the Ciskei. Her candidature was somewhat of a test case as she went to the Federal Theological Seminary of Southern Africa before any decision had been made, or was even considered, regarding women's ordination. She graduated with the Associateship of the Federal Theological Seminary qualification (a degree equivalent awarded in a context where private institutions at that time were not allowed to confer degrees). The Presbytery of the Ciskei was censured by the General Assembly for proceeding to promote her while there was no provision for the training and ordination of women. Further, she was allowed to remain in training while the General Assembly sent the matter of the ordination of women down to presbyteries under the Barrier Act (BPCSA 1975: 43). The purpose of this act (adopted from the Church of Scotland, 1697; Cox 1976: 385) was to prevent the denomination from making hasty and/or far reaching changes to church law without due consideration and consultation. In the same Assembly, the ordination of women as deacons was approved and that of women as elders sent down to presbyteries under the Barrier Act for discussion.

At the 1976 General Assembly, Majiza's name was forwarded to the Church Extension and Aid Committee for appointment on successful completion of her qualification (BPCSA 1976: 23). The matter of the ordination of lady elders was also raised at this time and Assembly failed to reach a definitive position. Yet, the matter of the training of women as ministers was remitted to presbyteries along with a Training for the Ministry *Memorandum on the Admission of Women into the Ministry*. In 1977, the BPCSA General Assembly took the momentous decision to 'admit women to the offices of elder and minister having the same status as men' (BPCSA 1977: 28).

Majiza was licensed by the Presbytery of the Ciskei on 8 January 1978 (BPCSA 1978: 17), sent to do her probationary period in Gooldville congregation in Venda and was ordained on 13 May 1978 (BPCSA 1978: 17). Venda was often the destination of candidates for the ministry who had challenged the system. However, she did particularly well there in a brief but faithful ministry, and was sent to Scotland in September 1980 to study for the BD degree at Edinburgh University (RPCSA 1979: 20; RPCSA 1980: 24) which she completed in 1983 (RPCSA 1983: 38). While there she, with another BPCSA minister, Rev. Cliff Leeuw who was also a bursar of the Church of Scotland, was threatened by agents of the South African Special Branch regarding statements made at public church meetings. Subsequently, she moved to Australia in 1984, apparently for security reasons where she pursued her ministry (RPCSA 1984: 40). Leeuw confirmed 'Rev. Majiza's fear for her life and her family's safety' (RPCSA 1984: 40). The General Assembly investigated the circumstances of Rev. Majiza'a irregular (i.e. without consultation with the RPCSA) departure to Australia but with little immediate success. The source of the harassment was clearly related to South Africa's apartheid policy against which Scotland's Anti-Apartheid Movement and the Church of Scotland had taken a clear stance in this regard. Missionaries on leave and students from South Africa were expected to speak at meetings on this issue and this included Majiza who was clear in her anti-apartheid position. Even within the church there were informers of the South African authorities and the Consul-General in Scotland spent a great deal of time and energy as an apologist for apartheid (the author took part in a debate with him on Scottish radio in 1988).

For a time, Majiza returned to South Africa with her husband, Graham, who was unable to find work. She was appointed General Secretary of the South Council of Churches in 1998 and was reinstated as a minister of the RPCSA. In 2002, she was appointed a minister in association at St Columba's Parkview (PCSA 2002: 22). Following this, they returned to Australia.

This facilitated the progress of women's ministry in the BPCSA although the next candidate Snowy Maomosi caused significant challenge until she withdrew her candidature. She graduated from FedSem with a Diploma in Theology (PCSA 1980: 170) but did not proceed to ministry.

The next two women candidates, Thokozani Mildred Ngcongo and Nokhalipa Vivienne Nonjojo, who completed their studies in 1988, were placed in congregations. Ngcongo served her entire ministry at Ugie congregation in Umthatha Presbytery until her death in 2015. Nonjojo served at Maclay congregation in Transkei Presbytery (RPCSA 1988: 36) until her resignation in 1998 (RPCSA 1998: 54). In 2004 she became a chaplain in the South African Defence Force (SANDF) (UPCSA 2004: 113) as have a number of others since.

A problematic situation arose in 1995 as the result of the presence of Rev. Sarah Holben from the Presbyterian Church of the USA (PCUSA). Ms Holben had been recruited by Rev. S. P. Xapile to assist in his HIV/Aids project, during a trip to the USA. There was no problem with Holben's sex. The issue was that she was introduced into the RPC irregularly as an 'assistant pastor' (RPCSA 1995: 17). A committee was established to investigate the partnership which existed between Xapile's congregation (J. L. Zwane and the PCUSA (1995: 3). The remit of the committee was later extended to include Holben's husband, Mr Robert Schminkey who was recognised 'as a representative of the PC [USA]' (BPCSA 1995: 65). In the following year, it was noted that Holben's term of office would expire at the end of the year (RPCSA 1996: 76). The growth of partnerships between congregations of the RPCSA and American congregations was formalised in 1997 when the General Assembly agreed 'that the Ecumenical Relations committee coordinates and oversees all partnerships in our church' (RPCSA 1997: 53). Thus, again the issue of women in ministry came to the fore (RPCSA 1997: min. 6676).

The next applications from women came in 1997 from Ms Bulelwa Ngebulana RPCSA 1997: 44). In 1999, she and Mrs Seani Mavhina (RPCSA 1999: 20) were accepted as candidates for the ministry. Several other women were referred to the Ministry Committee for consideration but none proceeded any further.

A matter which was significant in the decision to ordain women was 'the crying need for candidates for the Ministry' (BPCSA 1976: 18). At that time only forty-seven out of seventy-eight congregations had ministers (BPCSA 1976: 2–9). Nonetheless, the decision to ordain women was a courageous, yet pragmatic, step for a conservative black denomination with a strong patriarchal tradition. In a sense, although the ordination of women resulted from an attempt to hijack the system in Majiza's case, once the initial opposition was over, the acceptance of women was easily integrated into the ecclesiastical system. Although the growth of numbers of women in ministry was slow to begin with, numbers have increased progressively and women have become part of the accepted nature of the BPCSA.

Sandra Duncan, wife of Rev. Graham Duncan, studied during the 1980s at FedSem and graduated with distinction. She did not choose to offer for ordination despite considerable pressure from within the RPCSA.

Women's Christian Association (WCA) and Girls' Associations (GA)

The role of women throughout this period is important because of the part they played in the growth of African mission communities – 'In the teeth of opposition, they held on to a distinctive and fervent group solidarity which helped to sustain them in times of personal and communal upheaval' (Gaitskell 1995: 212). While the 1890s–1920s witnessed the 'real beginnings of numerical growth within mission communities' (Gaitskell 1995: 212) as well as secessions fronted by black leaders and pastors:

> The *manyanos* (women's associations) seem to have been part of a more general indigenization of religious initiative, particularly round the turn of the century. Lay movements of various kinds mobilized Africans to evangelise or enthuse their own people for Christianity. (Gaitskell 1995: 212)

Though not normally referred to as a leadership organization, the women's work of the mission and, subsequently, church certainly provided leadership in various ways though without power in the traditional sense of the word. The Women's Christian Association (WCA) was founded in 1893 (RPCSA 1993: 65) before the BPCSA was established. Its original name was the Bantu Presbyterian Women's Association (BPWA). It most likely has its roots in the 'Women's Guild' which was founded in 1887 by the General Assembly of the Church of Scotland on the initiative of Rev. Prof A. H. Charteris. Its aim is to 'to invite and encourage both women and men to commit their lives to Jesus Christ and to enable them to express their faith in worship, prayer, and action' (Wright 1993: men are now permitted to join).

It was a missionary's wife, Mrs Mary Doig, who led the initiative to establish the WCA, (Nzo 2017: 77). Missionary ministers' wives played an active and significant role in the WCA as Presidents of the association. This became their constitutional role. For instance, Mrs Dewar of Pietermaritzburg was the first President of the WCA. The first African President, Mrs Njikelana, was elected in 1936 (BPCSA 1973: 23). Mrs Maureen Summers, wife of Rev. John Summers, Principal of St Columba's College and President of the Federal Theological Seminary, was the national President. The associations expressed the indigenous face of the BPCSA especially in their forms of worship which were more attuned to the heart than to the intellect. Their worship indicated their pastoral concern and provided one way of enacting it. They led pastoral work, especially in times of crisis, such as bereavement, providing financial and spiritual help besides a ministry of presence. As a response to the plight of ministers' widows they established what was virtually a pension fund for them (BPCSA 1973: 24). They also contributed generously to church projects. This was a field where indigenous agency extended the mission of the church, beyond missionary control and influence. It demonstrated that indigenous peoples could work independently of missionary control.

The BPCSA WCA regularly reported on 'how the progress of the Kingdom of God could be furthered'. This was a missionary purpose consistent with the church's Constitution (BPCSA 1924: 55, (§VII) and became the prime focus of the WCA. The WCA conference held their annual meeting during the sitting of the General Assembly and the women were received at the closing sessions where they always brought contributions, *Isipo Somanyano*, for specific church projects (e.g. BPCSA 1924: 32), for example, the minster's pension fund and theological education. Although this was a distinctive African form of association, more so as it developed, missionaries' wives played a leading part in its witness. In time, a close and almost symbiotic link developed between the WCA and the General Assembly.

The women's association took an active interest in the mission work within the Zoutspansberg area of the Transvaal (BPCSA 1937: 64). Work grew steadily and this can be seen from the formation of a branch at Gordon Memorial mission, Natal in 1924 (BPCSA 1924: 53). An interesting decision is recorded in 1927 regarding uniforms, a subject of much historical debate which has hampered the work of mission: 'It was agreed that the WA brooch should be recognised as the only outward sign of the Association Membership and that uniforms be discouraged' (BPCSA 1927: 38). As time progressed, the wearing of distinctive black and white uniforms became the norm.

The WCA was committed to the support of the leper colony at Emjanyana (BPCSA 1930: 56), as was the General Assembly, as part of their missionary outreach.

In 1944 the WCA established a Bible Training Fund to enable women to undertake the course for the training of Bible women (BPCSA 1944: 20) who itinerate from village to village in rural areaas to teach Bible lessons and pray with the people. This was for women 'with Christian ideals and who ha[ve] shown interest in Church activities' (BPCSA 1944: 25). The centre for training was the Lovedale Bible School.

The WCA further developed this work among young women in the church by establishing a Girl's Association in 1954 (BPCSA 1937: 65). The GA was considered a preparation for membership in the WCA. Girls, as defined, here meant unmarried women and some women who did not marry retained their 'girls' status throughout their lives. The aims and objectives of the GA were similar to those of the WCA. The 1971 report (BPCSA 1971: 54–70), *Bantu Presbyterian Church of South Africa: Origin and progress*. In a section headed *Workers and their achievements: Minister and Elders* paid tribute to the sterling work of mission pursued by the WCA and the Girls' Association (GA) (1923–70).

In the BPCSA, gender issues were concerned with the role and place of women. A notable Presbyterian, Rev. Dr R. H. W. Shepherd, made the following comment on the role of women in the church:

> ... women make up the greater part of Christian congregations. Taking all in all women have been more devout believers in Jesus than men, and have followed their Master with a simpler faith. They have often a clearer vision of God. That may be simply due to the fact that women are not so coarse in thought as men. (quoted in Oosthuisen 1970: 125)

Despite earlier moves to include women in the eldership and ministry of the church (see Duncan 2019b: 4–6), it was decided that they were to be included in the representatives at presbytery, general assembly and assembly committee levels (RPCSA 1997: 63). To facilitate this process awareness workshops were to be held.

The WCA throughout South Africa was proactive in socio-political matters:

> From the 1950s, social and political pressures compelled religious organizations, including the *manyano*, to shift from a revivalist

emphasis to an emphasis of social protest. The *Asikweli* ('we will not enter') bus strike in 1953, and the Sharpeville tragedy of 1961 [sic 1960] gave new direction to the message of the *manyano*. (Sundkler & Steed 2000: 832)

Sundkler and Steed (2000: 821–2) further noted that the *manyano* were involved in political protests which:

> ... in the cities and to some extent in the countryrside soon took on sweeping dimensions ... The *manyano* women in their colourful uniforms participated and accompanied [African National] Congress speeches with hymn-singing. Later, they attended their own nightly church services with prayers for the success of the political campaign.

Despite all these different interests, the mainstay of the *manyano* women remains their Thursday afternoon prayer meetings which focus on worship prayer and preaching with a strong pastoral concern on mutual self-help. This is their lifeblood.

Evaluation

These women pastors do what people expect them to do as women *and* as pastors. They do not deny the conventional expectations people have of them as women, *and* they do not disrupt conventional wisdom about the power and authority of effective pastoral leadership. They live comfortably with both, even though a 'feminine female is supposed to be commensurate with, if not oppositional to, strong organisational and political leadership abilities':

> By embodying roles our social scripts say cannot be played by one person and roles that involve socialization processes that may be contradictory [referring to Jacquet 1978, 1989], they actually profoundly challenge unexamined assumptions about both women and clergy. In short, they *are* the best 'men' for the job and they *are women*. (Zikmund 1995: xi–xii)

Zikmund competently expresses the experience of most church members regarding ordained women ministers in the USA – that women appear to integrate seamlessly into the existing discourse without disrupting it, yet they unobtrusively promote their cause by the excellence of their commitment and service. However, Zikmund's assessment rings true also within the South African Presbyterian system.

> ... their leadership styles cannot be characterized along the lines of gender expectations, and yet, what they exceptionally are is conventional. They transgress neither vocational roles nor gender; they fulfil both. The combination is transgressive. (Purvis 1995: 85)

This combination crosses boundaries. By and large, the leadership of women ministers is not based on gender expectations. It is exceptionally conventional. Yet, it is not 'simply reinscribing patriarchal power and control' (Purvis 1995: 97). It goes beyond it.

The experience of having women in leadership in South African Presbyterianism is a positive one. The excellence of their faithfulness, responsibility and service is unchallenged. Once the ordination issue was resolved, they have simply got on with the job and pursued their calling and by the quality of their service they have demonstrated the delayed insight of the General Assembly in advocating for them to be ordained.

The fear, expressed in Murray's (1973: 10) paper that women would 'take over and completely feminise the institution' has not happened in the RPCSA context, nor in any other case globally. However, we may concur with Purvis' (1995: 96–7) assessment as a future prospective in the South African context regarding the embodiment by female pastors of traditional roles in ways that challenge tradition and are transgressive of gender expectations who:

> are part of a quiet revolution. They are not espousing or practicing radical social change; . . . on the one hand, self-consciously or not, . . . women . . . are not simply reinscribing patriarchal power and control. The transgressive role of traditional roles here is a subtle and effective agent of change. The ability . . . to live in the midst of incommensurate discourses and to continue to function so effectively in all of them, hold forth the promise of new discourses, even with some of the same old vocabulary.

In addition, the lay leadership expressed through the life and work of the *manyano* made a significant contribution to the development of the BPCSA through their distinctive form of evangelism blended with pastoral care both spiritual and material.

The experience of having women in leadership in ministry in South African Presbyterianism has been a positive one at all levels of the denominations involved. Now women are rarely referred to separately in terms of leadership in ministry. This has been a story of progressive integration as leadership was expanded and developed to all aspects of the denominations' lives. An integrated ministry has served the church well and will continue to do so into the future.

Conclusion: Indigenous Presbyterians and Missionaries – Transferring Contending Roles and Responsibilities

The Bantu Presbyterian Church of South Africa (BPCSA) was the first denomination to be formed as a result of the work of a foreign mission in South Africa that did not secede as a protest against various forms of oppression suffered at the hands of missionaries. Its gestation period was over 100 years but these were years of intense activity and faithfulness on the part of both missionaries and indigenous people. Historically, much more credit has been given to the missionaries than to the indigenous Christians and their PR model worked well in their favour to secure the funds that were required to promote and further their work among indigenous South African peoples.

It is impossible to write such a history without taking account of the secular context for the secular and sacred are integrated in real life. This is nowhere more true than in South Africa where one expression of Christianity both legitimised and promoted a heretical secular ideology, apartheid, while another focused on its essentially humanitarian nature; both of which views drew on scripture for support. One Christianised dimension of this coexistence of the sacred and the profane was the extension of evangelisation to include education, medical mission, agriculture and industrial education in the mission institutions as a means of both educating and maintaining peace among the indigenous people (as in Sir George Grey's reforms in the 1850s). This led to the coalition of colonialism, Christianisation, commercialism, civilisation and conciliation of the local population in different combinations at different periods and for different lengths of time. The missionaries were involved in all of these activities.

The missionaries arrived in South Africa during a troubled time, distinguished and characterised by racism, and had to struggle through and survive the 100 years Wars of Dispossession and the horrendous impact of the cattle-killing tragedy within a population which was under constant political, cultural and economic and social pressure. This continued into the twentieth century following the trauma of the South African War (1899–1902), leading to the formation of the Union in 1910, where the hopes and aspirations of black people were betrayed in favour of the appeasement of the Afrikaans people. This gave way in 1948 to the introduction of institutionalised racism in the form of apartheid when the

National Party came to power and continued until the birth of democracy in 1994.

Throughout this history, in common with most Christian denominations, the role of women has been consistent and supportive in a number of ways – spiritually, financially and evangelically, leading in time to their full recognition within the courts of the church and in its ordained ministry.

The missionaries did sterling work and made great sacrifices of themselves and their family members. Yet, despite their significant contribution to global mission, they produced paradoxical responses of conformity and resistance. This was largely the result of mission education. Some responded to this education by faithful conformity; others resisted, also through faithfulness, though not in accord with the missionaries' wishes or aspirations. Nonetheless, the mission was established and developed, leading in time to the formation of the BPCSA as an autonomous denomination. From there it continued to grow, still with the sometimes frustrating presence of missionaries until the 1980s. The missionary presence, particularly evident in the Mission Councils, both promoted and hindered the growth and development of their missionary intentions. Strangely, there was no resistance movement against the appointment of missionaries and most of those appointed were encouraged to remain so long as they wished. In one case, two mission partners were recalled for service within the RPCSA.

Historically, union was always a vexed issue which was complicated by the racial situation in the country. The PCSA had difficulty in accepting the maturity of black Presbyterian Christians as is seen in their separate missions policies for blacks and whites which kept black Presbyterian Christians in a subservient and dependent relationship to their sponsoring white congregations. While the church had an opportunity to express in word and action what it meant to be the body of Christ, it chose to follow the pattern of this world and support segregation either in action or by silence, while only a few challenged the status quo and often suffered for it.

It was this mature denomination that, having engaged in ecumenical relations with a number of other denominations during all of its life, following the advent of democracy in South Africa in 1994, approached the Presbyterian Church of Southern Africa with a view to union. In 1996, the General Assembly accepted the principle of union with the PCSA (RPCSA 1996: 59). The Draft Basis of Union was agreed in 1997 and from this time much missional energy was devoted to securing the union which was consummated on 26 September 1999 in Port Elizabeth.

All of the negative assessments of the BPCSA are premised on white understandings and interpretations of what constitutes church. Many assumed that the church in Africa should be a replica of the church in Scotland. In many ways this view has been perpetuated and even the emergence of a black theology of liberation, as can be seen in the incisive work of the late Prof Vuyani Vellem of the University of Pretoria and the University of South Africa (UNISA) and Dr Fundiswa Kobo of UNISA (Kobo 2018a, 2018b), has been eschewed by many black ministers.

In sum, despite all the vicissitudes endured by the BPCSA/RPCSA throughout the nineteenth and twentieth centuries, the 'Native experiment' has proved to be 'a triumph of realism' (Duncan 1997: 167).

Bibliography

African National Congress n.d., *A brief history of the African National Congress*, http://www.anc.org.za/show.php?id=206 (last accessed 13 May 2014).

Allen, R. (1962), *Missionary methods: St Paul's or ours?* Grand Rapids: Eerdmans.

Ashcroft to Lennox, 29 September 1914, file 'Synod' 1914–16, Lennox papers, Box F76–83, National Heritage and Cultural Studies (NAHECS), University of Fort Hare.

Ashcroft, F. and Houston, A. (1920), Report of Deputies, Edinburgh: Free Church of Scotland, 21 December 1920, PR3983, appendix 1:5, Cory Library for Historical Research, Rhodes University, Grahamstown.

Ashley, M. (1980), 'Universes in collision: A study of nineteenth century education in South Africa', *Journal of Theology for Southern Africa* 38 (March): 49–58.

Assembly of Divines (1646) [1995], *The Westminster Confession of Faith*, Glasgow: Free Presbyterian Publications.

Balia, D. M. (1991), *Black Methodists and white supremacy in South Africa*, Durban: Madiba.

Balia, D. M. (1994), 'New independent Methodist movements in Southern Africa', in Oosthuizen, G. C., Kitshoff, M. C. and Dube, S. W. D. (eds), *Afro-Christianity at the Grassroots*, Leiden: Brill: 23–36.

Bantu Presbyterian Church of South Africa 1923, 1925, 1928, 1930–1, 1931–2, 1934, 1935, 1936, 1937, 1938, 1939, 1940, 1944, 1948, 1952, 1954, 1958, 1959, 1960, 1971, 1972–9, 1980, 1984,1988, 1995, 1996, 1997, *Proceedings of the General Assembly, Incwadi yamaculo amaXhosa (Ehlaziyiwo): Egunyasiswe ngamabandla aseRhabe*, Lovedale: Lovedale Press.

Bantu Presbyterian Church of South Africa (1929), *Incwadi yamaculo AmaXhosa (Ehlaziyiweyo)*, Lovedale: Lovedale Press.

Bantu Presbyterian Church of South Africa (1957), Young Men's Christian Guild, *Imithetho yoMthandazo neNtlanganiso*, Lovedale: Lovedale Press.

Bantu Presbyterian Church of South Africa (1958), *Manual of the Bantu Presbyterian Church*, Lovedale: Lovedale Press.

Bantu Presbyterian Church of South Africa, Archives, Cory Library for Historical Research.

Bantu Presbyterian Church of South Africa (1958), *Manual of law, practice and procedure in the Bantu Presbyterian Church of South Africa (renamed) Reformed Presbyterian Church of South Africa*, Lovedale: Lovedale Press.

Bantu Presbyterian Church of South Africa (1971), *Souvenir programme*, Lovedale: Lovedale Press.

Bate, S. C. (2000), 'Points of contradiction: Money, the Catholic Church and a settler culture in Southern Africa, 1837–1920, Part I: The leaders of the mission', *Studia Historiae Ecclesticae* XXVI (no. 1): 135–64.

Bate, S. C. (2003), 'Creating a missionary vicariate: Economics in Catholic missionary culture, Part II: The economics of a new vicariate in Roman curial culture', *Studia Historiae Ecclesticae* XXIX (no. 1, June): 1–35.

Baur, J. (1994), *2000 years of Christianity in Africa*, Nairobi: Paulines Publications Africa.

Bax, D. S. (1997), *The Presbyterian Church of Southern Africa*, Johannesburg: PCSA.

Bean, L. and van Heyningen, E. (eds) (1983), *The letters of Jane Elizabeth Waterson, 1866–1905*, Cape Town: Van Riekeeck Society.

Beinart, W. (1994), *Twentieth-century South Africa*, Oxford: Oxford University Press.

Bellis, A. O. (1994), *Helpmates, harlots and heroes: Women's stories in the Hebrew Bible*, Louisville: Westminster/John Knox Press.

Best, T. (1992), *Living today towards visible unity: Faith and Order paper no. 142*, Geneva: World Council of Churches.

Betz, H. D. (1979), *Galatians*, Philadelphia: Fortress.

Black Community Project (BCP) (1976), *Transkei Independence*, Durban: Black Community Project.

Boegner, M. (1970), *The long road to unity: Memories and anticipations*, London: Collins.

Bosch, D. J. (1991, 2011), *Transforming mission: paradigm shifts in mission theology*, Maryknoll: Orbis.

Bredekamp, H. and Ross, R. (eds) (1995), *Missions and Christianity in South African history*, Johannesburg: Witwatersrand University Press.

Bridgman, F. B. (1903), 'The Ethiopian Movement and other independent factions characterised by a national spirit', paper read at the Natal Missionary Conference, *Christian Express* XXXIII (October: 150–2, November: 166–8).

Brock, S. M. (1974), 'James Stewart and Lovedale: A reappraisal of missionary attitudes and African response in the Eastern Cape, South Africa, 1870–1905', PhD thesis, Edinburgh: University of Edinburgh.

Bronner, L. L. (1994), *From Eve to Esther: Rabbinic reconstructions of biblical women*, Louisville: Westminster/John Knox Press.

Burchell, D. E. (1977), 'The origins of the Bantu Presbyterian Church of South Africa', *South African Historical Journal* 9: 39–58.

Burchell, D. E. (1979), A History of the Lovedale Missionary Institution, 1890–1930, MA dissertation, Natal University, Pietermaritzburg.

Burleigh, J. H. S. (1960), *A Church history of Scotland*, London: Oxford University Press.

Calvin, J. (1552), Letter XVII to Thomas Cranmer, Archbishop of Canterbury, retrieved from: http://reformationanglicanism.blogspot.co.za/2010/12/letter-xviicalvin-to-cranmer-archbishop.html (last accessed 21 November 2016).
Centre for Theology and Public Issues and New College, University of Edinburgh (CTPI) 2018, Commemorating 50 years of women's ordination in the Church of Scotland.
Cheyne, A. C. (1993), *The Ten Years' Conflict: the Disruption, an overview*, Edinburgh: Scottish Academic Press.
Christian Express (1898–1902), Lovedale: Lovedale Press.
Christian History sa. Perpetua: High society believer, http://www.christianitytoday.com/history/people/martyrs/perpetua.html (last accessed 5 March 2018).
Church of Scotland 1935, 1947, 1951, 1952, 1957, 1963, 1976, 1977, 1978, *General Assembly*, Edinburgh: Board of Practice and Procedure.
Church of Scotland (1969), *Westminster Confession of Faith (1647)*, Edinburgh: Blackwood.
Church of Scotland South African Joint Council (1971–81), Minutes of Council and Executive Committee, July 1972–May 1981, Grahamstown, Rhodes University, Cory Library for Historical Research (uncatalogued).
Claasen, J. W. (1995), 'Independents made dependents', *Journal of Theology for Southern Africa* 95: 15–34.
Cochrane, A. C. (1966), *Reformed confessions of the 16th century*, Westminster: Philadelphia.
Cochrane, J. R. (1987), *Servants of power: The role of the English-speaking churches in South Africa, 1906–1930*, Johannesburg: Ravan.
Coleman, S. and Elsner, J. (1995), *Pilgrimage Past and Present in the World Religions*, Cambridge, MA: Harvard University Press.
Comaroff, J. and Comaroff, J. (1991, 1997), *Of revelation and revolution: The dialectics of modernity on a South African frontier*, Chicago: University of Chicago Press.
Commission on Union, 6 February 192, Box 12, F91–100, NAHECS, University of Fort Hare.
Corrington, G. P. (1992), *Her image of salvation: Female saviors and formative Christianity*, Louisville: Westminster Press.
Council for World Mission (1999), *Inside Out*, no. 9:11.
Cowan & Dalmahoy to Simpson & Marwick, 3 June 1909, in file 'Synod 1909', Lennox correspondence, NAHECS, University of Fort Hare.
Cox, J. T. (1976), *Practice and procedure in the Church of Scotland*, Edinburgh: Committee on General Administration, Church of Scotland.
Cragg, G. R. (1960), *The Church and the Age of Reason, 1648–1789*, Harmondsworth: Penguin.
Cuthbertson, G. C. and Quinn, F. (1979), *Presbyterianism in Cape Town*, Cape Town, St Andrew's Church.

Cutthbertson, G. C. (1990), *Presbyterians in Pretoria*, Pretoria: St Andrew's Presbyterian Church.

Cuthbertson, G. C. (1991), '"Cave of Adullam": Missionary Reaction to Ethiopianism at Lovedale, 1898–1902', *Missionalia* 19, 1 April: 57–64.

Daneel, M. L. (1987), *Quest for belonging: Introduction to a study on African Independent Churches*, Gweru: Mambo Press.

Davenport, T. R. H. (1991), *South Africa: A modern history*, London: Macmillan.

De Gruchy, J. W. (1997), 'Grappling with a colonial heritage: The English-speaking churches under imperialism and apartheid', in Elphick, R. and Davenport, R. (eds), *Christianity in South Africa: A political, social and cultural history*, Cape Town: David Philip: 155–72.

De Gruchy, J. W. and de Gruchy, S. (2005), *The Church struggle in South Africa: 25th anniversary edition*, Minneapolis: Fortress.

De Gruchy, J. W. (2009), *Christianity and the modernisation of South Africa: A documentary history*, vol. II, Pretoria, UNISA Press.

De Villiers, J. H. G. (2011), *Presbyterians on the Koonap: 150th anniversary of the Church, 1861–2–11*, Adelaide: Moderator and Session.

Denis, P. and Duncan, G. A. (2011), *The native school that caused all the trouble: A history of the Federal Theological Seminary of Southern Africa*, Pietermaritzburg: Cluster.

Denis, P. (ed.) (1995), *The making of an indigenous clergy in southern Africa*, Pietermaritzburg: Cluster.

Devine, T. (2011), *To the ends of the Earth: Scotland's global diaspora*, London: Penguin.

Dewar, J. (1923), Committee on Creed and formula, Lennox papers, Box 12, F 91–100, NAHECS, University of Fort Hare, Plan of Union of the UFCoS, section on Administration of Missions, para, 6; minute 41,2(a) of General Assembly, Bantu Presbyterian Church of South Africa.

Donaldson, M. (1985), 'Missionaries and the Liberation of Women', *Journal of Theology for Southern Africa* 53, December (1985): 1–12.

Donaldson, M. (1990), 'History matters', *Presbyterian Life*, April: 7.

Dougall, J. W. C. (1963), *Christians in the African revolution*, Edinburgh: Saint Andrew Press.

Drummond, A. L. and Bulloch, J. (1975), *The Church in Victorian Scotland, 1843–1874*, Edinburgh: Saint Andrew Press.

Drummond, R. J. (1950), 'The significance of the United Presbyterian Church', *Scottish Church History Society*: 1–7.

Du Plessis, J. (1911), *A history of Christian missions in South Africa*, London: Longmans Green.

Duncan, G. A. (1997), Scottish Presbyterian Church Mission Policy in South Africa, 1898–1923, MTh dissertation, Pretoria: University of South Africa.

Duncan, G. A. (2002), 'The Reformed Presbyterian Church in Southern Africa – heritage and legacy', in Coertzen, P. (ed.), *350 years reformed*, Stellenbosch: CLF.

Duncan, G. A. (2003a), '350 years Reformed in South Africa: The contribution of the Reformed Presbyterian Church in Southern Africa', *HTS Teologiese Studies/Theological Studies* 59(1): 47–64.

Duncan, G. A. (2003b), '"Coercive agency": James Henderson's Lovedale, 1906–30', DTh thesis, Pretoria: UNISA Press.

Duncan, G. A. (2003c), *Lovedale – coercive agency: Power and resistance in mission education*, Pietermaritzburg: Cluster.

Duncan, G. A. (2004), 'Its end foreshadowed in its beginning: The closure of the Federal Theological Seminary', *Studiae Historiae Ecclesiasticae* XXX(1): 1–31.

Duncan, G. A. (2005), 'Historiography and ideology in the (mission) history of Christianity in South Africa', *Studia Historiae Ecclesiasticae* XXXI (1 June): 51–69.

Duncan, G. A. (2008), *Partnership in mission: A critical historical evaluation of the relationship between 'older' and 'younger' churches with special reference to the Church of Scotland*, Saarbrucken: VDM Dr Muller Verlag.

Duncan, G. A. (2012a), '"Pull up a good tree and push it outside"? The Rev. Edward Tsewu's dispute with the Free Church of Scotland Mission', *NGTT* 53 (1 & 2, March & June): 50–61.

Duncan, G. A. (2012b), 'The role of mission councils in the Scottish Mission in South Africa, 1864–1923', *Studia Historae Ecclesiasticae* XXXVIII (1 May): 217–34.

Duncan, G. A. (2013a), 'The origins and early development of Scottish Presbyterian mission in South Africa (1824–1865)', *Studia Historiae Ecclesiasticae* XXXIX (1 May): 205–20.

Duncan, G. A. (2013b), '"African churches willing to pay their own bills": The role of money in the formation of Ethiopian-type churches with particular reference to the Mzimba Secession', *African Historical Review* 45(2): 52–79.

Duncan, G. A. (2016a), 'Mission Councils: a self-perpetuating anachronism (1923–1971): A South African case study', *Studia Historiae Ecclesiasticae*, DOI: http://dx.doi.org/10.17159/2412-4265/2016/1315.

Duncan, G. A. (2016b), 'The formation of the Bantu Presbyterian Church of South Africa', *International Journal of African Historical Studies* 49(3): 329–60.

Duncan, G. A. (2016c), 'The migratory dimension of Scottish Presbyterianism in Southern Africa', *African Historical Review*, DOI.1080/17532523.2015.1130203: 85–114.

Duncan, G. A. (2017), 'To unite or not to unite? That is the question: A case study of Presbyterianism in South Africa, 1897–1923', *Acta Theologica* 2018 38(1): 37–60.

Duncan, G. A. (2018a), 'Tiyo Soga (1829–1871) at the intersection of "universes in collision"', *HTS Teologiese Studies/Theological Studies* 74(1): 4862.

Duncan, G. A. (2018b), 'Mission to Church – Church to mission?: The Bantu Presbyterian Church of South Africa: The first ten years, 1923–1933', *Missionalia* 46(3).

Duncan, G. A. (2019a), 'The Bantu Presbyterian Church in South Africa and Ecumenism, 1940–1999', *HTS Teologiese Studies/Theological Studies* 75(4).

Duncan, G. A. (2019b), 'South African Presbyterian women in leadership in ministry (1973–2018)', *HTS Teologiese Studies/Theological Studies* 75(1).

Dwane, S. (1989), *God, religion and culture: The idea of revelation and its consequences*, Lovedale: Lovedale Press.

Dwane, S. (1999), *Ethiopianism and the Order of Ethiopia*, Glosderry: Ethiopian Episcopal Church.

Elphick, R. and Davenport, R. (eds) (1997), *Christianity in South Africa: A political, social and cultural history*, Cape Town: David Philip.

Elphick, R. (1995), 'Writing religion into history: the case of South African Christianity', in Bredekamp, H. and Ross, R. (eds), *Missions and Christianity in South African History*, Johannesburg: Witwatersrand University Press: 11–26.

Elphick, R. (2012), *The equality of believers: Protestant missions and the racial politics of South Africa*, Pietermaritzburg: University of KwaZulu-Natal Press.

Encyclopædia Britannica sa. Montanism, https://www.britannica.com/topic/Montanism (last accessed 5 March 2018).

Erlank, N. (2001), '"Civilising the African": The Scottish mission to the Xhosa', in Stanley, B (ed.), *Christian missions and the Enlightenment*, Grand Rapids: Eerdmans: 141–68.

Etherington, N. (1979), 'The historical sociology of Independent churches in South East Africa', *Journal of Religion in Africa*, 10 (no. 2).

Farrell, B. (2011), 'Perspective 1', in Kim, K. and Anderson, A. (eds), *Edinburgh 2010: Mission today and tomorrow*, Oxford: Regnum: 69–72.

Finca, B. B. (2021), correspondence with author.

Foreign Mission Committee, Free Church of Scotland, Minutes, National Library of Scotland, Edinburgh (Cory PR 3983).

Free Church of Scotland n.d., *Free Church of Scotland*: Edinburgh, https://freechurch.org/about/history (last accessed 8 June 2021).

Friedman, S. (2014), 'The ambiguous legacy of liberalism: Less a theory of society, more a state of mind?', in Vale, P., Hamilton, L. and Prinsloo, E. (eds), *Intellectual traditions in South Africa: Ideas, individuals and institutions*, Pietermaritzburg: University of KwaZulu-Natal Press: 29–50.

Gaitskell, D. (1995), '"Praying and preaching": the distinctive spirituality of African women's church organizations', in Bredekamp, H. and Ross, R. (eds), *Missions and Christianity in South African History*, Johannesburg: Witwatersrand University Press: 211–32.

Glen Thorn Presbyterian Church (1990), *Tercentenary: Celebrating 150 years at the Glenthorn Presbyterian Church*, Adelaide: Moderator and Session.

Hanciles, J. J. (2008), 'Migration and mission: the religious significance of the North-South divide', in Walls, A. F. and Ross, C. (eds), *Mission in the 21st century: Exploring the five marks of global mission*, London: Darton, Longman & Todd: 118–29.

Hancock, K. (1968), *Smuts: The fields of force, 1919–1950, vol. 2*, Cambridge: Cambridge University Press.

Hastings, A. (1979), *A History of African Christianity, 1950–1975*, Cambridge: Cambridge University Press.

Henderson, J., Papers, Cory Library for Historical Research, Rhodes University, Grahamstown.

Henderson, J. (1902), 'Our Missions in South Africa', MS 14849, 1–2, Cory Library for Historical Research, Rhodes University, Grahamstown.

Henderson to Lennox, 7 April 1909, in file 'Synod 1909', Lennox correspondence, NAHECS, University of Fort Hare.

Lennox to Oldham, 11 December 1922, 'Personal 1919–1922', Lennox correspondence, Box 218–224, NAHECS, University of Fort Hare.

Hewat, E. G. K. (1960), *Vision and Achievement, 1796–1956: A history of the foreign missions of the churches united in the Church of Scotland*, London: Thomas Nelson & Sons.

Hinchliff, P. (1966), *The Church in South Africa*, London: SPCK.

Hobsbawm, E. (1962), *The Age of Revolution: Europe 1748–1848*, London: Abacus.

Hobsbawm, E. (1994), *Age of Extremes: The short twentieth century, 1914–1991*, London: Abacus.

Hofmeyer, J. W. and Pillay, G. J. (eds) (1994), *A history of Christianity in South Africa, vol. 1*, Pretoria: Haum Tertiary.

Holcomb, J. (2014), 'Influential women of the Reformation', https://www.christianity.com/church/church-history/influential-women-of-the-reformation.html (last accessed 5 March 2018).

Hunter, C. F. D. (1983), 'Some aspects of the African mission policy of the Presbytery of Adelaide/Port Elizabeth with special reference to the origin and development of the New Brighton Mission Church, 1898–1962', PhD thesis, Grahamstown: Rhodes University.

Hyam, R. and Henshaw, P. (1993), *The lion and the springbok: Britain and South Africa since the Boer War*, Cambridge: Cambridge University Press.

Imvo Zabantsundu [IZ] (1923), 7 August.

International Missionary Council (IMC) (1939), *The world mission of the church: Findings and recommendations of the meeting of the International Missionary Council, Tambaram, India, Dec. 12–19, 1938*, London: IMC.

International Missionary Council (1952), *The missionary obligation of the Church, Willingen, Germany*, London: Edinburgh House Press.

Isichei, E. (1995), *A History of Christianity in Africa: From Antiquity to the Present*, London: SPCK.
Jacquet, C. H. Jr (1978), 'Women ministers in 1977', a report of the Office of Research, Evaluation and Planning, New York: National Council of Churches.
Jacquet, C. H. Jr (1989), 'Women ministers in 1986 and 1977, a ten-year view', *Yearbook of American and Canadian Churches*.
Jafta, D. N. (1971), 'The impact and development of literature on the Xhosa people', in Pahl, H. W., Jafta, D. N. and Jolobe, J. J. R. (eds), *Xhosa literature: Its past and future*, Lovedale: Lovedale Press.
Jensen, A. (1996), *God's self-confident daughters: Early Christianity and the liberation of women*, Louisville: Westminster Press.
Kaffir Express, June 1871, UNISA Press.
Kairos Theologians (1986), *The Kairos Document: Challenge to the Church*, Johannesburg: Skotaville.
Kalu, O. U. (ed.) (2005), *African Christianity: An African story*, Pretoria, Department of Church History, University of Pretoria.
Kalu, O. U. (1981), 'Doing church history in Africa today', in Vischer, L. (ed.), *Church History in ecumenical perspective*, Papers and Reports of an International Ecumenical Consultation held in Basle, October 12–17: 77–91.
Kamphausen, E. (1995), 'Unknown heroes: The founding fathers of the Ethiopian Movement in South Africa', in Denis, P. (ed.), *The making of the indigenous clergy in Southern Africa*, Pietermaritzburg: Cluster Publications: 83–100.
Kidd, B. (1894), *Social evolution*, London: Macmillan & Co.
Kim, K. and Anderson, A. (eds), *Edinburgh 2010: Mission today and tomorrow*, Oxford: Regnum.
Kobo, F. A. (2018a), 'A womanist exposition of pseudo-spirituality and the cry of an oppressed African woman', *HTS Teologiese Studies/Theological Studies* 74(1), 4896, https://doi.org/ 10.4102/hts.v74i1.4896.
Kobo, F. A. (2018b), 'Black women's bodies as reformers from the dungeons: The Reformation and womanism', *HTS Teologiese Studies/Theological Studies* 74(3), 5015, https://doi. org/10.4102/hts.v74i3.5015.
Lamar, H. and Thompson, L. (eds) (1981), *The frontier in history: North America and South Africa Compared*, London: Yale University Press.
Lamola, J. M. (1988), 'Towards a Black church: A historical investigation of the African Independent Churches as a model', *Journal of Theology for Southern Africa* 1(May): 5–14.
Landau, P. S. (2010), *Popular politics in the history of South Africa, 1400–1948*, Cambridge: Cambridge University Press.
Lea, A. (1926), The Native Separatist Church, in Taylor, J. D. (ed.), *The Native Separatist Church Movement in South Africa*, Johannesburg: Juta.
Lennox, J., Papers, Howard Pim Library, University of Fort Hare.

Lennox, J. (1911), *Our missions in South Africa: Missions of the United Free Church of Scotland*, Edinburgh: UFCoS.
Lennox, J., sa. Correspondence, Howard Pim Library, University of Fort Hare.
Lennox, J., 28 July 1898–14 April 1904, Lennox correspondence, Howard Pim Library, University of Fort Hare.
Lennox to Stewart, 28 February 1904, D65/48,23A [ix], J. W. Jagger Library, University of Cape Town.
Lennox to PCSA General Assembly, 20 September 1915, 'Synod 1914–1916', Lennox correspondence, NAHECS, University of Fort Hare.
Lennox to Soga, 27 November 1920, Commission on Union, Lennox correspondence NAHECS, University of Fort Hare.
Lennox to Ashcroft, 30 August 1922, Letterbook, Mission Council, Howard Pim Library, University of Fort Hare.
Lennox to Henderson, 29 September 1922, Henderson correspondence, Cory Library for Historical Research.
Lennox to Soga, 25 November 1922, Letterbook, Synod of Kafraria, Howard Pim Library, University of Fort Hare.
Lennox to Oldham, 11 December 1922, 'Personal 1919–1922', Lennox correspondence, Box 218–24, NAHECS, University of Fort Hare.
Lindsay to Stormont, 20 October 1898, MS 14303, Stormont papers, Cory Library for Historical Research.
Luka-Mbole, J.-C. (2013), 'The significance of Bible translations for African theological education', in Phiri, I. and Werner, D. (eds), *Handbook of Theological Education in Africa*, Oxford: Regnum: 508–22.
Macgregor, http://www.mcgregorvillage.co.za/history/ (last accessed 20 July 2015).
McIntosh, H. (1993), *Robert Laws: Servant of Africa*, Edinburgh: Handsel Press.
Mackenzie, J. M. (2007), *The Scots in South Africa: Ethnicity, identity, gender and race, 1772–1914,* Manchester: Manchester University Press.
Mackie, J. D. (1964), *A history of Scotland*, Harmondsworth: Pelican.
Magesa, L. (2013), *What is not sacred?: African spirituality*, Maryknoll: Orbis.
Majiza, C. M. (2018), 'Celebrating four decades of women in the ordained ministry', Presentation at the UPCSA General Assembly, 11 July 2018, Emseni Retreat Centre, Benoni.
Maluleke, T. S. (1995), 'Some legacies of 19th century mission: The Swiss Mission in South Africa', *Missionalia* 23 (no. 1, April): 9–29.
Maluleke, T. S. (1997), 'Truth, national unity and reconciliation in South Africa', in Guma, M. and Milton, A. L. (eds), *An African challenge to the church in the twenty-first century,* Johannesburg: South African Council of Churches: 109–32.
Manaka, S. P. (1996), 'A century of Christian witness of the Reformed Presbyterian Church in South[ern] Africa', unpublished paper, Turfloop: University of the North.

Marks, S. (1970), *Reluctant rebellion: The 1906–1908 disturbances in Natal*, Oxford: Clarendon.
Marrty, M. E. (1964), *Church unity and church mission*, Grand Rapids: Eerdmans.
Matlala, S. (2016), *Presbyterianism and ecumenism, a good friend: The biography of Reverend Mitši Abraham Maja*, Polokwane: Kwarts Publishers.
Maxwell, I. D. (2001), 'Civilisation or Christianity? The Scottish debate on mission methods', in Stanley, B. (ed.), *Christian missions and the Enlightenment*, Grand Rapids: Eerdmans: 123–40.
Meiring, P. (1999), *Chronicle of the Truth Commission: A journey through the past and present – into the future of South Africa*, Van der Bijl Park: Carpe Diem.
Millard, J. M. (1994), 'New independent Methodist movements in Southern Africa', in Oosthuizen, G. C., Kitshoff, M. C. and Dube, S. W. D. (eds), *Afro-Christianity at the grassroots*, Leiden: Brill: 23–36.
Millard, J. A. (1995), 'A study of perceived causes of schism in some Ethiopian-type churches in the Cape and Transvaal, 1884–1925', DTh thesis, Pretoria: UNISA Press.
Millard, J. A. (1999), *Malihambe – Let the Word spread*, Pretoria: UNISA Press.
Mission Council of South Africa, Relation of Mission Councils to Bantu Presbyterian Church, FMC note 2154, 1923, Lennox papers, Box 12, F91–100, NAHECS, University of Fort Hare.
Mofokeng, T. (1997), 'Land is our mother: A Black theology of land', in Mongezi Guma and Leslie Milton, A. (eds), *An African challenge to the Church in the twenty-first century*, Johannesburg: South African Council of Churches: 42–56.
Mostert, N. (1992), *Frontiers: The Epic of South Africa's Creation and the Tragedy of the Xhosa People*, London: Jonathan Cape.
Moyo, F. (2015), *The Bible, the bullet and the ballot: Zimbabwe: the impact of Christian protest in socio-political transformation, ca. 1900–2000*, Eugene, OR: Pickwick.
Muirhead, A. (2015), *Reformation, dissent and diversity: The story of Scotland's churches, 1560–1960*, London: Bloomsbury, T. and T. Clark.
Müller, R. (2011), *African pilgrimage: Ritual travel in south Africa's Christianity of Zion*, London: Routledge.
Murray, D. E. (1973), 'A background study paper for the Ministry Committee of the PCSA', Johannesburg: PCSA.
Mzimba to Smith, 29 May 1893, National Library of Scotland, ms. 7798.
Mzimba, P. J. (1898), Letter of resignation, Howard Pim Library, University of Fort Hare. Presbytery of Kaffraria Minute Book, meeting of 15 April 1898.
Mzimba, P. J. (1904), SANAC, vol. II.
National Library of Scotland, Letterbooks of the Free Church of Scotland, Edinburgh.

Newbigin, L. (1958), *One body, one gospel, one world*, London: International Missionary Council.
Nkumanda, S. S. (2009), 'A history of the man of God Pambani Jeremiah (P. J.) Mzimba, founder of the Presbyterian Church of Africa: 1850–1911', unpublished paper.
Ntantala, P. (1992), *A life's mosaic: The autobiography of Phyllis Ntantala*, Cape Town: David Philip.
Nussbaum, S. (ed.) (1994), *Freedom and independence*, Nairobi: OAIC.
Nzo, M. (2017), 'The Bantu Presbyterian Church in South[ern] Africa: Its origins and history', unpublished manuscript.
Oosthuizen, G. C. (1970), *Shepherd of Lovedale*, Johannesburg: Hugh Keartland.
Overseas Ministries Study Centre (1977), 'Henry Venn, 1796–1873', *International Bulletin of Missionary Research*, 2 April: 16–19.
Peires, J. B. (1989), *The dead will arise: Nongqawuse and the great Xhosa cattle-killing movement of 1856–1857*, Johannesburg: Ravan Press.
Pobee, J. S. and Ositelo, G. (1998), *African initiatives in Christianity: The growth, gifts and diversities of indigenous African Churches – a challenge to the ecumenical movement*, Geneva: WCC.
Pons, E. S. n.d., *The Southern and Central Streams of Presbyterianism in Africa*, Kitwe, Zambia: PCSA.
Presbyterian Church of South Africa 1915, 1922, 1924, 1925, 1927, 1934, 1973, 1975, 1980, 1983, 1987, 1990, 1991, 1999, *Blue Book: Proceedings of General Assembly*, Johannesburg: PCSA.
Presbyterian Church of South Africa (1891–), Archives, William Cullen Library [WCL], University of the Witwatersrand [Wits], Johannesburg.
Pretorius, H. and Jafta, L. D. (1997), '"A branch springs out": African Initiated Churches', in Elphick, R. and Davenport, R. (eds), *Christianity in South Africa: A political, social and cultural history*, Cape Town: David Philip: 211–26.
Purvis, S. B. (1995), *The stained-glass ceiling: Churches and their women pastors*, Louisville: John Knox Westminster Press.
Reese, R. (2010), *Roots and remedies of the dependency syndrome in world missions*, Pasadena: William Carey Library.
Reformed Presbyterian Church in Southern Africa, 1979–82, 1983, 1984, 1985, 1988, 1989, 1993, 1995, 1996, 1997, 1999, Proceedings of the General Assembly of the Reformed Presbyterian Church in Southern Africa, Lovedale: Lovedale Press.
Reformed Presbyterian Church in Southern Africa, archives, Rhodes University, Grahamstown, Cory Library for Historical Research, Schenk WR 1977.
Reformed Presbyterian Church in Southern Africa (Khabela, M. G., Soga, D. M. and Mdlalose, J. V.) (1995), REFORMED PRESBYTERIAN CHURCH IN SOUTHERN AFRICA: Submission to the Truth & Reconciliation Commission Special Faith Hearing.

Roberts, A. W. (1904), SANAC, 1904, vol. II, 11.095.

Robertson, R. (1994), 'The union that fell through', unpublished paper, Cape Town.

Robertson, W., http://www.geni.com/people/William-Robertson/600000 0000866071008 (last accessed 20 July 2015).

Rohr, R. (2011), *Falling upward: A spirituality for the two halves of life*, San Francisco: Jossey-Bass.

Ross, A. (1986), *John Philip (1775–1851): missions, race and politics in South Africa*, Aberdeen: Aberdeen University Press.

Ross, K. R. (2008), 'The legacy of James Dougall', *International Bulletin of Missionary Research* 32(4): 206–9.

Rouse, R. and Neill, S. (eds) (1967), *A history of the ecumenical movement, 1517–1948*, London: SPCK.

Rousseau, J. J. (1762), *The Social Contract*, available from: https://www.sparknotes.com/philosophy/socialcontract/summary/ (last accessed 7 February 2010).

Russell, L. M. (ed.) (1985), *Feminist interpretation of the Bible*, Louisville: Westminster Press.

Ryan, C. (1990), *Beyers Naudé: Pilgrimage of faith*, Cape Town: David Philip.

Saayman, W. A. (1984), *Unity and mission: A study of the concept of unity in ecumenical discussions since 1961 and its influence on the world mission of the church*, Pretoria: UNISA Press.

Saayman, W. A. (1996), *A Man with a Shadow: the life and times of Prof ZK Matthews: A missiological interpretation in context*, Pretoria: UNISA Press.

Saayman, W. A. (2007), *Being missionary, being human: An overview of Dutch Reformed mission*, Pietermaritzburg: Cluster.

St Andrew's Kirk Session Minute Book (1843), Cape Town: St Andrew's Presbyterian Church.

Schrage, W. (1988), *The ethics of the New Testament*, Philadelphia: Fortress.

Selope Thema R. V. (1953), 'How congress began', *Drum*, July, http://www.scribd.com/doc/206854093/African-National-Congress-A-Documentary-History-of-the-Struggle-Against-Apartheid-in-South-Africa (last accessed 15 May 2014).

Shepherd, R. H. W. (1937), *The Separatist Churches of South Africa* (1937: 455) in Millard, J. A. (1995), 'A study of perceived causes of schism in some Ethiopian-type churches in the Cape and Transvaal, 1884–1925', DTh thesis, UNISA, Pretoria.

Shepherd, R. H. W. (1940), Lovedale: *South Africa, 1824–1955*, Lovedale: Lovedale Press.

Shepherd, R. H. W. (1945), *Lovedale and literature for the Bantu*, Lovedale: Lovedale Press.

Shepherd, R. H. W. (1971), *Lovedale, South Africa: 1824–1955*, Lovedale: Lovedale Press.

Shepherd, R. H. W. (1972), 'A difference in methods', in Wilson, F. and Perrot, D. (eds), *Outlook on a Century: South Africa 1870–1970*, Lovedale: Lovedale Press.

Shiferaw, Y. (2012), 'Migration', in Melake M. K. Merahi, *Christianity in Ethiopia III*, Addis Ababa: Merahi.

Sikhutshwa, D. V. (1939), *South Africa Outlook*, December.

Sikutshwa, D. V. (1946), *Formation of the Bantu Presbyterian Church*, Lovedale: Lovedale Press.

Sjollema, B. (1982), *Isolating Apartheid*, Geneva: World Council of Churches.

Smith to Weir, 28 October 1904, in file 'Mission Council 1902–1905', Lennox correspondence, NAHECS, University of Fort Hare.

Soga, T. (1862), 'Gxuluwe and the bushmen', in Williams, D. (ed., 1983), *The journal and selected writings of the Reverend Tiyo Soga*, Cape Town: A. A. Balkema.

Soga to Lennox, 15 November (1920), 'Commission on Union', Lennox correspondence, NAHECS, University of Fort Hare.

South African History Online (2012), 'States of Emergency in South Africa: The 1960s and 1980s', available from: https://www.sahistory.org.za/topic/state-emergency-south-africa-1960-and-1980s (last accessed 25 February 2019).

South African History Online (2016), 1976-1983-mass-democratic-movements https://www.sahistory.org.za/article/1976-1983-mass-democratic-movements (last accessed 23 April 2021).

South African Native Affairs Commission (SANAC) 1903–1905 [Lagden Commission], *Minutes of evidence taken in the Cape Colony*, vols II, IV. Cape Town: Cape Times Limited, Government printers.

South African Outlook (1973), November.

Stanley, B. (ed.) (2001), *Christian missions and the Enlightenment*, Grand Rapids: Eerdmans.

Stanley, B. (2009), *The World Missionary Conference, Edinburgh 1910*, Grand Rapids: Eerdmans.

Stapleton, T. J. (1994), *Maqoma: Xhosa resistance to colonial advance*, Johannesburg, Jonathan Ball.

Stewart, J. (1894), *Lovedale: South Africa*, Edinburgh: Andrew Elliot, Stewart Papers, University of Cape Town Library, BC 106: C167.

Stewart, J. (1896), *Monthly Record of the Free Church of Scotland*, 21 April.

Stewart, to Roberts, 26 December 1902, private collection of Roberts papers, Mr P. van Lill.

Stewart, J. (1904), SANAC, vol. IV.

Stockwell, S. (ed.) (2008), *The British Empire: Themes, and perspectives*, Oxford: Wiley-Blackwell.

Stormont, D. D. (1902), The Ethiopian churches of South Africa, Stormont papers, Grahamstown: Cory Library for Historical Research (no further details available).

Stormont, D. D., Papers, Rhodes University, Grahamstown, Cory Library for Historical Research.
Stuart, Rev. W. (1899), Burnshill in Editorial, *CE*, XXIX, 344, 2 February.
Sundkler, B. G. M. (1961), *Bantu prophets in South Africa*, London: Oxford University Press.
Sundkler, B. G. M. and Steed, C. (2000), *A history of the Church in Africa*, Cambridge: Cambridge University Press.
Switzer, L. (1993), *Power and resistance in an African society: The Ciskei Xhosa and the making of the South Africa*, Pietermaritzburg: University of Natal Press.
Synod of Kaffraria of the Free Church of Scotland (1894–1906), Minutes, Howard Pim Library, University of Fort Hare.
Thema, R. D. (2021), *The origin and development of the Reformed Presbyterian Church mission station within Mamabolo Location of the northern Transvaal*, Polokwane: RD Thema.
Thomas, D. G. (1984), 'Ecumenism and indigenisation in the churches of South Africa, 1904–1975', Master's dissertation, Johannesburg, University of the Witwatersrand.
Thompson, A. (2008), 'The Empire and the British State', in Stockwell, S. (ed.), *The British Empire: Themes, and perspectives*, Oxford: Wiley-Blackwell.
Thompson, T. J. (2000), *Touching the heart: Xhosa missionaries to Malawi, 1876–1888*, Pretoria: UNISA Press.
Thompson, T. J. (2012), *Light on darkness? Missionary photography in the nineteenth and early twentieth centuries*, Grand Rapids: Eerdmans.
Trible, P. (1985), 'Postscript: Jottings on the journey', in Russell, L. M. (ed.), *Feminist interpretation of the Bible*, Louisville: Westminster Press: 147–9.
United Free Church of Scotland (1927), *Manual of practice and procedure*, Edinburgh: UFCoS.
UPCoS n.d., United Presbyterian Church, https://www.britannica.com/topic/United-Presbyterian-Church (last accessed 8 June 2021).
UPCoS, Minutes, Department of World Mission: Church of Scotland, Edinburgh.
Vale, P. (2014), 'Introduction', in Vale, P., Hamilton, L. and Prinsloo, E. (eds), *Intellectual traditions in South Africa: Ideas, individuals and institutions*, Pietermaritzburg: University of KwaZulu-Natal Press: 1–25.
Van Der Spuy, D. (1971), 'The origins, growth and development of the Bantu Presbyterian Church of South Africa', BD thesis, Grahamstown: Rhodes University.
Van Dyk, H., et al. (2001), 'Population mobility in Africa: An overview', in Miriam de Bruijn et al., *Mobile Africa: Changing patterns of movement in Africa and beyond*, Boston, MA: Brill: 9–26.
Van Zyl, H. E. (1985), 'The letters of Jane Elizabeth Waterson, 1866–1905' (book review), *Presbyterian Life*, January: 6.

Vellem, V. S. (2013), 'The "Native Experiment": The Formation of the Bantu Presbyterian Church and the Defects of Faith: Transplanted on African Soil', *Missionalia* 42, 3, August: 146–63.
Villa-Vicencio, C. and Grassow, P. (2009), *Christianity and the colonisation of South Africa: A documentary history, vol. I*, Pretoria, UNISA Press.
Vischer, L. (ed.) (1981), *Church History in ecumenical perspective*, Papers and Reports of International Ecumenical Consultation held in Basle, 12–17 October.
Walls, A. F. (1996), 'The evangelical revival, the Missionary movement in Africa', in Walls, A. F., *The missionary movement in Christian history*, Maryknoll: Orbis: 79–101.
Walls, A. F. (1996), *The missionary movement in Christian history: Studies in the transmission of faith*, Edinburgh: T. and T. Clark.
Walls, A. F. (2002), *The cross-cultural process in Christian history*, Edinburgh: T. and T. Clark.
Walls, A. F. (2008), 'Afterword: Christian mission in a five-hundred-year context', in Walls, A. F. and Ross, C. (eds), *Mission in the 21st century: Exploring the five marks of global mission*, London: Darton, Longman & Todd: 193–204.
Walls, A. F. (2014), 'Mission and Migration: The Diaspora Factor in Christian History', in Chandler Him and Amos Yong (eds), *Global Diasporas and Mission*, Oxford: Regnum: 19–37.
Weatherhead, J. L. (ed.) (1997), *The Constitution and laws of the Church of Scotland*, Edinburgh: Board of Practice and Procedure, Church of Scotland.
Wells, J. (1909), *Stewart of Lovedale: The life of James Stewart*, London: Hodder & Stoughton.
Westminster Confession of Faith 1647 (1969), *The Confession of Faith*, Edinburgh: Blackwood.
Williams, D. (1978), *Umfundisi: a biography of Tiyo Soga 1829–1871*, Lovedale: Lovedale Press.
Williams, D. (1983), *The journal and selected writings of the Reverend Tiyo Soga*, Grahamstown, Cape Town: A. A. Balkema.
Williams, R. (2008), 'Foreword', in Walls, A. F. and Ross, C. (eds), *Mission in the 21st century: Exploring the five marks of global mission*, London: Darton, Longman & Todd: xi–xii.
Wilson, F. and Perrot, D. (eds) (1972), *Outlook on a century: South Africa, 1870–1970*, Lovedale: Lovedale Press.
Wilson, M. (1974), 'Naboth's Vineyard (2)', *South African Outlook* 114 (1243, November): 179.
Wilson, M. (1976), 'Missionaries: Conquerors or Servants of God?', address given on the occasion of the opening of the South African Missionary Museum, 30 January 1976 (King William's Town, South African Missionary Museum, 1976): 7.
World Council of Churches (1960), Bantu Presbyterian Church of South

Africa, Report of the Study Committee of the Bantu Presbyterian Church of South Africa, JSTOR Primary Sources, 12-07-1960, contributed by World Council of Churches Consultation (Cottesloe, Johannesburg, 7–14 December, 1960), Bantu Presbyterian Church of South Africa.

Wright, D. F. (1993), 'Woman's Guild', in Wright, D. F. (ed.), *Dictionary of Scottish church history and theology*, Edinburgh: T. and T. Clark.

Wuthnow, R. (2014), *Rough country: How Texas became America's most powerful bible-belt state*, Princeton: Princeton University Press.

Xapile, S. P. (1994), 'Unity negotiations between the Bantu Presbyterian Church and the Presbyterian Church of Southern Africa (1959–1971)', Cape Town: University of Cape Town.

Xapile, S. P. (1999), 'The quest for unity between the Bantu Presbyterian Church of South Africa and the Presbyterian Church of South Africa: 1959–73', DTh thesis, University of Stellenbosch.

Zikmund, B. B. (1995), 'Foreword', in Purvis, S. B., *The stained-glass ceiling: Churches and their women pastors*, Louisville: Westminster/John Knox Press: vii–xii.

Index

Abrahamic model, 4
Adamic, 4
Adams College, 154
African Initiated Churches (AICs), 1, 42, 140
African Methodist Episcopal Church, 78
African Traditional Religion (ATR), 1
Alice, 23, 79, 168, 204, 223
Alice Lenshina, 204
All Africa Council of Churches (AACC), 156
Alliance of Black Reformed Christians in South Africa (ABRECSA), 156
amaXhosa, 18, 19, 24, 31, 64, 215
Anderson, Rufus, 20, 21, 32, 89, 100, 190, 221, 222
Ashcroft, Rev. Frank, 53, 54, 96, 107, 108, 110, 111, 114, 116, 125, 176, 215, 223
Association of Southern African Theological Institutions (ASATI), 154

Bantu Education Act (1953), 186, 188
Bantu Presbyterian Church of South Africa (BPCSA), 1, 2, 6, 19, 55, 65, 89, 105, 124, 161, 205, 212, 215
Bantu Presbyterian Church of South Africa: Origin and progress, 183
Barrier Act, 159, 205
Bax, Rev. Douglas, 86, 88, 91, 95, 153, 216
Bennie, John, 22, 23, 24, 180
Bernard, Rev. Neil C., 164
Black Consciousness, 31, 33, 36, 37, 39, 40, 42, 119, 121
black nationalism, 39, 40
Black Theology of Liberation, 150
Blyden, Wilmot Edward, 39

Blythswood Institution, 24, 25, 46, 54, 67, 102, 111, 113, 188
Bokwe, John Knox, 27, 75, 106
Brandt, Bowling & Tagg, 172
Brownlee, 22, 23, 30, 34, 40, 47, 138
Burnshill Mission, 1, 170
Burnside, Janet, 32

Cameron, Dr A. T., 168
Campbell, Rev. Ewan, 168
cattle-killing movement (1856–7), 19
Chalmers, Rev. J. A., 31
Chalmers, Rev. Thomas, 10, 12, 31, 32, 33, 35, 37, 39, 40, 41, 42, 43
character formation, 19
Christian Council of South Africa, 138, 157, 180
Christian Express, 57, 66, 67, 93, 94, 179, 216, 217
Christian fundamentalism, 201
Church Associations, 129, 178
Church of Scotland, 6, 8, 9, 12, 13, 14, 23, 24, 26, 32, 44, 46, 51, 57, 61, 62, 63, 66, 71, 74, 76, 77, 78, 79, 80, 82, 83, 88, 90, 96, 97, 98, 99, 100, 105, 110, 111, 119, 120, 124, 126, 128, 130, 136, 137, 138, 141, 151, 156, 161, 162, 163, 165, 167, 168, 169, 170, 171, 172, 173, 177, 178, 182, 185, 203, 204, 205, 206, 208, 215, 217, 219, 221, 223, 225, 228, 229, 230
Church of Scotland South Africa Joint Council (CoSSAJC), 161
Church of the Province (Anglican), 151, 152
Church Theology, 195
Church Unity Commission, 152, 155, 160
churches of European origin (CEO), 5, 56

'Claim of Right', 12
Cluster of Theological Institutions, 154
Commission on Union, 54, 95, 103, 109, 110, 113, 114, 116, 118, 119, 125, 217, 223, 227
Committee on Priorities & Resources, 155
Constitution of the Bantu Presbyterian Church of South Africa, 81
Cook, Rev. Prof. Calvin, 137, 168, 173
Cottesloe Consultation 1960, 157, 189, 190
Crawford, Victor, 168

Davidson, Rev. J., 52, 90
Deborah, 202
Department of Bantu Administration, 186
dependency, 19, 20, 21, 72, 83, 118, 126, 128, 131, 132, 134
Dewar, Mrs, 208
Dewar, Rev. James, 119, 138, 208, 218
'Disruption', 8, 12, 23, 71
Doig, Mrs Mary, 208
Don, Rev. J. D., 45, 68, 69, 75, 90, 94
Dougall, Rev. James, 162, 163, 218, 226
Duff, Alexander, 24, 44, 45, 46
Duncan, Rev. Graham, 19, 22, 24, 25, 26, 28, 31, 34, 37, 52, 54, 57, 58, 72, 73, 80, 86, 88, 96, 97, 98, 126, 127, 133, 134, 140, 162, 163, 165, 166, 168, 170, 171, 174, 175, 176, 182, 207, 209, 214, 218, 219, 220
Duncan, Sandra, 207
Dutch Reformed Church, 85, 86, 99, 190, 193

Ecumenical Relations Committee, 155, 156, 159
Ecumenism, 137, 139, 140, 141, 143, 145, 147, 149, 151, 153, 155, 157, 159, 220, 228
Edinburgh World Missionary Conference, 1910, 19
Education, 19, 26, 32, 115, 126, 127, 154, 172, 178, 181, 186, 188
Ellesmere Farm, 166
Emjanyana, leper colony, 127, 209
Ethiopia, 36, 39, 60, 220, 227

Ethiopian Church Movement, 21
Ethiopianism, 52, 57, 59, 60, 62, 78, 82, 218, 220
Evangelical Bible Seminary of South Africa, 154
Evangelical Presbyterian Church, 152
Evangelicals, 8, 9, 10
Evangelists, 127, 177

Federal Theological Seminary of Southern Africa (FedSem), 154
Finca, Rev. B. B., 27, 150, 155, 157, 159, 190, 195, 196, 221
Finca, Rev. Titus P., 150
Forced Removals, 191
Foreign Mission Committee, 44, 47, 53, 54, 55, 62, 77, 93, 98, 99, 109, 125, 130, 132, 133, 135, 136, 162, 163, 164, 165, 221
Forgan, Robert, 133
Forts, 16
Fraser, 203
Fraser, Rev. Donald, 81, 168, 203
Fraser, Rev. Dr Ian, 203
Free Church of Scotland (FCoS), 8, 12, 23, 44, 98

Gavin, Rev. William, 131
General Missionary Conference (1904), 59
Girls' Association, 128, 129, 178, 209
Glasgow African Missionary Society (GAMS), 23
Glasgow Missionary Society (GMS), 11, 23, 137
Glenthorn congregation, 24, 46, 130, 141, 144, 145, 221
Gooldville, Venda, 205
Gordon Memorial Mission, 25
Gossip, Rev. James, 166, 168, 169
Govan, Rev. William, 9, 31, 32, 126, 179
Grey, Sir George, 16, 26, 34, 191, 203, 212
Group Areas Act of 1950, 186
Gush, G. A., 180

Hamill, Fiona, 168
Henderson, Dr James, 3, 27, 28, 49, 50, 51, 55, 81, 89, 93, 94, 95, 99, 100,

101, 102, 103, 104, 105, 106, 109, 110, 114, 116, 138, 219, 221, 223
highland clearances, 8
History of Christianity, 1, 221, 222
Hliso, Rev. Joash Yoash, 146, 152
Holben, Rev. Sarah, 206, 207
Horton, James Africanus, 39
Houston, Mr Andrew, 54, 96, 110, 111, 215
Hutton & Cook, 168

Igcibira, 23
imperialism, 5, 6, 33, 89, 164, 218
Imvo Zabantsundu, 59, 140, 222
imvuselelo (revival), 128
inculturation, 13, 28, 42, 126
Incwadi Amaculo AseRabe (1929), 40
independency, 19, 20
Institute for Contextual Theology, 194
integration, 6, 32, 139, 147, 161, 162, 163, 164, 165, 166, 167, 168, 169, 171, 173, 211
Integration Committee, 167, 169
International Missionary Council, 163, 222, 225

Jabavu, J. T., 59
James Stewart, Dr, 9, 15, 27, 28, 29, 31, 38, 45, 50, 52, 62, 64, 65, 72, 87, 93, 99, 101, 103, 126, 138, 179, 216, 230
Jane Waterston (1843–1932), 204
John Street UP Church, Glasgow, 32
Joint Council, 136, 143, 144, 145, 146, 161, 166, 167, 168, 169, 170, 171, 172, 173, 177, 217
Jongilanga, Chief D. M., 172

Kairos Document (1986), 194
Kala, J. M., 74, 75, 76
Kerr, Dr Alexander, 138
Khabela, Dr Gideon M., 33, 34, 40, 196, 226
Khala, Milton M., 172, 173
Khonyane, 1
Kimpa Vita (Donna Beatrice), 204
Kincaid, Rev. James, 168
Kingcome, Harry A., 168
Kobo, Rev. Dr Fundiswa, 214, 222
Koyi, William, 27, 28

Ladies' Kafrarian Society, 46
Laing, James, 31
land, 5, 7, 12, 13, 14, 15, 16, 17, 18, 22, 27, 31, 34, 35, 36, 37, 38, 39, 55, 57, 58, 63, 69, 74, 77, 82, 87, 104, 117, 132, 134, 141, 151, 153, 168, 169, 171, 176, 182, 189, 190, 191, 193
Land Act (1913), 87
Leeuw, Rev. Cliff, 206
Lennox, Rev. John, 2, 24, 35, 46, 48, 50, 51, 53, 68, 73, 77, 89, 91, 93, 94, 95, 99, 100, 101, 102, 103, 104, 105, 106, 107, 108, 109, 110, 113, 114, 116, 117, 118, 119, 125, 138, 139, 176, 215, 217, 218, 221, 223, 224, 227
Levison, Mary, 203
Lindsay, Dr, 52, 68, 89, 104, 223
liturgy, 22, 60, 120, 128, 161, 178
Livingstonia, Nyasaland (Malawi), 204
London Missionary Society (LMS), 11
Lovedale Bible School, 177, 178, 209
Lovedale Missionary Institution, 1, 45, 188
Lovedale Native Congregation, 46, 74, 76
Lovedale Press, 25, 88, 169, 172, 177, 179, 180, 215, 216, 217, 220, 222, 226, 227, 230
Lundie, Rev. J., 49, 113, 117

Ma Nku, 204
Maja, Rev. Abraham N., 196, 224
Majiza, Rev. Charity, 205
Makiwane, Rev. Elijah, 26, 27, 64, 68, 106
Malan Mission, 49
Mama, Rev. Holfort, 106, 144, 147
Mandela, Nelson, 159
Manual of the Bantu Presbyterian Church 1958, 119
Maomosi, Snowy, 206
Maqoma, 14, 15, 228
Mary, 202
Mary Magdalene, 202
Matanzima, Chief Kaiser D., 194
Mavhina, Rev. Seani, 207
Mcoteli, Rev. G. T., 195
Mdlalose, Rev. Vusumuzi John, 196, 226

Memorandum of Native Ministers and Officebearers, 106
Mennonites in the USA, 156
Methodist Church of South Africa, 152
Mfecane (Difiqane), 5
Mfengu, 25, 37
Mgunana, Shadrack, 27, 28
Mgwali, 23, 24, 25, 34, 35, 37, 41, 52, 191
Mgwali Girls' School, 25
Migration, 4, 191, 221, 227, 230
Miller, Dr A., 24, 46, 51
Mission, 1, 2, 4, 7, 13, 18, 19, 22, 23, 24, 25, 26, 28, 34, 40, 44, 45, 46, 47, 48, 49, 50, 51, 52, 53, 54, 55, 56, 57, 62, 63, 64, 67, 69, 71, 74, 77, 78, 80, 82, 83, 91, 92, 93, 94, 95, 97, 98, 99, 100, 101, 103, 105, 106, 107, 108, 109, 110, 111, 112, 113, 114, 115, 116, 117, 119, 120, 121, 122, 123, 124, 125, 127, 130, 131, 132, 133, 134, 135, 136, 138, 139, 144, 146, 148, 151, 155, 157, 161, 162, 163, 164, 165, 166, 167, 168, 169, 171, 173, 174, 175, 176, 177, 178, 181, 183, 194, 195, 213, 216, 217, 218, 219, 220, 221, 222, 223, 224, 227, 229, 230
Mission Council of Kaffraria, 46, 48, 127
mission councils, 7, 28, 29, 46, 47, 53, 55, 56, 125, 126, 176, 177, 219
mission hospitals, 167
Mission Stations, 24
missionaries, role of, 45, 47, 50, 58, 71, 75, 98, 103, 118, 126, 161, 166, 176, 206, 212, 218, 230
Missionaries' Committee, 161, 166
Missionary Movement, 124
Moderate, 9
Moir, Rev. Iain, 1
Moir, Rev. W. B. J., 61, 62, 67, 68, 168, 169, 170, 171
money, 60, 65, 69, 72, 73, 74, 75, 77, 78, 79, 80, 81, 82, 83, 84, 90, 130, 162, 165, 192, 219
Mpamba, Rev. William, 24, 27
Mure, Rev. R., 105, 106
Mzimba Secession, 13, 49, 57, 68, 69, 71, 73, 75, 77, 79, 80, 81, 83, 88, 93, 97, 103, 104, 105, 106, 115, 116, 121, 140, 219
Mzimba, Rev. Pambani J., 13, 26, 27, 46, 49, 57, 60, 61, 62, 63, 64, 65, 68, 69, 71, 72, 73, 74, 75, 76, 77, 78, 79, 80, 81, 82, 83, 88, 93, 97, 98, 103, 104, 105, 106, 113, 115, 116, 119, 121, 124, 140, 141, 142, 219, 225

Natal Mission Council, 46, 53, 94, 108
National Committee on Theological Education, 154
Native Affairs Commission (1903–5), 59
Native assistants, 125
Native church, 54, 96, 167
'Native Experiment' option, 100
Ndibongo, Rev. W. P. T., 141, 143, 146, 190
negritude, 33, 37, 40, 42
Nessie Knight Hospital, 166, 170
Ngcobo, Rev. Samuel B., 170, 173, 195, 196
Ngcongo, Rev. Thokozani Mildred, 206
Ngebulana, Rev. Bulelwa, 207
Ngqika, 15, 16, 22, 30, 37
Nissen, Rev. Chris, 195
Njikelana, Mrs, 208
Njikelana, Rev. S. W., 49, 105, 143, 208
Nonjojo, Nokhalipha Vivienne, 206
Nonquawuse, 34
Ntintili, Mapassa, 27, 28
Ntsikana, 27, 31, 40, 103

Oldham, J. H., 105, 114, 125, 176, 221, 223
Operation Faithshare, 165
Overseas Council of the Church of Scotland, 1

Pan Africanist Congress (PAC), 188
Pan-Africanism, 40, 59
partnership in mission, 19, 126, 134, 161
pass laws, 189
passive resistance, 187
pastoral care, 45, 50, 64, 127, 128, 129, 178, 202, 211

Index

patronage, 12
PCSA Church Extension Committee, 92, 139
PCSA Colonial Committee, 91, 92, 139
PCSA Federal Council, 91, 139
Philip, Rev. John, 17, 22, 226
Phillip, Elizabeth J., 168, 169
Phoebe, 202
Pholela Institution, 25
Pilgrim's Progress, 30, 40
Pirie mission, 23, 191
Pollock, Rev. J., 111
'Practice and Procedure' of the UFCoS, 119
Presbyterian Church of Africa (PCA), 46, 100, 151
Presbyterian Church of South Africa (PCSA), 46, 49, 61, 97
Presbyterian Church of the USA, 156, 206
Presbyterianism, 5, 6, 7, 22, 57, 85, 96, 100, 118, 140, 149, 204, 211, 218, 219, 220, 224, 226
Presbytery of Kaffraria, 3, 24, 48, 51, 54, 62, 63, 64, 65, 68, 69, 72, 73, 75, 78, 91, 96, 104, 107, 110, 112, 114, 117, 225
Presbytery of Mankazana, 95, 117, 141
Presbytery of Natal, 24, 157, 169
Presbytery of the Ciskei, 1, 88, 143, 170, 205
Prisca, 202
Programme to Combat Racism, 192, 197
Promotion of National Unity and Reconciliation Act (1995), 196
Property and Assets Holding Committee, 171
Prophetic Theology, 195

Read, James, 22, 78
reconciliation, 196, 226
Reformed Presbyterian Church of Southern Africa (RPCSA), 6
Roberts, Alexander, 59, 76, 79, 102, 226, 228
Robertson, Rev. Rob, 86, 146, 226
Robson, Rev. George, 52, 53, 94
Ross, Rev. John, 8, 10, 11, 21, 23, 24, 46, 47, 73, 102, 138, 179, 216, 220, 221, 226, 230

Saayman, Prof. Willem, 1, 2, 12, 13, 29, 33, 39, 40, 42, 43, 82, 107, 174, 193, 227
St Columba's College, 154, 208
St Joseph's Scholasticate Seminary, 154
Sammon, Dr A. M., 169
Schminkey, Robert, 207
school people (*amakholwa*), 134
Scots Confession (1560), 7
Scottish Enlightenment, 8
Scottish mission, 6, 7, 11, 17, 24, 42, 52, 62, 71, 104, 115, 137, 140, 142, 147, 162, 174, 177, 191, 203, 204, 220
Scottish Missionary Society, 11
secessions, 7, 22, 58, 59, 69, 70, 73, 97, 98, 102, 105, 107, 115, 119, 123, 126, 207
Sharpeville tragedy of 1961, 210
Shepherd, Dr R. H. W., 14, 25, 26, 38, 72, 82, 88, 91, 100, 103, 114, 119, 121, 126, 133, 135, 138, 139, 179, 180, 204, 209, 225, 227
Sikhutshwa, Rev. D. V., 92, 146, 227
Sililo, Rev. M., 117
Smith, Dr George, 16, 46, 62, 101, 102, 225, 227
Social Responsibility Committee, 194
Soga, Rev. de, 196
Soga, Rev. de Villiers M., *196*
Soga, Rev. T. B., 30, 31, 32, 33, 34, 35, 36, 37, 38, 39, 40, 41, 42, 43, 95, 103, 110, 114, 118, 125, 128, 133, 134, 135, 141, 176, 189, 196, 198, 223, 226, 227
Somerset, Lord Charles, 16, 24, 46
South African Council of Churches, 138, 157, 168, 171, 197, 224, 225
South African Council on Theological Education, 154
South African Native College, 126, 138, 181
South African Natives' National Congress (SANNC), 59
South African Outlook, 146, 179, 180, 228, 230

South African War (1899–1902), 87, 212
Standing for the Truth Committee, 194
Stanford, Robert D. N., 173
State Theology, 195
States of Emergency, 193, 228
Stevenson, Matthew Inglis, 166, 168, 169, 170, 171, 172, 173, 184
Stormont, Rev. D. D., 3, 10, 73, 75, 78, 102, 104, 223, 228
Stuart, Rev. William, 68, 74, 101, 117, 123, 175, 228
Summers, Mrs Maureen, 190, 208
Summers, Rev. John, 208
Supreme Court of the Cape Colony, 74
Synod of Kafraria, 3, 46, 47, 49, 54, 63, 64, 65, 66, 67, 68, 78, 91, 94, 95, 96, 101, 103, 106, 107, 110, 111, 112, 115, 116, 117, 118, 139, 223, 228

Temperance, 127, 184
The Transkei Mission, 24, 52, 108
Theological Education, 154
Thom, Rev. George, 22
Thomson, Rev. W. R., 8, 16, 22, 23, 24, 28
Three-Self Principle, 45, 89
Tiyo Soga, 26, 27, 30, 31, 33, 34, 35, 36, 37, 39, 41, 42, 43, 82, 135, 191, 194, 220, 227, 230
Transkei Mission Council, 24, 46, 49, 51, 52, 53, 108
Transkei National Independence Party, 194
Truth and Reconciliation Commission (TRC), 196
Tsewu Secession, 63, 69
Tsewu, Rev. Edward, 57, 59, 61, 62, 63, 64, 65, 66, 67, 68, 69, 98, 219
Tsonga Presbyterian Church, 151, 157
Tutu, Bishop Desmond, 171
Tutura, 23, 34
Tyali, 15
Tyamzashe, Rev. Gwayi, 24
Tyhumie, 23

umjikelo (fund-raising revival), 128
Union of South Africa (1910), 87
Uniondale, 33
'United Church' option, 99
United Congregational Church, 152, 157, 160
United Democratic Front (UDF), 156
United Free Church of Scotland, 13, 136, 138
United Presbyterian Church of Scotland, 26, 138
Uniting Presbyterian Church in Southern Africa (UPCSA), 6
'universes in collision', 81
University of Fort Hare, 3, 25, 73, 146, 154, 172, 181, 182, 215, 223, 225
University of Natal, Faculty of Theology, 154, 228

Van der Kemp, 22
Vellem, Rev. V. S., 86, 111, 150, 213, 229
Venn, Henry, 20, 21, 45, 89, 100, 225
Vika, Rev. Gladwin T., 167, 170, 184, 186, 187
voluntary societies, 10, 11, 137

War of the Axe (1846), 31, 32
Warneck, Gustav, 100
Wars of Dispossession, 15, 18, 32, 212
Wauchope, Isaac Williams, 27, 28
Westminster Confession of Faith 1645, 200
Whither Bantu Presbyterian Church?, 167, 186
Wildridge, Mr, 51
Wilkie, Dr Arthur, 138, 144
Willingen Conference, 1952, 163
women, 5, 7, 11, 34, 47, 53, 54, 55, 56, 102, 108, 116, 121, 129, 142, 177, 178, 183, 189, 191, 196, 200, 201, 202, 203, 204, 205, 206, 207, 208, 209, 210, 211, 213, 216, 217, 220, 221, 222, 223, 224, 226, 231
Women's Christian Association (*uManyano*), 102
Women's Guild, 208
World Alliance of Reformed Churches (WARC), 156

World Council of Churches (WCC), 156, 163, 190, 192
World Missionary Conference, Edinburgh in 1910, 107

Xhosa Bible, 40, 180

Young Men's Christian Guild (*amaDodana*), 102

CPSIA information can be obtained
at www.ICGtesting.com
Printed in the USA
BVHW010002210622
640070BV00018B/37